■ *CORPORATE PHYSICIANS*

Corporate Physicians

BETWEEN MEDICINE AND MANAGEMENT

Diana Chapman Walsh

YALE UNIVERSITY PRESS
New Haven and London

Copyright © 1987 by Yale University. All rights reserved. This book may not be reproduced, in whole or in part, including figures, in any form (beyond that copying permitted by Sections 107 and 108 of the U.S. Copyright Law and except by reviewers for the public press), without written permission from the publishers.

Designed by Nancy Ovedovitz and set in Baskerville type by Eastern Graphics. Printed in the United States of America by Edwards Brothers Inc., Ann Arbor, Michigan.

Library of Congress Cataloging-in-Publication Data
Walsh, Diana Chapman.
   Corporate physicians.
   Bibliography: p.
   Includes index.
   1. Medicine, Industrial. 2. Occupational health services. I. Title. [DNLM: 1. Occupational Medicine. 2. Role. WA 400 W224p]
RC963.3.W33   1987   658.3′82   87–6096
ISBN 0–300–03902–6 (alk. paper)

The paper in this book meets the guidelines for permanence and durability of the Committee on Production Guidelines for Book Longevity of the Council on Library Resources.

10 9 8 7 6 5 4 3 2 1

CONTENTS

Preface, vii

PART ONE
Introduction

1. Challenges, 3

PART TWO
A Profession Evolving

2. Origins and Evolutionary Threads, 27

3. In Search of Professional Identity, 42

4. The Corporate Medical Director, 63

PART THREE
Inside the Corporation

5. Clinicians in Corporations, 93

6. The Population as Patient, 117

7. Doctors of Corporations, 136

8. Can There Ever Be a More Strategic Role?, 174

PART FOUR
Conclusion

9. Lessons, 207

Appendix 1: Company Physicians and Others Quoted
  in Chapters 4 through 9, 229
Appendix 2: Profile of Interviews, 233

References, 239

Index, 259

■ PREFACE

This book—like the professional specialty it portrays—straddles two separate worlds: medicine and management. Both were changing appreciably during the decade spanned by this research, and it seemed a propitious time to conduct a searching inquiry into the past and potential roles of physicians in corporate settings. My interest in the subject grew out of explorations on the general theme of industry and health care conducted at the Boston University Health Policy Institute in collaboration with its director and my colleague, Richard H. Egdahl, M.D. The more clearly he and I came to understand the corporate perspective on employee health, the more puzzled—and intrigued—we became by the shadowy figure of the corporate doctor.

The exploration presented certain logistic problems that influenced the methodologic approach. I began with a general notion of a particular population I wanted to study: the "leadership" of corporate occupational medicine in the United States. I also had in mind a general problem: how did those leaders view their roles, their profession, and its future; what problems did they perceive; what solutions were they pursuing? More important, I wanted to be in a position to assess how their particular constructions of problems and solutions might be functional and dysfunctional for themselves, their profession, the clients they served, and for the public interest.

With this general task in mind, I needed to define a leadership pool and then learn as much as I could about the content of these leaders' jobs, as well as the larger context. My sample was not random but purposive, taking account of the corporate affiliation, geographical location, and reputation of possible respondents. Those I interviewed earliest suggested others who they thought would be informative, and from these recommendations I gradually accumulated my sample.

The terrain I had chosen to explore was largely uncharted. The problem might have been suitable for conventional participant observation, except that the population of interest was widely dispersed and seldom functioned as the kind of group most accessible to the participant observer. When the profession was functioning that way, in annual meetings and educational seminars, I tried as often as possible to be there. Although useful as a rough test of the external validity of information I was gleaning from interviews, observing professional meetings was seeing my subjects out of the context of their jobs, divorced from the day-to-day reality which was my principal interest.

I considered conducting a mail survey of the population or a random sample of it and even developed and pretested a comprehensive survey instrument. But I deferred, feeling that my research questions demanded a probing, interactive approach that would be difficult to build into a structured questionnaire, however administered. I needed to learn about the corporate physician's world and world-view. This I set out to do in a series of unstructured interviews, using an interview guide.

I began with a few recognized leaders in the field, probing their own experiences and concerns on the job, their views of the critical issues facing their profession as a whole, and their sense of who the other leaders were. During this stage, I also interviewed informed observers of occupational medicine from academia and organized labor and a few corporate managers to whom physicians report. Between February 1978 and October 1982, I conducted the 127 interviews listed in the appendix. They averaged about an hour and a half each and included, in 29 different firms, 37 with occupational physicians. All were employed by corporations except one university health service director and the medical director of a sizable quasi-public agency interviewed for comparison. All held full-time appointments in a single organization. Only one was a woman, and no minorities were represented. Profiles of the firms appear in the appendix.

I did not tape-record the interviews but took careful notes, which I always reviewed and augmented for transcription within hours of the interviews. The direct quotations in the text are thus reconstructed from extensive field notes. Some of my respondents would gladly have spoken for the record but others requested anonymity. For consistency and simplicity, I use pseudonyms throughout.

A little more than half of the interviews were conducted during a second phase of the research. After completing many of the exploratory interviews, I organized a conference in December 1980, including as active participants sixteen top corporate medical directors and five senior managers of corporate physicians. I wrote a background paper for that conference and subsequently synthesized the proceedings for a 1983 book entitled *Corporate Medical Departments: A Changing Agenda?* By then I had become convinced that there were underlying conflicts in corporate physicians' roles about which I was learning too little in my interviews and interactions with them. I was sure the conflicts accounted for some of the profession's acknowledged problems: difficulty in recruiting new talent, in attracting patients, and in influencing management. But I needed a more systematic way to characterize the conflicts.

I therefore set out in phase two to learn more through intensive case studies at five selected companies. They are described in the appendix. The profiles are elliptical because to gain access I assured respondents that I would reveal neither their identities nor those of their companies. Adapting techniques developed by Kahn and his coauthors (1964), I conducted a structured interview with the corporate medical director at each firm, developing in that initial interview a list of the essential people with whom he interacted in his job. Through the corporate medical director's office I then arranged meetings with these other managers and conducted structured interviews with them, each lasting about an hour. At the end of the process, usually on a second or third day-long visit to the firm, I reinterviewed the corporate medical director.

This process yielded a total of fifty-five interviews at the five firms. Safety, industrial hygiene, benefits, industrial relations, personnel, counseling, nursing, and medical staff perspectives were represented, as well as, in every case, at least one manager an echelon or more above the corporate medical director. One of the two unionized firms arranged for me to interview a labor representative; the other demurred. In the three non-union firms, I had to rely on anecdote and word of mouth to gauge the employee's perspective, which is, therefore, not well represented in the study.

The object of the interviews was to ascertain: (1) how the corporate medical director perceived his role and the potential contribution he could make to the corporation; (2) whom he felt the need to interact with in order to carry out his responsibilities; and (3) how those other "role senders" saw his role, his potential contribution, and his performance. The material in part III derives in large part from these interviews.

The approach outlined above was labor-intensive and not very efficient. In retrospect, however, I still view it as a reasonable way to have proceeded, under the circumstances. While I was conducting this study, Ralph W. Hingson at the Boston University School of Public Health and I were designing and beginning to implement a randomized controlled trial of alternative treatments for alcoholics identified on the job. For two years I moved back and forth between the two research designs— one (the randomized trial) as experimentally tight as is feasible in the social sciences, the other (the exploratory case studies) considerably looser.

Both have merits and limitations. The randomized trial is strong on internal validity but rigid and limited in its generalizability. The qualitative approach is more fluid but internally less valid. On balance it seemed to me that an exploratory study such as this one required flexibility more than elegance of design. To have fixed too early on a more sharply defined problem—for example, a single aspect of the corporate medical director's role—would have obscured the complexities that have emerged as fundamental to the role. To have narrowed the population—perhaps focusing exclusively on one industry type—would also, I believe, have simplified but diminished the study.

It was my good fortune to have gained access to a sizable number of firms in a variety of industries, each adding a new dimension to my understanding of the corporate physician's complex and changing role. Gaining that access was a challenge in itself, owing to pressures on respondents' time and their apprehensions about outside researchers. It was necessary to discover and break into a sociometric network. I made a concerted effort to win the trust of informants without compromising my independence and objectivity. I assured them that I would be fair, would protect anonymity, and would be discreet, especially when moving from person to person in a single firm.

Successful students of occupations, Hughes has written, are those who achieve a kind of "emancipation . . . a very delicate balance between detachment and involvement" (Hughes 1971:420). Maintaining that equilibrium in a field as polarized as occupational medicine was a constant struggle. At times it led me in the text to engage in careful balancing of competing perspectives. I hope, in the end, that this has been a sympathetic and perceptive treatment of the corporate physician's role, but also a critical one. At this point, it seems to me that the study as undertaken has been well suited to the sort of exploration, deep description, and analysis and hypothesis-generation that culminate in chapter 9. Testing and refining those hypotheses will call for a more formal design.

As scholars often do, I have accumulated debts of various kinds, few fully repayable. I owe a debt of gratitude to the many sources of information for this study, including but not limited to the eighty-two individuals who granted me personal interviews. Eight corporate physicians and two senior managers were, at one stage or another, especially generous in sharing their insights and experiences; Robert N. Beck, H. Dean Belk, Gilbeart Collings, Jr., Anthony A. Herrmann, Dorothea Johnson, Rebecca N. Parkinson, Norbert J. Roberts, Lloyd B. Tepper, Glen Wegner, and Leon J. Warshaw are among those I owe a debt that cannot completely be repaid.

Many academic colleagues made a difference in discussions during the course of the research. Alasdair MacIntyre, Michael Gordy, Fred K. Foulkes, and James E. Post stand out within this group. At an early stage Nicholas A. Ashford, Harvey M. Sapolsky, Deborah A. Stone, and S. M. Miller provided useful advice. Alfred M. Whittaker kindly sent me a copy of his unique book, *Occupational Health in America*, no longer in print. At another stage, Paul Starr shared relevant portions of the then unpublished manuscript of his seminal work, *The Social Transformation of American Medicine*. Willis B. Goldbeck has been a friend and teacher throughout the decade encompassed by this inquiry. Conversations with Gershon Fishbein, Leonard Glantz, George A. Goldberg, Anthony Robbins, William Patterson, Kent Peterson, and Allen Xenakis had an impact too.

Other colleagues at Boston University and elsewhere have shaped my thinking on this problem in many different ways, as have participants in our regular biannual conferences on industry and health, sponsored originally by the Robert Wood Johnson Foundation and now by the Pew Memorial Trust. William J. Bicknell, long a coworker and friend, read parts of an early draft and provided a perceptive critique. So did Peter Conrad, Frances Hanckel, Thomas Murray, Lloyd Tepper, Eve Spangler, Gladys Topkis, and Irving Zola. Fran Defren first showed me the basic construct that ultimately led to the model in figure 8.1, and the *Harvard Business Review* permitted me to reprint it from a 1982 article I published with them.

Three special mentors helped me anchor this widely ranging work in their respective disciplines: sociology, management, and medicine. They read countless drafts (some over 700 pages long) and supplied indispensable advice and counsel. Sol Levine—an extraordinary teacher, sociologist, and university professor—challenged assumptions, provoked intrapsychic debates, spun out hypotheses, offered new leads and lines of inquiry, and gave the project a shape it would never have assumed without his decisive input. Always accessible and supportive in every important way, he was also intellectually exacting. I'm not sure I consistently met the high standards he obliquely set, but the way he did it surely made me want to try. I hope his influence will endure for the rest of my career. Jules Schwartz, a professor of management policy, was a tough and intelligent reader of several drafts who was generous with his criticism and encouragement. The debts I owe Richard H. Egdahl— surgeon, biomedical researcher, academic and medical administrator, mentor, and friend—can hardly be reckoned, much less repaid. First, he made the project possible, and then he made it fun. His creative impact on the inquiry—as well as on my intellectual growth within it—has been profoundly constructive and helpful.

Polishing the many iterations of the manuscript might have consumed another decade (and produced untold angst) without the remarkable efficiency and the thoughtful ministrations of a succession of special coworkers I can never adequately thank; Lisa Stearns-Doherty, Susan Duschl Cornelius, Amy Pett, Janet Marantz, Melissa McWhinney, Maureen Shea, Maura D. Shaw Tantillo, and Sue Ware helped in myriad ways. The unique support of Antonette Doherty and Susan Kelleher has been a crucial constant in my working life for which I'm deeply grateful.

Funding from several sources, notably the Commonwealth Fund, the National Institute on Alcohol Abuse and Alcoholism, and the General Electric Foundation, has enabled me to pursue other research that has enriched my understanding of the corporate physician's world. Dan Merrigan's sensitivity and administrative skill and Ralph Hingson's energy and ingenuity prevented those other research endeavors from engulfing this one; their friendship prevented those other projects from engulfing me.

By simply assuming that I would complete anything I began, my parents have helped me do so. Last and foremost are Chris and Allison. The pseudonyms they (sometimes inadvertently) supplied are the least of it. This project disrupted and intruded on Allison's ten-year transition from toddler to teenager. Extraordinary forbearance has bespoken unflagging love. They just keep repaying me the debts that I owe them.

■ *PART ONE*
Introduction

1 ■ Challenges

Work drives a wedge of paradox into the core of modern life. At times the indispensable adhesive binding a fragile life together, at other times, like a caustic acid, work corrodes interpersonal relations and poisons the wells of identity, motivation, and self-worth. If it is often less extreme than this in its impact on individual experience, work is seldom any less central an element in the human condition. As many struggle simply to tolerate a day at a time in menial, routine, and dehumanizing jobs, nearly all workers believe at some level that work ought to be stamped with deeper meaning.

Such a belief is deeply rooted in Western thought, appearing at least as far back as the "Protestant ethic," which transforms all legitimate occupations into intrinsically valuable "vocations" (Green 1959). A belief in the redemptive quality of work, in turn, sustains the "spirit of capitalism" and, with it, modern industrial enterprise (Weber 1930). Herein lies the paradox: at one and the same time the industrial revolution moves work to the center of the moral universe but also restructures it in such a way as to render its meaning increasingly opaque. In response to this paradox, Karl Marx supplied a theory of work in which self-actualization, personal growth, responsibility, and respect can be taken as necessary desiderata for judging blue- and white-collar work no less than for evaluating the experiences of upwardly mobile careerists (Gruenberg 1980). Irrespective of ideological stripe, anyone concerned about work must confront problems variously referred to as the alienation of labor, the issue of anomie, the dilemma of job satisfaction, the quality of working life.

Two images inform these discussions of work. On the one hand, professions are the occupations that represent work at its best: intrinsically interesting, socially and financially rewarding, autonomously organized. In contrast, bureaucratic jobs are often portrayed as highly routinized,

4 ■ INTRODUCTION

ineffective, dependent, and stultifying. The modern corporation and the profession of medicine represent these two conflicting visions of work. They are also among the most intensively studied, from an extraordinarily wide range of disciplinary and ideological perspectives. Yet one intriguing nexus between these two worlds—the physicians corporations employ—has attracted remarkably little sustained and systematic attention by detached observers.[1]

Important in their own right as part of an unusual and difficult form of medical practice, the roles of company-employed physicians inform two kinds of question concerning the transcendent meaning of work. Looking back, these roles reveal problems in the relations between employer and employee. The company doctor system, historically grounded in nineteenth-century industrial welfare capitalism, has long been one of the mechanisms employers use in the social control of labor. Looking ahead, these roles foreshadow adjustments to be made in the organization of medical practice, as the solo practice system succumbs to bureaucratic forms. Predictions are now being made that by the turn of the century half or more of the nation's physicians will have become salaried workers (Rich 1986); the potential implications for the practice of medicine are just beginning to be plumbed (Starr 1982). As agents of an employer and as themselves employees, then, company doctors can tell a lot about how it is to work in the two institutions they span: the modern business enterprise and the profession of medicine.

What they tell can make a difference from a practical standpoint as well. That the profession of occupational medicine is poised at a crossroad right now will become increasingly clear as we trace the historical

---

1. Relevant writings fall into the following broad categories: (I) Textbooks and trade books on occupational medicine, of which Schilling (1981), Zenz (1975, 1980), Levy and Wegman (1983), and Rom (1983) are among the best, often include prescriptive chapters on the "role of the corporate physician." Less current but useful are Shepard (1961) and Wolf, Bruhn, and Goodell (1978). Other professionally directed trade publications that treat legal and ethical dimensions of occupational health include LaDou (1981), Lee and Rom (1982), Roberts (1978a), Ashford (1976), and Goldsmith and Kerr (1982). (II) Professional spokespersons publish on the corporate physician's role most frequently in the *Journal of Occupational Medicine*, occasionally in the *Archives of Environmental Health*. (III) Studies of occupational physicians by outside investigators are rare. Stern's 1946 work still stands as one of the most comprehensive. Goldstein and Goldstein conducted such a study in the 1960s (see Goldstein and Goldstein 1967; Goldstein, Northwood, and Goldstein 1960). More recently Vivienne Walters (1982, 1984, 1985) began publishing the results of her study of twenty-three doctors employed by ten companies in the province of Ontario. Also see a collection on "divided loyalties in medicine" organized by the Hastings Center and published in *Social Science and Medicine* 23 (1986). (IV) In addition, there are lively and large sociological literatures on professionals in organizations, the profession of medicine, and the problem of social control. The most relevant works are referenced throughout the text. (V) Finally, descriptive or journalistic treatments of the company physician's role occasionally appear in professional and popular publications. See, for example, Altman (1979), Abrams (1976), Woods (1978), Prescott (1977), and Hales (1979).

forces that have driven its past. Choices that are made in the next several years will open or foreclose important opportunities for advancing public policies in health and improving corporate management of productivity.

To hear the things that company doctors have to tell, we need to place them in theoretical and historical context, then to observe them closely as they go about their everyday work. This book attempts those tasks. It deals with all sorts of occupational physicians, but principally those in the full-time employ of large corporations: physicians dependent for their livelihood on the employer who pays their patients' salaries too. In particular, it focuses on corporate medical directors and others with different titles but comparable responsibilities at the corporate level for the development and oversight of health policies, procedures, and practices of large business firms operating multiple sites. It identifies challenges and contradictions embedded in this form of medical practice and looks for evidence of change: are there compelling reasons to anticipate that this profession's future will diverge sharply from its checkered and often desultory past?

Company physicians have been medicine's man-in-the-middle, like the shop foreman whose misfortune it is to owe allegiance to bosses above and workers below (Kahn et al. 1964:19). Foremen find ways to adapt to or manipulate their situations; corporate physicians do too. But lacking predictable rules of role, company physicians have to work at the accommodation: seldom is it as straightforward for them as it is for private physicians, whose primary obligation to their patients seems relatively clear-cut.

The difficulty of the challenge is evident in the shortage of doctors ready to take it on. Valid statistics are elusive, further signaling the specialty's orphan status; but no more than five thousand in all, less than 1 percent of all active American physicians, practice occupational medicine—a proportion that table 1.1 suggests has been declining in the past two decades with the growth in the number of physicians. Until recently it was virtually unheard of that a young physician fresh out of training would opt directly for occupational medicine, so invisible was this alternative in medical school curricula and residency programs. Within the past five years, anecdotal evidence and impressionistic accounts suggest that this has started to change. Still, occupational medicine remains a backwater, even though the full-time physicians in American corporations oversee a diversity of health programs for at least ten million employees.[2] The work is widely perceived as tedious and routine, but many examples show that it need not be so. While limitations on the content or

2. This is a very crude estimate, arrived at by tallying the total number of employees in the *Fortune* 500 companies that apparently had medical directors in 1985, based on an analysis of the membership directory of the American Occupational Medical Association.

Table 1.1
Physicians Reporting to the American Medical Association That Their Primary Medical Specialty Is Occupational Medicine

Year	Occupational physicians	As percent of all active physicians
1968	2,702	0.91
1969	2,746	0.90
1970	—	—
1971	—	—
1972	2,506	0.74
1973	2,374	0.69
1974	2,365	0.66
1975	2,555	0.63
1976	2,322	0.60
1977	2,149	0.55
1978	2,351	0.57
1979	2,356	0.57
1980	2,358	0.50
1981	2,623	0.54
1982	2,587	0.51
1983	2,648	0.50

Sources: Calculated from statistics in *Distribution and Medical Licensure in the U.S.*, annual volumes (Chicago: American Medical Association) and *Distribution of Physicians, Hospitals, and Hospital Beds in the U.S.*, annual volumes (Chicago: American Medical Association).

scope of a company physician's job have posed undeniable problems in the past, the structure, not the content, of this form of practice is the real source of strain.

The Structures of Medical Practice

In a theoretically pure form of medical practice, the physician and patient jointly pursue the goal of restoring or maintaining the patient's health; no outside interests intrude with confounding or competing goals. Contemporary medicine deviates from this ideal in at least three important ways (Mechanic 1978:114–17).

First, the financing of health services through third-party payers, a pattern established in the United States after World War II, complicates the original dyad with an additional set of interests, those of the payer. At the same time, however, insurance may in some circumstances simplify the exchange between patient and physician by removing cost as a serious constraint on the clinical disposition of the case. This enables the physician to recommend a comprehensive course of treatment without worrying about whether his patient has the wherewithal to pay.[3] The resulting incentives, however, may result in overtreatment, from which the physician may benefit financially, whether or not the patient's interests and comfort are well served.

If the payer then faces escalating costs and seeks to contain them, the physician or the patient may be held to account in some new way, but normally the two remain more or less in their original roles and in the same basic relationship. The provider's independence of the payer may be a matter of degree, and the social distance between physician and patient may be more or less wide (Bloom and Wilson 1979), but the usual arrangement extends the payer's authority little beyond paying (or refusing to pay) for a course of treatment the physician and patient have jointly negotiated, implicitly or explicitly.

In a second departure from the simple idealized model, the physician works for a bureaucratic organization (Stevens 1971; Mechanic 1976). Complex organizations have multiple goals (Perrow 1977), as do their diverse constituents. These goals may begin to encroach on a specific physician's single-minded attention to a particular patient's needs. A large urban hospital, for example, pursues missions in research and medical education that may on occasion color the clinician's assessment of the preferred course of treatment for an individual patient. The impact of any one such encroachment of a conflicting goal will vary with the circumstances and with the organization. But theorists and empirical researchers have until recently generally agreed that even in extremely bureaucratic medical organizations—where physicians may lose some

---

3. I use the masculine pronoun throughout when I need a generic one, as a convenient but not altogether satisfactory accommodation to the reality that our language is "man made" (Spender 1980). Doing so masks the important fact that several impressive women were and are leaders in this field. Alice Hamilton is the most preeminent example (see Hamilton 1943; Sicherman 1984). Her example has been followed by Harriet Hardy, a colleague of Hamilton who became a prominent occupational physician in her own right and a member of the faculty of the Massachusetts Institute of Technology (see Hardy 1983). The issue of women in occupational medicine is an interesting sidelight of this study. The field beckons women because it can be practiced on a part-time schedule or on a predictable schedule within which child-bearing and child-rearing can more easily be accommodated than is true of many other specialties. On the other hand, it is practiced in what has been a male domain, where women corporate physicians trying to gain credibility as "managers" are burdened with a double negative stereotype—as physicians and as women. Two of the physicians in this sample were women, but their perspective *as* women was not a focus of the study. It would be interesting to pursue, especially in light of the fact that where medicine is not a high-prestige specialty, as in the Soviet Union, women tend to be much more strongly represented than they are in the United States. As one of the lower-prestige medical specialties in the United States, occupational medicine would, by analogy, be expected to have more than its share of women, an empirical question this study does not address.

measure of control over the *terms* of their work (hours, space, pay, staffing, and the like)—they have tended to retain the decisive say in major judgments concerning the definition and treatment of the patient's needs, that is, in crucial aspects of the *technical* content of work.[4]

The institution's ancillary goals, moreover, usually relate in some way to the medical-care mission, which is generally expected to retain preeminence in the organization's value structure. In true conflict, the physician, therefore, should theoretically tilt toward the individual patient, who is believed also to have the market protection of the freedom to choose (himself or through an intermediary) whether, when, and where to seek out a physician's service and to accept or reject the advice proffered (Freidson 1970a). He has recourse to "exit," if not always to "voice" (Hirschman 1970). This holds even in managed care systems (such as health maintenance organizations) where he has the opportunity, once a year, to express his displeasure and disenroll from a health plan that has been in some way less than satisfactory.

The third and most radical departure from the original two-party relationship occurs when medicine is practiced in the service of an organization whose principal function is entirely nonmedical. While many contemporary physicians practice in settings nearly or fully as bureaucratic as a modern corporation, few are integral members of an organization whose overriding mission or manifest function is something other than—even at times antithetical to—health and health-care delivery. This ancillary status is the problem facing physicians in occupational medicine: military medicine, sports and aviation medicine, and corporate occupational practice. They, more than other physicians in the United States, occupy a force field in which it must be asked whether pressures from the organizations they serve rival or outweigh pressures from the profession they represent. From this it would seem to follow that physicians' practice settings can be arrayed along a simple hypothetical continuum, with organizational norms dominant at one pole and professional norms at the other.[5] On such a continuum, the full-time practice of medicine in a corporation would be expected to fall near the organizational pole. In solo or small group practice, even in increasingly bureaucratic medical delivery systems, the basic mission is patient care, more or less attenuated by the survival demands of the organization and its personnel. In the corporation, by contrast, the basic mission is profit, and a secondary medical mission must seek a management rationale.

    4. Freidson (1970a), Larson (1977), Spangler (1986), and others make this distinction. Charles Derber explores it deeply in the contrast he draws between the "post-industrial thesis" concerning the role of the organizational professional and the "proletarianization thesis" (Derber 1982).
    5. I am indebted to Sol Levine for suggesting this formulation.

In the analogous if perhaps somewhat more extreme case of military psychiatry, Daniels found that the "priorities and values of the military system become the crucial factor" defining practice (Daniels 1969, 1972, 1975). They convert the psychiatrist into an "impersonal administrator, responsible *for* the welfare of patients, rather than *to* the patient himself" (1972:147), and even distort the practitioner's basic theoretical understanding of psychopathology. The military psychiatrist develops a theory of practice (known as "combat psychiatry") that minimizes a soldier's psychiatric symptoms and strongly enjoins him to adapt to the situation, ostensibly for his own good. Since the "spread of symptomatology" through an army could have serious repercussions for a war effort, this theory provides a rationale that shields military psychiatrists from conflict with their employing organization.

Although tailored to the exigencies of war, the theory is generalized to peacetime circumstances and is communicated by military psychiatrists in their normal consultations throughout the organization. These adaptations, Daniels argues, render military psychiatrists "unfit in many ways for traditional practice" among civilians (1972:146), although psychiatrists face "similar organizational pressures" in hospitals, prisons, and schools (Murray 1986; Toulmin 1986; Arnstein 1986; Gellman 1986; Callahan and Gaylin 1978).

If conflicts of interest become more overt as one moves along the continuum away from the professional pole, it would be an oversimplification to portray the physician's professional norms as necessarily standing in opposition to the organization's controls. As Daniels's military psychiatrists reveal, and as Derber has cogently argued, "the sustaining of a distinct professional reference group is not necessarily incompatible with a complete acquiescence to or identification with organizational goals," a process he labels "ideological cooptation" (Derber 1982:185).

Adopting a circumscribed organizational persona offers a way to deal with the conflict in a situation that would otherwise be intolerably ambiguous. Joseph Ben-David showed in his study of Israeli physicians in bureaucratic organizations that the role conflicts were palpable enough to influence decisions about practice style. The subset of his sample who were "satisfied" used devices to wall off the conflict. They "tried to create for themselves a closed circle of their 'own' patients" or emphasized "the scientific nature of their work" within the context of the organization's demands (Ben-David 1958:263).

This issue of the tension between professional and organizational norms is generic to professional practice within bureaucratic organizations. In a study of military chaplains, Burchard looked for and found signs of role conflict in the incompatibility between their calling and the military's mission. Some argued away the conflicting elements, while others compartmentalized the incongruent behaviors in which they were forced to engage, refusing to recognize the conflict at all. Both devices enabled them to accept the organization's ultimate ends (Burchard 1954:528–35). Kaplan reviewed writings on scientists in organizations and saw "tension between organizational controls and the scientists' traditional emphasis on autonomy" as a central theme in the literature. The typical response, the studies reported, was for scientists to "become acculturated to the goals and interests of their organization" (Kaplan 1965:95).

The issue is growing in importance because, as Everett Hughes predicted, the "superegos" of professions have been moving into complex organizations (1965:12). During the first half of the twentieth century, the number of professionals on salary increased by an order of ten, almost three times the growth rate in the overall supply of professionals of all kinds (Derber 1982:5). Only recently, however, have physicians as a group begun to exhibit a marked trend toward salaried practice. As concerns are raised about what this may portend for the medical profession, occupational medical practice stands out as one of few long-established examples from which relevant lessons can be drawn. Occupational medicine, in turn, is best understood in the larger context of professionalism in large organizations.

Professionals in Organizations

The problem of professional practice within a bureaucracy has a long lineage of scholarship originating with the premise that professionals would bring to organizations a set of externally derived standards and norms as a guide to their practice (Parsons 1951) and that these would clash with the need of all complex organizations to assure "dependency of role performance" by requiring certain behaviors (Kahn et al. 1964: 13). Trained to think and act independently and (in some cases) licensed individually by the state, professionals were presumed to give up some autonomy in agreeing to serve an employer's goals and adapt to organizational standards of conduct.

Although early sociologists saw professionalization as antithetical to bureaucratic forms of control (Scott 1966), more recent writers have begun to portray professions and bureaucracies as quite compatible in many ways (Davies 1983; Larson 1977). In calling attention to Max Weber's largely overlooked views on professions, Ritzer (1975) shows that for Weber bureaucratization and professionalization were mutually reinforcing factors rationalizing life in the West. American scholars, Ritzer argues, have been overly influenced by the special (and "in many ways aberrant") case of the physician in private practice.

Empirical studies have focused on the disaffection felt by scientists and engineers in industry (Marcson 1960; Kornhauser 1963; Bailyn and Schein 1980; Larson 1977) and have documented tensions over the selection of research projects, especially when the scientist wants to pursue questions too basic to serve the immediate financial interests of his firm. Industrial engineers, like military psychiatrists, tend to skirt these conflicts by recasting their professional goals in terms of the organization's needs (Goldner and Ritti 1967; Larson 1977). These rationalizations can become quite elaborate, as one study showed in its examination of the moral detachment developed by a group of military scientists and engineers during the Vietnam War (Shevitz 1979).

Although there are certainly parallels to corporate medical directors in the situations of engineers and other industrial scientists, the latter group has the advantage that its expertise fits in the organization's "technical core" (Thompson 1967), where it produces its products. Those who write about the "proletarianization" of free professionals argue that engineers have always been creatures of large organizations; as a group they never developed much of a cottage industry of their own and never fully controlled the products and the processes of their labor (Derber 1982). In her definitive study of the rise of professionalism, Larson (1977) uses engineering to illustrate the organizationally subordinated profession in its extreme form. Partly for this reason, chemists and other research scientists in industry were, in early sociological writings on the subject, considered "professionals" only in a loose sense of that term. More recently it has been acknowledged that many professionals in the United States and most in Europe have long been employees (Dingwall and Lewis 1983).

Definitions of a profession by American sociologists have emphasized the power aspect: the privileged status of the "free" or "consulting" professional in relation to organizations and the state. This special status derives from certain features distinguishing professions from other occupations: an esoteric body of knowledge, mastered through prolonged and rigorous training, and an implied "avowal or promise" (Freidson 1970a) to serve the broad public interest. Medicine and law are the two classic cases.

Studies of corporate lawyers have stressed conflicts of interest associated with difficulty identifying the specific client within the corporation—the individual who embodies or can stand in for the corporation-as-client, thus the one to whom inside counsel owes ultimate allegiance (Auerbach 1984). Like industrial engineers, staff counsel become "company men through and through" (Spangler 1986:70). Their status is low relative to the outside legal profession, and they practice a kind of "preventive law," advising management on inchoate situations too trivial to warrant the expense of outside counsel, which often feel like a waste of their professional time (Spangler 1986). In this and other respects that will become clear, they strongly resemble company physicians. Still, medicine has characteristics that set it apart.

Medicine has long enjoyed the status in American sociology of the quintessential profession: the one that provides the blueprint for members of aspiring occupations to consult in designing "professional projects" to upgrade their own status (Wilensky 1964). More than the other two traditional professions (law and the ministry), medicine draws strength from a close association with modern science and technology and exhibits a complex division of labor, a pyramid atop which physicians are said to sit in an unchallenged position of dominance (Freidson 1970b).

Not so in corporate medical practice. There, to a degree unimaginable in the most bureaucratic of hospitals or health institutions, the physician is accountable to an employer. This employer can exert legitimate control over the physician's own conduct as well as over that of his patients, and indirectly through him, over them. Indirect control is exerted, for example, when an employee's health status becomes an issue in his employer's decisions about his future with the firm. The situation complicates the roles of both physician and patient. The physician-employee may at times have to balance interests of his patients against those of his employer; the worker-patient may at times have to weigh concerns about his health against the value of his job (Goldstein and Goldstein 1967; Walters 1985).

Occupational Medicine as an Agency of Social Control

To the third party in this situation (the employer) is now attached a web of intersecting relationships centered around what Kingsley Davis (1949) describes as the "property rights" through which an employer may claim "the right to demand certain kinds of behavior" from his employees. As a consequence, the purely volitional quality in the patient's seeking of help (and the physician's proffering it) cannot always be assumed, an observation that has led the courts in the past repeatedly to conclude that there is no effective physician-patient relationship in the occupational setting.[6]

---

6. Belair (1981) reviews the court record. Courts in California, Maryland, Michigan, Minnesota, New York, Ohio, Texas, and Washington "have held that occupational physicians and their employee/patients do not have a doctor-patient relationship or, at the least, do not have the normal doctor-patient relationship. To date, not one reported decision has held that occupational physicians and their employee/patients have a doctor-patient relationship" (123–24). Also see U.S. Department of Labor 1980b:35234–35.

No matter what degree of rectitude individual occupational physicians are able to exhibit, the structure of occupational medicine subjects its practitioners to competing, and occasionally contradictory, expectations. It divides the loyalty of corporate physicians and gives them coercive authority over their patients, something most other professionals lack in their dealings with clients. Whether and how they exercise that authority is an empirical question, but that they possess it is theoretically irrefutable, and empirically available. Formal company policy statements often make direct or oblique reference to a disciplinary role for the medical department. The following drug abuse policy illustrates the direct approach:

> If a supervisor has a reasonable basis for suspecting drug use because of an employee's behavior on the job, or if an employee admits to or is observed being a user off the job but is not subject to dismissal under this policy, the employee should be referred to the medical department for examination. Should the employee refuse to visit the medical department, the supervisor must point out that such refusal constitutes insubordination and the employee may be subject to disciplinary action.[7]

A more oblique recognition of the medical department's disciplinary function is contained among the formal operating principles of another company's occupational health and safety program. After stating, as a first principle, that "the professional staff should be ethical, capable, and alert to advances in medicine and changes in the social, legal, and economic aspects of medical care," the document goes on to recommend to operating units that "the participation of employees in the health maintenance program shall be on a voluntary basis wherever this is compatible with their own safety and that of others, as well as with applicable legal regulations." It is the occasional incompatibility of voluntarism with these overriding considerations that can draw the medical program into a coercive role or can place the individual's needs in the penumbra of larger organizational purpose.

For occupational medicine, this intrusion of organizational needs creates what has been termed the problem of "dirty work." Everett Hughes (1962) observed that every occupation has certain dirty work that must be done. Those who do it are often isolated from the occupational mainstream, to exonerate the "good people" from responsibility for the dirty work carried out in their midst. This may provide a clue to the historical isolation of industrial physicians.

One kind of dirty work from which the profession of medicine needs

---

7. This and the quotation in the next paragraph are quoted directly from corporate policies, given me on the condition that I not reveal the names of the companies.

to distance itself, in order to protect the patient-oriented value system it projects to win public trust, is "social control" work. Parsons (1951) recognized that social control is an integral function of medicine, especially where more direct political and legal sanctions cannot be invoked. Medicine has "an officially approved monopoly on the right to define illness" (Freidson 1970a:5), and illness, once legitimized, confers on the sick person privileges and exemptions from normal social responsibilities. "The physician often serves as a court of appeal, as well as a direct legitimizing agent" (Parsons 1951:436). Lest physicians be tainted as agents of social control, the institution of medicine assumes the ideological position that the individual patient's welfare always come first in the ethical clinician's mind.

But the structure of corporate medicine removes this ideological veil. The industrial physician's clear accountability—not only to an individual patient but also to a corporate employer—brings his social-control role into full view. He may be called upon, for example, to make a medical determination on which will hinge the decision whether an employee will receive some kind of "secondary gain" (Parsons 1951) (such as early retirement with disability payments) or suffer some kind of penalty (such as reassignment to a less desirable job, or outright termination). Allegations have been made that employers have on occasion altered a worker's job status on fictional medical grounds.[8] Even without this clear breach of the profession's ethical code, the corporate physician's necessary involvement in the application of a medical yardstick to decisions in the employment context places him in a situation unlike that of the private practitioner, a situation in which he has "coercive sanctions at [his] command" (Parsons 1951). These are the situations that typically ignite complaints from representatives of unions or special interest groups that corporate physicians are "indentured" (Nader 1973:xi), that they "fail to make common cause with the worker" and are "tools of the boss" (Samuels, 1977:153), and that the "ghettoized" (Berman 1978:5) "company doctor system" ought to be entirely replaced with one in which the physician serves at the behest of the employee, not the employer (Glasser 1976; Mazzocchi 1981).

In these situations, the conflict is close to the surface. A deeper problem for occupational medical practice—still related to social control—

---

8. The hearing record for the Occupational Safety and Health Administration's rulemaking on a right-to-access regulation includes a reference to this practice (see U.S. Department of Labor 1980:35226). In a textbook on occupational medicine, the former corporate medical director of Metropolitan Life Insurance Company confronts the issue head on: "It must also be admitted, to our great embarrassment, that under the older concept, the physician was sometimes expected by the employer to find medical reasons to disqualify those suspected of being 'troublemakers'" (Shepard 1961:16–17).

arises from the possibility that the only moral justification for anything less than full protection of an individual employee's health is the utilitarian calculus, foreign to the clinical ideal, of a greater good for a greater number: the unemployment or the loss of a socially useful product that could result from closing a high-risk industrial operation. A poignant articulation of this perspective was offered by a victim of angiosarcoma, a rare liver disease associated with occupational exposure to vinyl chloride. Approaching death, Pete Gettlefinger interpreted his own fate in a utilitarian framework:

> I think about this a lot—it's helped me a whole lot—the fact that we got 6,500 guys in the United States makin' a livin' workin' with polyvinyl chloride ... and a million ... makin' a livin' in plastics. And I feel that our industry must survive. ... It has economically given millions of people things that they couldn't have. If it wasn't for plastics, now, the price of wood would be so expensive that the average man couldn't afford to have a rockin' chair like this one. ... And, yet, that's killin' people. It may kill me. Look how much safer it's made an automobile or at the safety features in the home. So far now they only got 28 dead. ... It's so important for the industry to survive—for the employees that work with it. You've got to look at everyone's viewpoint. I can't say that I'm one of the lucky guys, but I must say that as long as we have put products on the market that has helped the average person economically—that must be weighed against all that's bad too (Agran 1977:51–52).

Even if the good should outweigh the bad in this balancing of incommensurables, the risk falls inequitably on a subset of those who may enjoy the benefit. In this context, occupational medical programs can be conceived, cynically perhaps but not unreasonably, as serving the function of "cooling out the mark," in Goffman's (1952) brilliant metaphor. Cooling out the mark (the victim of a confidence game) involves an effort to keep his anger "within manageable and sensible proportions." This is accomplished by guiding him to a definition of the situation that "makes it easy for him to accept the inevitable and quietly go home. The mark is given instruction in the philosophy of taking a loss" (Goffman 1952:99). Gettlefinger spoke like a mark who had been cooled out, and the account of his final months makes clear that his equanimity came in large part from his conviction that "I've got the best [doctors] doin' their best. What else could they do?" (Agran 1977:50).

To the extent that the cooling-out task does fall to the corporate physician, even if only indirectly or symbolically, it both violates basic notions about medicine's curative role (its manifest function) and vulgarizes one of its most powerful latent functions, countering what Powles calls "the existential threat that disease poses to the individual" (Powles 1974). "Through explanation, ritual, and symbols—those doctor-patient interactions which do not alter the course of events but which both parties nevertheless feel to be worthwhile—the patient's situation is defined, ambiguity is reduced, and reassurance—as doctors call it—results" (Powles 1974:36). A fine line separates Powles's "helping-to-cope" side of medicine, oriented toward mitigating the patient's worry and suffering, from Goffman's "cooling-out" side, oriented instead toward deflecting the mark's justified sense of outrage to minimize his disruptiveness. Helping to cope serves the patient; cooling out serves the operation (or the organization). But it is the need to draw this line on a case-by-case basis that has created many of the conflicts in the corporate physician's role.

The structure of occupational medicine raises in bold relief the issue of social control of deviant behavior through the agency of modern medicine. But it also raises a corollary issue concerning the social control of medical work—that is, the issue of professional autonomy. If medicine is one agency through which employers control the behavior of their employees, how is control exerted over the behavior of the physicians who are serving to some extent as agents of the employer's control?

Social Control of Medical Work

Nearly all studies tracing the movement of professionals into organizations arrive at control of their work as a central concern. Questions that emerge from the literature speak fundamentally to control: how much autonomy do organizational professionals have, how much authority and power, who sets priorities for them, defines the terms, conditions, and even the content of their work, how much influence can they exercise inside the organization, and how much visibility and mobility can they retain on the outside?

Derber (1982) reviews this literature and extracts two opposing theories that lead to very different predictions about what the future may hold. "Postindustrial" theory (Bell 1973) sees professionals accreting exceptional power. Theorists from diverse perspectives share this general view of professionals as a rising "new class" (Gouldner 1978), in some visions basically benign in its social impact (Bell 1973; Galbraith 1967), in others more malign (Gouldner 1978; Illich 1975, 1977; Lasch 1978), but in all seen as a new governing elite in possession of what the new economic order makes the most strategic commodity: technical knowledge and expertise. The second theoretical construct frontally contradicts the first. It holds that professionals are being gradually "proletarianized," reduced to wage laborers, "increasingly subordinate, like any other workers, to their employers" (Derber 1982:3; McKinlay 1982). By specifying different types of "proletarianization" (ideological versus technical), Derber finds a middle course between the two extremes. He argues that organizational professionals lose ideological control over their work (that is, they accept the organization's ends) but for the most part retain control in the technical domain (that is, maintain the ability to select the means). Still he grants that a great deal remains to be learned about "the meaning and implications of the new dependent employment for the organization and identity of professional workers" (1982:167). A problem that continues to cloud the picture is how precisely to define the concept of control. The corporate physician's special situation reveals where traditional definitions have fallen short.

Sociology has developed two basic conceptions of the social control of physicians' work. Neither one alone fully captures the complexities of occupational medicine. The first emphasizes the socialization of recruits entering the profession. Embodied in the seminal work of Merton, Reader, and Kendall (1957), this perspective was employed and at the same time challenged in the work of Becker and his colleagues (1961), showing that behavior is as situationally specific as it is socialized. Recently extended again by Bosk (1979), the socialization perspective is no longer an either-or proposition but does presume that at least some of what goes on during a physician's training stays with him or her and shapes subsequent behavior throughout an entire career.

As an exemplary contribution to this line of research, Bosk's study illustrates both the strengths and the weaknesses of the approach. It uses ethnographic techniques to examine the ways in which senior surgeons recognize and correct the errors young physicians make during a period of indoctrination. In setting the stage, Bosk identifies the confusion he says has weakened previous research on social control, owing to a failure to distinguish among different types of control. To clarify the concept, he discusses two dimensions of control, its formality and its locus (internal versus external), and arranges these in a four-way matrix or typology of social control.

This typology is helpful but leaves in shadow a problem that comes to light in the corporate physician's situation. "Internal control" in Bosk's scheme is internal either to the individual practitioner or to some undefined reference group. This ambiguity takes care of itself in the closed system of Bosk's inquiry. His group consists quite simply of the house staff and attending physicians on two surgical wards of an urban medical center he calls "Pacific Hospital." Bosk skillfully examines the process through which the younger surgeons learn to conform to group standards or face sanctions, the severity of which reflects the perceived seriousness of the particular "technical" or "normative" error. Bosk's most striking finding is that the more damaging errors are not the narrow "technical" ones but the breaches of "normative standards of dedication, interest, and thoroughness" (Bosk 1979:190). Normative failure is the surest way a young surgeon can jeopardize his long-term career prospects, by signaling to the attending physicians that he is ethically unfit. Otherwise, the controls Bosk discovers are relatively mild (hence the book's title, *Forgive and Remember*) and are observed to function only within the confines of the training period. They may appear formally or informally, internally or externally, but they influence the physician's long-term performance only to the extent that he internalizes them. Internalized rules are the essential mechanism of the "socialization" school.

The danger of counting too much on these internal controls becomes evident when one begins to speculate on what guideposts Bosk's physicians would take from their experience at Pacific Hospital if they were then to move on to a basically different practice situation, such as a corporate medical department. Would any of the Pacific rules apply in this different setting? If not, what would be the source of controls on professional performance? The fact that very few physicians train specifically for corporate practice (the vast majority enter the specialty in mid-career)[9] makes this more than idle speculation.

A shortcoming of the Bosk formulation, resting as it does on the influence of the immediate work group, is that work groups can be both ambiguous and ephemeral. To be sure, the controls applied during a period of indoctrination may endure for a time. Some may even influence permanent career tracks. But whether they can be expected to generalize into a lifetime of professional performance is a sociological issue Berger states well: "Identities are socially bestowed. They must also be socially sustained, and fairly steadily so" (Berger 1963:100).

The reigning alternative to the "socialization" approach dwells on the sustaining social structure that holds identities in place. Parsons developed the structural paradigm for viewing medical care; his theories have been refined by Freidson, among others. Bosk faults Freidson (together with his followers in the "professional dominance" school) for giving short shrift to "the substantial amount of control that is built into the system through socialization, work routines, and normal relations with colleagues" (Bosk 1979:21). Parsons's structural functionalism highlighted norms as control mechanisms, but Freidson (1970a) is more interested in explaining how a profession remains autonomous, how it manages to escape meaningful control from the outside society. He views autonomy as a profession's "most strategic and treasured characteristic," indeed the *sine qua non* supporting an occupation's claim to professional status. Freidson shows how the profession of medicine won this autonomy when the state conferred on it formal legal authority in return for an "avowal or promise" to engage in self-regulation. Social control at the

---

9. This statement rests mostly on anecdotal information. For a discussion of career patterns and choices, see chapter 9. Also see Walters (1982), whose data support this point.

macro-social level is waived in favor of control on a slightly lower plane, under the aegis of a profession as an organizational entity. It has recourse on this plane only to coarsely discriminating controls (certification of training and licensure of individuals), which provide one-time standards for training and admission to practice but serve poorly as concrete criteria against which to measure individual performance on a continuous basis.

Only at a lower level of analysis, where smaller-sized groups work in everyday settings, does Freidson find physicians actually exerting effective control of performance through informal policies of referral and boycott. While these policies enable practitioners to keep their own referral networks clean and to protect their own patients, they fall short of fulfilling the profession's social contract to monitor the integrity of overall practice and protect an uncritical public.

Again, the case of the corporate physician stretches this formulation. Freidson explicitly limits his attention to medicine as a consulting profession (as distinct from a learned one). Consulting professions depend for their survival on attracting clients "by providing services that are expected to solve problems." These clients may come through different gates. Specialists rely on their colleagues to send them referrals, while general practitioners count on word-of-mouth from satisfied customers. Their two types of practice, then, are colleague- and client-controlled, but the ability to attract clients is the universal criterion. Boycott and referral serve as effective control mechanisms because in order to survive economically, physicians must attract clients. Corporate occupational medicine introduces a different dimension. The corporate physician is not dependent for his livelihood on attracting and holding a patient population. But he is still a consulting professional, still expected to solve problems. The basic question becomes who is the client—that is, whose problems is the professional there to solve? To colleague- and client-control is now added the possibility of various types of organizational control.

To embrace these complexities in the concept of social control, further elaboration is needed along the lines that Bosk began. His "internal controls" may be intrapsychic or internal to the individual (acquired through socialization); they may emanate from a small work group (as he observed at Pacific Hospital); they may be internal to a specialty group of the larger profession, located outside the immediate organization in which the work takes place; or they may be even more diffuse professional controls, and nevertheless be "internal" to the professional group, in Bosk's and Freidson's sense of the self-imposed controls of an autonomous occupational group. The external controls are the residual category, depending on how widely the group is defined, but including, at a minimum, political or economic controls imposed from outside the profession, through formal or informal regulatory mechanisms. To unravel the interaction in occupational medicine between professional and organizational controls, the problem must be addressed not only in the context of day-to-day work routines—the material Bosk and other ethnographers develop so well—but also in the broader professional and sociopolitical context analyzed so effectively by structuralists such as Freidson. This, then, is the task at hand.

Part II of this book places occupational medicine in historical context, with special reference to ways in which sociopolitical and professional developments have imposed external controls on the context and scope of practice. In chapter 4 I describe the institution of occupational medicine and the structure and organization of corporate practice in its contemporary form. Part III moves in closer for a more detailed view of the corporate physician's work. It begins with a conceptual model that classifies the work of corporate physicians into four major sectors of activity: two medical, two managerial. Subsequent chapters develop the sectors individually, emphasizing differences in the demands they make, the controls they impose on the work of company physicians, and the degree to which they engage these physicians as agents of the organization's control over other employees. Part IV concludes with inferences for theory and practice.

The empirical research on which much of the analysis draws involved fifty-six months of formal data collection, in a series of 127 face-to-face interviews with 37 highly placed physicians practicing in 29 American corporations. The companies ranged in number of employees from under 4,000 to over 400,000, but averaged over 72,000. Those companies that appeared on the *Fortune* 500 listing were all ranked among the top 250 in total dollar sales in 1982, and 7 ranked among the top 10. They represented a wide range of industry types.

Interviews were held also with other relevant representatives of management, labor, the government, and academia, both during the early exploratory phase of the research and as part of a second phase involving intensive case studies. These were conducted at 5 firms, ranging in size from 17,000 to 200,000 employees, producing, among other major products, metals and metal products, chemicals and photographic equipment, office equipment, computers, and energy. For the case studies, interviews were conducted with representatives of all the major disciplines or functional units involved in corporate health programming. The object was to characterize as fully as possible the role pressures, conflicting expectations, and sources of external control being brought to bear on the corporate medical director in the course of his work. Respondents sharing this sensitive information were assured confidentiality for themselves and their firms; this material appears in the text chiefly as anonymous or pseudonymous quotations.

Although the formal aspect of the research ended in 1983, frequent ongoing interactions with numerous corporate physicians have continued to suggest new insights and extensions of the analysis. The study thus spans a decade from 1977 to 1987 and captures the world of the corporate physician through that ten-year window. The world it captures is parochial in other ways as well. The sample was skewed, intentionally but not systematically, in favor of companies with a strong reputation in employee health. A beginning hypothesis of the study was that conditions seemed right for a fundamental redefinition of the central roles and missions of corporate occupational physicians. With this in mind, I thought it made sense to try to find leaders who might be charting a new course. At the same time, however, in the hope of avoiding a seriously distorted view, I conducted interviews in some corporations that paid less attention to health, and made an effort to attend a representative sample of the profession's conventions and meetings. That a parallel study, conducted in Canada by Vivienne Walters, reached a number of conclusions corroborating findings reported here offers reassurance that the findings are not entirely idiosyncratic (Walters 1982, 1984, 1985).

Nevertheless, it must be emphasized that an exploratory study designed in this way will produce tentative conclusions still needing validation in more systematic studies. And the findings will be limited in their generalizability. They cannot be expected to apply to other large firms not included in the sample or to the many smaller firms that employ the majority of American workers. For their importance to workers' health, these smaller, less prosperous, lower-profile employers are of substantially greater concern than are the affluent, public-relations–minded largest corporations. So this study speaks only indirectly to the broad policy question of how American industry in general can and should organize to protect the health of American workers.

Nor can the findings be read as an exoneration of corporate conduct with respect to employee health. The extensive and blistering literature on the more general topic of corporate accountability for the harm arising out of work stands apart from the present study and should be evaluated on its own terms.[10] There are growing numbers of documented cases, and even some criminal prosecutions, in which crucial health in-

---

10. Among the better-known works criticizing corporate conduct vis-à-vis employees' health are Agran (1977), Berman (1977, 1978), Brodeur (1974, 1977), Davidson (1970), Epstein (1978), Goldsmith and Kerr (1982), Mancuso (1976), Page and O'Brien (1973), Randall and Solomon (1977), Stellman (1977), Stellman and Daum (1973), Stone (1975, 1977), Wallick (1972), and Yodaiken and Robbins (1980).

INTRODUCTION

Table 1.2
The Preeminent Corporate Employers[a] of Physicians

Company	Full-time physicians[b]	Employees[c]	Industry type
General Motors Co.	114(63)[d]	750,000[e]	Automobile
AT&T	80(19)[d]	332,000	Communications
E.I. Dupont	70	108,000	Chemical
IBM Corp.	52	250,000	Communications
Ford Motor Co.	45	165,000	Automobile
General Electric Co.	44	220,000	Aircraft/electronics
Eastman Kodak	33	79,000	Chemical
Chrysler	26	122,900	Automobile
Exxon	22	66,000	Oil/petrochemical
Metropolitan Life	21	36,000	Insurance
Mobil Oil	17	38,000	Oil/petrochemical
Allied-Signal	16	106,000	Chemical
Dow Chemical	15[f]	49,800[j]	Chemical
Boeing	14	95,000	Aircraft
Caterpillar Tractor	14	38,000	Machinery
American Cyanamid	14	22,300	Chemical
Union Carbide	14[f]	98,400[j]	Chemical
United Technologies	13	125,000	Aircraft/electronics
Chevron	13	41,400	Oil/petrochemical
Amoco	12(16)[d]	40,700	Oil/petrochemical
ARCO	12	35,000	Oil/petrochemical
New York Telephone	12[f]	—[g]	Communications
U.S. Steel (now USX)	12[f]	88,800[j]	Metals
ALCOA	10	27,000	Metals
Shell Oil	9	35,000	Oil/petrochemical
ITT	8[f]	110,000	Conglomerate
Monsanto	8	50,000	Chemical
Bethlehem Steel	8	33,000	Metals
Westinghouse Electric	8[f]	126,000[j]	Electronics
Mountain Bell	7[f]	—[g]	Communications
Proctor & Gamble	6	44,000[g]	Consumer products
Reynolds Metals	6	25,000	Metals
Conoco	6[f]	—[g]	Oil/petrochemical
FMC Corp.	6[f]	27,100[j]	Machinery
Upjohn Co.	5	15,000	Pharmaceutical
Illinois Bell	4[h]	20,000	Communications
Rohm & Haas	2[h](25)[d]	8,000	Chemical

Summary by industry type	Companies	Physicians
Automobile	3	185
Chemical	8	172

Table 1.2 (*continued*)

Summary by industry type	Companies	Physicians
Communications	5	155
Other[i]	4	120
Oil/petrochemical	7	91
Aircraft/electronics	4	79
Metals	4	36
Machinery	2	20
Totals	37	858

a. A short manpower survey was sent in summer 1986 to corporate medical directors of the 37 American companies with more than five U.S.-based physicians listed as members of the American Occupational Medical Association, 1986 membership directory. Of those, 31 replied.

b. Except when otherwise noted, the number of full-time physicians is that reported by the corporate medical director in response to the survey in summer 1986.

c. U.S. employees, unless otherwise specified, as reported in the survey.

d. Number in parentheses is part-time physicians employed on a regular basis (four or more hours/week).

e. Includes Canadian employees.

f. Nonrespondent to survey; number of physicians is tallied from AOMA directory.

g. Not available.

h. Included in survey because AOMA directory listed more than 5 physicians.

i. Consumer products, conglomerate, insurance, pharmaceutical.

j. Number of employees taken from *Fortune* (April 29, 1985); it may be the case that employees working outside the U.S. are included in this figure.

formation was withheld from employees, study results were suppressed or distorted, and workers were deliberately deceived by company-employed experts. There are cases, too, of complicity by company doctors in their employers' censorship of information and callous disregard for workers' health (U.S. Department of Labor 1980b; Magnuson 1978; Brodeur 1974, 1986; Page and O'Brien 1973). This study sheds little light on the extent of those abuses, which do, however, contribute to the stigma that all corporate physicians have had to carry.

Despite these inevitable limitations, a study focusing on some of the leading corporations in America has overriding advantages for understanding the roles company physicians can and do play. On this question, it can be argued, it is the behemoths that count. As table 1.2 reveals, sizable companies that dominate economic and political life are the ones that employ the largest numbers of corporate occupational physicians. They exercise the greatest care in selecting qualified candidates and offer them not only generous compensation packages but also opportunities for professional development and interaction with medical peers

(Walters 1985:69). It is therefore safe to assert that if the giant corporations and the physicians in their employ cannot work out a mutual accommodation, no one will. For policy we need to know how this accommodation can be reached, and with what effect on the major interests at stake—employees, unions, employers, stockholders, the medical profession, and the public. For theory we want to ask who accommodates and controls whom, what forces are decisive in the existing balance of power, and what the preconditions would be for significant change to occur. Is the past prologue, and if so, how?

PART TWO
A Profession Evolving

2 ■ Origins and Evolutionary Threads

A specialty of occupational medicine began to coalesce in the United States during the 1900s, an epiphenomenon of the safety and health movement promoting worker's compensation laws to cushion the impact of rising industrial accident rates (Somers and Somers 1954). These rates had been building momentum from the close of the Civil War, followed as it was by a wrenching burst of industrial development (MacLaury 1981). The legal and organizational roots of the movement for industrial safety reached back into nineteenth-century Europe and the gradual social and political awakening, initially with England's industrial revolution, to the plight of factory workers, particularly women and children.

The intellectual and scientific ancestry of occupational medicine dated back to ancient times, when concern tended to center on "aristocratic hygiene," not the health "of those who had to work for a living" (Rosen 1958:37), least of all that of the slaves who performed the most degrading and dangerous jobs (Schilling 1981:3).

It has taken a continuous interplay of industrial development, scientific observation, and political intervention to shape modern occupational medical practice and the still stunted roles available to physicians within corporations. War has been a wild card. It attracts attention to the conservation of scarce manpower in order that industrial production can be sustained while much of the workforce has gone to the front. And the rehabilitation of injured soldiers brings into national prominence another of the occupational physician's preoccupations: returning workers to their jobs. Upsurges in the economy, when they create labor shortages, as well as periods of labor organizing and unrest foster a climate more favorable to investments in either conserving or seeming to show concern for the health of people at work.

This combination of driving forces underscores the very slow and cyclical pattern of progress in the field. Technological changes alter the nature of work, creating new hazards, which are eventually recognized by medical science, itself diversifying both technologically and organizationally. Social reformers bring the dangers to public attention, and legislation generally follows in due course, but seldom quickly, owing to the resistance it engenders from powerful vested interests. The legislation attempts to enlarge the employer's accountability for the health hazards of work, and the social response reflects a given context of both ideologies and organizational capabilities in management and in medicine and prevailing notions about the proper role of government in the two spheres.

The interwoven threads in the evolution of occupational medicine can be said, broadly speaking, to form two central strands. One is medical. It includes both the scientific understanding of the associations between work and health and the social organization of the medical enterprise. The second is managerial. It includes technological and economic transformations in the form and content of work, as well as protean conceptions of the social accountability of an employer for the impact of the business enterprise on the health of its employees, and sometimes on the wider community as well.

To inquire seriously into the history of occupational medicine in the United States is to confront the inescapable conclusion that progress has been painfully slow. The balance of power has always weighed strongly on the employer's side, and barriers to effective action have much more often been political and economic than technical or scientific (Smith 1986).

The central threads in occupational medicine can be traced through five reasonably discrete but overlapping periods. These followed a longer "precursor" period during which rudimentary scientific and legal foundations were laid before the United States exhibited a serious interest in health and safety at work.

Limited interest began to stir in a period, commencing around the turn of the century, when a few firms hired surgeons to treat victims of industrial accidents. This was just prior to the agitation for worker's compensation laws, modeled on developments in Europe and sparked by the rising accident rate documented in statistics collected from the 1870s on by state bureaus of labor (MacLaury 1981). Lasting about a decade and a half, this period coincided with the rapid economic and technological growth of American industry initiated as early as Reconstruction and strengthened by the expanding railroad system.

The second major period, beginning around 1915, set the stage for the discipline of industrial medicine. Worker's compensation statutes were passed, and manpower shortages during World War I created a social and economic milieu within which industrial physicians could begin to define the lineaments of a somewhat broadened role that extended beyond surgical repair of injuries into medical care as well.

During the Depression years—the third critical period—organized medicine closed ranks to protect the economic interests of the private practitioner, and "contract practice" surfaced as a major issue. Industrial medicine, struggling to gain respectability, found itself bounded on two sides by the effects of the nation's economic crisis. On one side stood the survival tactics of the wider medical profession in a hostile economic milieu; on the other, the indifference of industrialists to safety and health in a buyers' labor market, where workers felt fortunate to have any job at all and government placed economic recovery above other social priorities.

A fourth period was ushered in by the New Deal and the outbreak of World War II. Like World War I, the conflict raised the profile of industrial physicians as potential contributors to the war effort (Selleck and Whittaker 1962). At the same time, though, the war, like the Depression, deflected attention within the business sector away from marginal issues such as occupational safety and health (Ashford 1976). The postwar period found the specialty growing in numbers but still scrapping for a modicum of professional recognition. A partial victory was won in the form of board certification in 1955.

A fifth period began in the 1960s with events leading up to the passage of the Occupational Safety and Health Act (OSHA) of 1970. With this and other landmark federal legislation, the specialty's issues began finally to reach the national agenda. The rapid modernization and expansion of industry during the postwar period had exposed weaknesses in the patchwork of laws and regulations on the state level that governed safety and health on the job as well as the compensation of injured workers. Grassroots organizing efforts by environmentalists and labor leaders culminated in the enactment of OSHA, which fundamentally altered the rules of the game for occupational physicians in ways that continue to unfold.

The Precursor Period Defines Public Health

In this, as in many other branches of medicine, Hippocrates was there first. His *Airs, Waters, and Places*, from the fifth century B.C. (Jones 1948), established a relationship between the environment and health and specifically mentioned occupation as relevant to the practice of medicine.

Hippocrates' appreciation for the whole person living in harmony with a total environment has been eclipsed in contemporary medicine by what Dubos (1959) calls "the doctrine of specific etiology" that flows from the germ theory of disease. The schism Dubos analyzes between the curative ("health restored") and preventive ("health preserved") branches of medicine has had particularly profound implications for the occupational physician, whose mission belongs so clearly in the Hippocratic tradition undermined by the germ theory (Dubos 1959:129–69). Occupational physicians must by definition concern themselves with the patient's interaction with the working environment and his functional ability to perform a social role. The germ theory of disease, in contrast, moved the frontiers of medical science into laboratories peopled by bench scientists who were worlds removed from other workers and their jobs (Smith 1986).

The "father of occupational medicine" was very much a child of Hippocrates. Bernardino Ramazzini, a sixteenth-century Italian physician, codified knowledge for the field at a time in post-Renaissance Italy when feudalism was giving way to economic forms presaging capitalism. Metal-working and other trades (apothecary, midwifery, baking, milling, pottery-making) were expanding rapidly, as was mining, one of the oldest and most hazardous of occupations (Rosen 1958:37, 45–46). Driven by scientific curiosity but also a reformer's sympathy for the common man, Ramazzini assimilated the bits of evidence that had accumulated over the years, leavened them with his own extensive clinical observations, and published the first compendium of known and suspected associations between diseases and occupations. This was in 1713. Ramazzini's treatise was entitled *De Moribus Artificum Diatriba* (The Diseases of Tradesmen). Its importance lay not only in the classification of diseases associated with some forty different occupations, but also in its emphasis on preventive intervention and its admonition to all practicing physicians to ask on every patient's first visit, "What occupation does he follow?" and to learn about the hazards "in shops, mills, mines, or wherever men toil" (Rosen 1958: 95; Johnstone and Miller 1960: 3). Ramazzini placed the responsibility on medical science "to cultivate industrial medicine as a specialty in order that workers could earn their living without bodily injury" (Stern 1946:5). Like Hippocrates, Ramazzini considered gathering and weighing environmental and occupational evidence an essential part of any competent physician's task.

Although slow to exert the influence it ultimately did have, Ramazzini's work was translated during the mid-1700s into English, German, and French. It was published and republished, paraphrased, and updated repeatedly throughout the eighteenth century, which saw a growth of interest in associations between aspects of the physical and social environment (including work) and specific forms of illness (Lilienfeld and Lilienfeld 1980).

The mid-1800s brought the "greening of epidemiology" (Lilienfeld and Lilienfeld 1980:27) by uniting the germ theory of disease, gaining adherents at the time, and the inductive logic developed earlier by Francis Bacon during the scientific revolution of the 1600s. One of the earliest applications of this logic in unraveling the etiology of disease was in Pott's 1775 investigation of scrotal cancer among chimney sweeps (Pott 1775). He observed an association and was able to recommend a solution without any understanding of the underlying mechanism of disease (Wolinsky 1980).

This mode of problem solving was, according to McKeown (1976: 144), the single most important (and perhaps the only important) contribution science and technology made to the "modern improvement in health" from the seventeenth century onward. Epidemiological investigations of environmental conditions during the eighteenth and early nineteenth centuries fixed the targets for the great sanitary reforms which did result in the virtual conquest of epidemic infectious disease. The rise of capitalism in England, and later on the European continent and in the United States, brought rapid urbanization, the growth of an industrial proletariat, and enormous dislocations, attended by an alarming rise in the rates of cholera, tuberculosis, typhoid, typhus, yellow fever, smallpox, and other infectious diseases. Railroad networks were laid and the factory system was constructed; the social problems sullying these achievements gave rise, between 1830 and 1875, to the great sanitary reform movement and the origins of modern public health.

Like Pott, the eighteenth-century reformers acted on a limited and often flawed conception of the subtleties of the disease process. Although, as Dubos argues, "scientific medicine and the germ theory have been given all the credit" for the reformers' accomplishments, it rightfully belongs instead to "the campaign for pure food, pure water, and pure air based not on a scientific doctrine but on philosophical faith . . . and the attempt to recapture the goodness of life in harmony with the ways of nature" (Dubos 1959:151).

Hippocrates and Ramazzini addressed the physician in his clinical role; only incidentally did they suggest its expansion into reformist activities. But self-conscious social reformers, moved by the egregious working and living conditions accompanying the early industrial revolution, created the institutions—and the philosophical rationale—that would establish the modern practice of public health, and with it the clinical subspecialty foreseen in Ramazzini's writings. Thus, the events that finally did lead to the widespread dissemination and the elaboration of Ramazzini's observations were, in their orientation, more social and pragmatic than scientific or medical. This theme resurfaces frequently in the history of occupational health (Coye, Smith, and Mazzocchi 1984; Smith 1986).

Directed at the privations of the industrial revolution, the public health movement established a "theory of social action in relation to health" (Rosen 1958:225). Its major elements included the observations that poverty breeds disease and that contagion among the poor crosses class and community boundaries. Thus, Dr. Thomas Percival, whose exposes of working conditions in Ratcliffe textile mills led the British Parliament to enact the first of a series of factory acts, was originally commissioned by the town to investigate an outbreak of typhus. He and the other reformers were able to demonstrate that the health of the entire community was jeopardized by the inhuman conditions in and around the mills.

Gradually, the movement created the collective will and the organizational capacity to define public health as at least in part the responsibility of the state. The German-speaking nations elaborated this concept of state intervention (or "medical police") (Rosen 1979) early and wholeheartedly, resting as it could on the authoritarianism and paternalism of "enlightened absolutism" prevailing there at the time. The economic liberalism of England and the United States required a more oblique and tortuous justification for state intervention, acerbically summarized by Waldron: "Diseases were unpleasant, but more important, they were inefficient. Children who died young could not be employed, and when adults were sick, the quality of their work suffered. More deaths meant less production" (1978:6). So inspired, Parliament enacted a series of statutes which slowly propelled nineteenth-century England away from an entirely laissez-faire and fragmented town-by-town approach to the protection of workers' health, but rarely did changes take place in the absence of a public outcry from powerful vested interests intent on diluting the influence of the legislative process.[1]

Significance of the Precursor Period

The piecemeal construction of a state apparatus in Great Britain for the regulation of safety and health at work, together with the philosophical rationale originating in France, influenced thinking and action throughout Europe and in America. The industrial revolution was destroying the social fabric and creating economic, political, and social upheavals on a worldwide scale (Hobsbawm 1962). Questions were being raised in many quarters about the kind of society being forged by the engines of industrial growth and how people were faring in it. Workers were be-

---

1. Rosen observes that "all the important acts were preceded by agitation and public inquiries and were enacted into law in the face of determined opposition. On the whole, the development of factory and mine legislation between 1830 and the end of the century reflects little credit on the coal owners, the manufacturers, and their spokesmen" (Rosen 1958:268).

ing enfranchised (Great Britain's Second Reform Bill of 1876 gave the vote to all male householders) and trade unionism was beginning to gain legitimacy (an 1873 act provided English unions their first legal protections).

The sanitary reforms were an integral part of this more general ferment, and the issues they urgently raised concerning the health effects of work were seen in this broad social context. Occupation was but one of the social factors bound up with poverty and squalor destroying the working classes' health. In this larger context, the human capital argument advanced by the public health advocates made good sense. To prosper, England *did* need to do a better job of conserving the energy and vitality of the working masses. The state therefore did need to set and enforce standards of workplace safety. And there was a clear role in this overall enterprise for physicians. They were needed to investigate the causes of disease and to inspect the health of workers who were vulnerable or exposed to extreme risk.

But the human capital case did not yet apply to industry as a sector of the total society. Employers could and did work their untrained employees to the point of exhaustion or death, thereupon easily replacing them with a new cohort of cheap recruits.[2] So there was not yet a clear role for physicians within any but the most enlightened or paternalistic business firms. Rare were the employers in eighteenth- and nineteenth-century England who retained the part-time services of a physician; when they did it was as an adjunct to a general (and for the time unorthodox) policy of humanitarianism toward employees (Schilling 1981:14).

An Early Role for Surgery and the "Company Doctor System": 1900–1915

On the American frontier, employers in railroading, lumbering, and mining operations in remote locations had little choice but to arrange for some basic medical services to handle frequent injuries and emergencies. Although the precise dates are unknown, the Pennsylvania Railroad had an arrangement for physician services some time before the Civil War, and the Baltimore and Ohio probably did too. The mining industry was the first to employ physicians on anything approaching a full-time basis, as early perhaps as the late 1700s (Selleck and Whittaker 1962:58). One history of occupational medicine in western Pennsylvania

---

2. Brown makes the chilling connection between the industrialists' view of their employees as a form of human capital and the slaveowners' view of their human chattel. He asserts that, like employees, "slaves were provided with medical care [primarily because of] the tremendous economic investment they represented to slave owners" (Brown 1979:113).

cited evidence that the care provided by these early company physicians fell short of community norms and observed that many of these "strictly 'contract doctors' operating on a head fee basis . . . gave a reputation to occupational medicine which took years to overcome" (Hazlett and Hummel 1957:46).

As a rule, the few companies around the turn of this century that did sponsor medical programs for their workers were seeking to entice physicians to settle in isolated areas by guaranteeing them an income. This income the employers raised through automatic payroll deductions. Workers were offered no option but to make the contribution, nor did they have access to any alternative source of medical care. These and successive generations of early medical programs often came to function as instruments of "welfare capitalism" (Brandes 1976), where employers in remote areas controlled the community's entire social and political infrastructure (public schools, housing, churches, even the police) in an effort to bind workers to the company as literally the only game in town. One rationale was the need to organize these basic community services where they did not yet exist, but they were also profitable and, more important, a deliberate hedge against unionization. Even the best-intentioned programs were tainted to some degree by the implicit paternalistic assumption that the employer needed to provide direct services, rather than higher wages, because employees would lack the good sense to invest in their own health and welfare (Shain, Suurvali, Boutilier 1986:15).

Despite the generally negative experiences workers had with the early company doctors, a few physicians are said to have made outstanding contributions even in the late 1800s—to have served "with distinction" as surgeons designated by employers to treat the casualties occurring in iron works, steel mills, and mines (Hazlett and Hummel 1957:31). Arrangements varied, but the majority were private practitioners on call, some paid a part-time salary, others a fee per case or per capita, none paid very well by the standards of the time and by no means all paid by taxing workers' wages. They treated the accident victims in their own offices or in local hospitals, some of which set up special wards to handle the growing caseload.

Two pioneers in American occupational medicine, Dr. Alvin Schoenleber and Dr. Alice Hamilton, raise in separate reminiscences a two-sided question that has dogged the field: why does a business enterprise hire a physician, and why, for his or her part, does a physician elect to practice in a corporate setting? During his world travels as an employee of Standard Oil Company of New Jersey over a twenty-five-year period beginning in 1919, Alvin Schoenleber frequently was asked the first part of the question: "I didn't know that oil companies employed doctors," people would say to him; "What on earth do you do to earn your pay?" (Schoenleber 1950:1). Alice Hamilton herself posed the other side of the question. Looking back at the state of industrial medicine in America some thirty years after she entered the field in 1910, she observed that "for a surgeon or physician to accept a position with a manufacturing company was to earn the contempt of his colleagues" (Hamilton 1943: 4). Although she later frequently remarked on the tremendous progress she had witnessed over a relatively short span of time, never in her very long career did Dr. Hamilton function as a company physician; instead she always approached industry from the perspective of an independent investigator and social reformer. Schoenleber, by contrast, served with self-proclaimed zest as a full-time career employee of Standard Oil of New Jersey.

Answers to this reflexive question of motives for the field as a whole are as diverse and idiosyncratic as they are for these two pioneers. For the field, the evolution of worker's compensation is an important underlying factor. The story has repeatedly been told, and glaring defects in the system have frequently been analyzed. Of interest here are ramifications for the practice of medicine within a corporation. Somers and Somers (1954) set the context in early twentieth-century America.

The Rising Tide of Industrial Accidents in The "Dangerous Trades"

Industrial accidents were taking an accelerating toll, being documented by muckraking journalists and the awakening union movement. In the former category, Crystal Eastman's influential study for the Russell Sage Foundation was published in 1910 and became a popular bestseller. It showed, in a graphic "death calendar" on the frontispiece, that work was killing people routinely, day in and day out: the 526 deaths recorded that year among workers in a single county in western Pennsylvania were represented by red crosses distributed at the rate of at least one every day over the entire year, and as many as 50 on the worst day (Eastman 1910). In the latter category, the American Foundation of Labor president, Samuel Gompers, testified in 1910 before the Senate Committee on Conservation that "since coal mining began in 1820 the loss of life in the mines has exceeded our fatalities in war and the sacrifice still goes on at the rate of two or three full regiments yearly" (Gompers 1910:665). The accident rate peaked around 1907, the year the Somerses cite as the beginning of serious reaction among Americans "to the challenge of occupational disability" (Somers and Somers 1954:15).

The major events comprising that "serious reaction" during the opening years of the twentieth century included a parade of state and then federal legislative initiatives, patterned on the English factory laws and seeking to protect the most vulnerable groups of workers, again singling out women and children (Stellman 1977). A few also required employers to correct the most blatantly harmful working conditions. Led by Massachusetts's 1877 factory act, most of the industrial states had by the turn of the century enacted some form of legislation restricting the freedom of employers to pursue profit with no regard for the safety of workers (Ashford 1976:47); however, all the state laws had gaping holes (MacLaury 1981). The muckraking journalists of the Progressive era exposed weaknesses in the state response and tallied the toll of human suffering.

Alice Hamilton, whose investigations of working conditions in the "dangerous trades" rank among the important early events, documents in her autobiography the industrialists' avarice that enabled the death and disease rates, especially among poor immigrant labor, to reach appalling proportions (Hamilton 1943). The gradual public reaction embodied a double goal: to minimize injuries and illness attending work and to compensate as fairly as possible those injured on the job or the survivors of those killed.

The second goal reflected strains that the rising accident rate placed on established legal mechanisms for parceling out responsibility. Employers had had a virtually impenetrable wall of common law defenses, erected on the foundation of Lord Abinger's 1837 doctrine of the "assumption of risk." An injured worker was unable to recover damages from his negligent employer if he, himself, or a fellow employee had been in any way negligent, or if the injury had resulted from a hazard of which he should have been aware because it inhered in his job. Choosing that job was in Lord Abinger's view tantamount to voluntarily assuming the risks (Somers and Somers 1954:18). This edifice began to crumble as the accident rate rose and ultimately was replaced by state worker's compensation laws. They acknowledged that modern work is inevitably hazardous and, therefore, replaced the moral and legal concepts of individual fault with a social policy allocating the costs of accidents to the employer, for whom they were then to become a cost of doing business.

With the rising accident rates and the advent of worker's compensation statutes, a shadowy role for medicine in the workplace began to emerge and to assume a form that foretold its own future struggles. Physicians were needed to attend to industrial accidents in order to accelerate the convalescence and return-to-the-job of workers injured in the line of duty. Starr observes that as the railroading industry drove westward in the late 1800s it developed extensive medical programs that spawned a subspecialty of "railway surgery." These programs "were motivated not only by the special hazards of railroad work, but also by the interest of companies in protecting themselves from lawsuits" (Starr 1982: 201).

The ends of medicine in this context were more palliative than preventive. Remarkable preventive successes were achieved by the industrial safety movement, led chiefly by the engineers. In this effort, the post-accident ministrations of physicians (mainly surgeons) were incidental. The engineers also succeeded in preempting part of the role that industrial medicine might have played. "Safety first" was there first in many of the large industrial firms. It filled a niche in the corporate structure and relegated medicine to an ambiguous status where palpable results would be far more difficult to demonstrate than they were in the heady days of the "safety first" campaigns. In some of the older industrial firms, infighting still prevents effective cooperation between the safety and the medical staffs. And all modern corporate medical departments still struggle to one degree or another with the problem of how to produce identifiable or measurable results, how, in Freidson's words, to craft "an empirically demonstrable outcome" (Freidson 1970a).

Whereas accident prevention was basically a problem of engineering, coupled with worker education and motivation, the one health-related task to which medicine could claim exclusive license at this early stage was the certification of health status, in some views the profession's quintessential function (Freidson 1970a). This, more than preventing accidents to obviate compensation claims, explains the genesis of occupational medicine. When the industrial-accident problem led to the creation of relief and benefit associations, beginning with an association established in 1886 for workers of the Pennsylvania Railroad, a rationing device was needed to differentiate worthy from frivolous claims.

In concept, these associations go back to the very birth of the union movement in colonial America. The newer associations varied in their structures and functions, but all needed the services of physicians to verify the legitimacy of claims, and many required a physician's examination as a prerequisite for participation.

The new function, according to Hazlett and Hummel, accounts for the "phenomenal" growth of industrial medicine between 1900 and 1915. This was prior to the widespread dissemination of worker's compensation laws, which were analyzed, designed, and promoted by state investigatory commissions that met between 1909 and 1930 in over thirty separate jurisdictions. By 1908, most states had passed laws restricting in some way the employer's common-law defenses. But it was not until 1917 that the U.S. Supreme Court lifted the shadow of unconstitutionality from the principle of worker's compensation. By 1920 all but six (southern) states had passed worker's compensation legislation, but it took until 1948 for all political jurisdictions to adopt the principle in one form or another (Somers and Somers 1954:33–34).

Thus the advent of industrial medicine is not fully explained by the presumed incentive for employers to prevent illness and injury, resulting from the passage of state worker's compensation laws. There was also the practical problem of having to deal with an increasing number of private insurance claims—a problem that made "both physicians and industrialists . . . aware of the need for some kind of medical service for employees" (Hazlett and Hummel 1957: 69–70).

A Physician for the Situation

The kind of medical service demanded by the mounting pressures for processing insurance claims anticipated problems the profession continues to face. Already, the industrial physician had agreed to weigh competing interests in a total situation rather than act in the isolated interest of an individual patient. If the physician's job were simply to prevent and treat injuries and illnesses, thereby saving his employer some of the costs of compensation, his judgments could normally be guided by a sincere and single-minded calculation of the best interest of his patient, the worker. Complexities might arise should someone in management disagree with an employee's own assessment of his readiness to return to work, but even this discussion would take place against a backdrop of concern for that particular employee's personal health and welfare.

But the processing of claims takes place against an altogether different backdrop. The object is to ferret out potential fraud in the worst case, or, in the best, to protect the common pool of funds from the inadvertent harm caused by too many individuals rationally pursuing their own self-interest (Hardin 1968). This weighing of competing interests implies a role for the industrial physician analogous to the notion of a "lawyer for the situation," expounded in 1916 by Justice Louis D. Brandeis when his ethics were being called into question (Hazard 1978:58). A lawyer for the situation serves more than one client in a single transaction, acting as a mediator, arbitrator, or orchestrator for all the parties. He no longer has the unequivocal "rules of role" to tell him where his loyalties lie. Instead he has choices to make between the interests of his several clients:

> He is advocate, mediator, entrepreneur, and judge, all in one. He could be said to be playing God. Playing God is a tricky business. It requires skill, nerve, detachment, compassion, ingenuity, and the capacity to sustain confidence. When mishandled, it generates the bitterness and recrimination that results when a deep trust has been betrayed. (Hazard 1978:65)

The recriminations that have swirled around occupational medicine over the years are therefore not merely the result of difficulty in shaking the "very bad reputation" earned at the turn of the century by unscrupulous and lazy "contract doctors" (Hazlett and Hummel 1957:73). They reflect a more fundamental structural issue inhering in a role that requires its incumbents to "play God." Difficult choices bedevil the physician certifying claims, each of which he must consider in light of the possibility that an inappropriately liberal ruling could contribute to the depletion of the pool before an even more deserving or needy applicant has experienced his mishap or filed his claim. As if to verify the complexity of this new role, early industrial physicians seem implicitly to have granted, with Brandeis, that "a lawyer [or physician] for the situation has to identify clearly his role as such" (Hazard 1978:65). Thus, physical examinations were justified during this period as a condition of participation in the relief and benefit societies but, for the most part, not yet as a condition of employment.

Sears, Roebuck and Company did initiate a program of physical examinations in 1908, but it was conceived in classic public health terms, the object being "to discover and isolate those with tuberculosis." Although the company's new medical director, Harry E. Mock, M.D., "quickly became convinced of the economic as well as the medical value of thorough examinations and complete case records," the subject "remained for many years the source of bitter controversy with both labor and management" (Selleck and Whittaker 1962:60).

In his appreciation of the *medical* value of complete case records, Dr. Mock was aligning himself with the British public health reformers, for whom careful documentation and analysis of illness patterns were dogma. In his *economic* rationale, he was looking for the tool that was needed to carve as secure a niche in the business enterprise for preventive medicine as was being established for safety by the engineers. This perspective was enunciated clearly by John B. Lowman, M.D., director of the Cambria Iron Company Hospital, in a 1916 *Pennsylvania Medical Journal* article quoted by Hazlett and Hummel (1957:106–07) as "one of the great pioneer works in the field of preventive medicine in industry."

Emphasizing the value of physical examinations in preventing industrial injuries, Lowman claimed to have persuaded management and labor "what a paying investment it was, not only from a humanitarian point of view but through remuneration as well." He admitted that "at first there was some objection by the men and some refusal to be examined" but said that when they were "told that no one was to be discharged and of the good derived from same, not only for their own protection but also for the protection of others, they fell right into line and at present we have no trouble whatever." He rested his case on an enumeration, from the employer's perspective, of five reasons for conducting periodic physical examinations of employees:

(1) Safety first and prevention of accidents. The number of preventable accidents will decrease as the physical standard is increased; (2) The importance to the employer of knowing the condition of his men; (3) That suitable

employment is found for those unfortunate enough to have physical defects which debar them from their normal vocations; (4) The rejection of the unfit, but not without free medical consultation, and recommendation for their regeneration; (5) Economic value to the company because of the greater freedom from falsified claims and freedom from indemnities and compensation required in accidents due to impaired vision, hearing and other disabilities of the workingman, who injures himself as well as his fellow workman. (Hazlett and Hummel 1957:107)

As a benchmark expression of the rationale for preventive medicine in industry, Lowman's case for periodic examinations adumbrates difficulties that have persisted for years. He advanced two separate arguments, one directed at employers, the other at employees, and the two are at least partially inconsistent. So that employees would undergo the examinations, he claimed that "no one was to be discharged," but keeping this promise would make the first, fourth, and fifth of the employer's objectives in supporting the program difficult or impossible to meet through the mechanism of periodic examinations of employees already on the payroll. Those three objectives suggest that "the importance to the employer of knowing the condition of his men" extends beyond aggregate or statistical impressions to specific knowledge of the health status of individual men, who, if they saw this list of the employer's objectives, might be well advised to demur when offered an examination.

Significance of the Surgical Period

The contours of a role for medicine as management began to appear during the surgical phase. First, physicians were needed to provide early treatment of the injuries that were occurring in epidemic proportions. If they did this well, they could reduce the incidence of wound infections, spare injured employees the horrifying and sometimes lethal ride to the hospital in a crude horsedrawn ambulance, and presumably shorten the convalescence and reduce the employer's costs. In this there was the beginning of a preventive role, although of a secondary nature. The safety engineers and employee motivators cornered the primary prevention market and substantially reduced the prevalence of accidents. The rates remained high enough, however, to leave for the physicians and surgeons a meaningful role in mitigating the harmful sequelae.

Second, there was also a beginning appreciation of a subtle but real place for medicine in the primary prevention of accidents. The "safety first" campaigns consisted in part of engineering improvements to separate agent from host in the traditional public health paradigm. But passive protection was a relatively minor part of the strategy, which reflected the full complement of empirically derived change theories, including education, motivation, exhortations from opinion leaders, pressures from peers, all reinforced by a liberal sprinkling of incentives. Creating a safety-conscious climate in the plant was central to the strategy, and that required convincing employees of the employer's genuine concern for their welfare on the job. If he did not care, why should they? A medical program in the plant, staffed by a qualified physician, could serve as a symbol and an agent of the employer's concern and as a motivating factor in the effort to encourage employees to take greater responsibility for their own safety.

Third, physicians in industrial settings were trying to gain support for a program of periodic examinations of workers. This could be rationalized as part of accident prevention to the extent that the weak could be sorted out of the labor force (or moved to jobs better suited to their limited physical capabilities). But giving preferential treatment to those who cannot carry their share of the load raises thorny issues of equity that remain unresolved to this day. It seems unlikely that the pioneers found ways around this problem, nor does the historical record of this period provide evidence of more than lip service to this notion of fitting the man to the job. The notion, however, developed in later years into one of the cornerstones of the practice of industrial and then occupational medicine. A different rationale for periodic examinations—to detect tuberculosis and other communicable diseases—harked back to the previous period of public health interventions. It also established for industrial physicians a health mission to which they had clear title, in contrast to the safety mission, where their role was ancillary at best.

Finally, there emerged in this early period a clear case of role conflict. In the adjudication of claims for compensation, initially under the voluntary welfare programs and subsequently under worker's compensation laws, the physician no longer acted as the stalwart champion of his individual patient. This, and the initial function of sorting strong from weak employees, diluted whatever impact the industrial physician could have as a symbol of the employer's genuine concern for the welfare of his workers. It created the conflicted role that took the discipline seven decades to formally recognize and begin to sort out in a code of ethical conduct, adopted in 1976 (American Occupational Medical Association 1976).

Handicapped in several important ways—in its origins in the paternalism of welfare capitalism, in its low status by association with patients who were working men, in its involvement with salaried or contract practice and prepayment experiments (the anathema of organized medicine), in the variable quality of the performance of its practitioners, and in its structured ambivalence—the small nucleus of a new profession set out to gain respectability. War, it turned out, would be a major boon.

3 ■ In Search of Professional Identity

The Civil War unleashed the American industrial revolution and opened the way for a new profession of industrial medicine. World War I gave the profession a glimpse of a higher plateau to which World War II would actually move it. It is well known that organized labor has managed repeatedly to consolidate its gains during war-stimulated periods of increased industrial activity, manpower shortage, and national unity. Organized industrial medicine has reaped similar indirect benefits from the exigencies of war. Not only does manpower conservation become a national preoccupation during war time, but physicians who serve in the military are exposed to an institutional form of practice that may have greater appeal than they would have anticipated.[1] Medical knowledge is advanced, and rehabilitation and vocational placement of returning veterans become moral obligations. World War I brought the federal government for the first time into the "business of providing medical care for the armed services on a large scale" (Stevens 1971:132).

War Confers the Basis for a Socially Accepted Function: 1915–1929

In 1916, when the war was already underway, but before America had entered it, a group of about 125 physicians and surgeons formed the

---

1. Military medicine is an analogue of occupational medicine or, more precisely, a subtype. Both seek to fit the man to the job, to support him medically in it as long as possible, and to arrange for the repair of any damage he suffers in the line of duty. Impressionistic evidence suggests that many corporate physicians have served a term in the military before joining a corporation. There are no available data against which to test the strong impression that military service is more likely to be found in the background of a corporate occupational physician than in that of a private practitioner, but this would be an interesting hypothesis to pursue. (For writings on military medicine see Daniels 1972, 1975.)

American Association of Industrial Physicians and Surgeons (AAIP&S). Preeminent among their goals was to raise the standard of practice in their field and thereby, it was hoped, to enhance its prestige. At that time, according to the association's official history published a half-century later, "Men in plant practice were commonly the object of professional scorn." They were "poorly paid, respected neither by management nor by labor," and often "of mediocre ability, performing routine work acceptably but with little awareness of its potentials. The field, by and large, was uninviting, unrewarding." The association's founders, according to this official history, were "exceptions to the rule of mediocrity in plant practice at the time." These physicians and surgeons were "for the most part young" and "attracted to industrial practice by the new emphasis on safety, public health, and hygiene." Indeed, "their stature was the more pronounced because of the scarcity of medical talent in the industrial field" (Selleck and Whittaker 1962:59).

Held in conjunction with the sixty-seventh annual meeting of the American Medical Association, the charter session of the AAIP&S (and the parent organization's conference) was "pervaded by a sense of world crisis and the imminent need for preparedness for war" (Selleck and Whittaker 1962:77). Conservation of the nation's labor force assumed a new salience: not only did a fighting force have to be sustained, but domestic workers would be called upon to initiate "new unfamiliar procedures" of industrial production, often involving the large-scale use of poisonous substances that the United States had previously been able to purchase from Germany (Hamilton 1943:184). Alice Hamilton had been dispatched in 1915 to investigate the newly fitted munitions plants along the Atlantic seacoast; she describes in her autobiography the "very shocking conditions" she found there, owing to employers' neglect as well as that of her medical colleagues, and to the workers' ignorance of the hazards to which they were being grossly overexposed.

It was not until the United States finally entered the war, Hamilton said, that she began to see worker safety accepted as a topic of legitimate study and concern. She later wrote of that entry into the war: "For me the most important change was . . . the new interest taken by my own profession in the protection of munition workers. . . . And that interest has never died down, on the contrary it has increased with the increasing complexity of methods of manufacture" (Hamilton 1943:197). The pressures of war and the technological requirements of munitions production awakened the medical profession to the new problem of industrial toxins, although it was several decades before recognition spread beyond a very few specialists (Coye, Smith, and Mazzocchi 1984). But also, Hamilton felt, these pressures began to awaken at least some industrial managers to the more general lesson of the value of conserving human resources. Once employers recognized "large labor turnover" as "not only wasteful but an unsatisfactory method of dealing with dangerous processes in industry," she argued, "industrial medicine had at last become respectable" (Hamilton 1943:198).

Respectability grew in part out of the medical profession's technical development, which enhanced its ability to achieve what Starr terms "therapeutic competence" (1982:16). Hamilton, for example, was able to make a few concrete recommendations for improving the control of toxins released in the production of munitions, although the conditions remained exceedingly dangerous and casualties high.

Hamilton's toxicological interests did gain some adherents during the war, but industrial medicine retained its surgical orientation well into the postwar period.[2] Surgery had come a long way from the turn of the century, when a distinguished pioneer recalled that his choice of surgery over medicine as a young intern had been viewed "as the equivalent of a social error" (Stevens 1971:11). The ascent of surgery reflected technical developments—anesthesia and antisepsis—as well as the organizational advantages of an expanding hospital system and the organizing genius of a charismatic leader (Stevens 1971:85–92). Industrial physicians were looking for a combination of technical and organizational wizardry to establish their specialty so firmly that they, like the surgeons, might look back at the end of their careers and laugh at the recollection that their choice of specialty could have been considered ill advised. They found no such formula. One of the nation's most eminent corporate medical directors, interviewed in 1979, voiced regret that neither his medical school classmates nor his father had come to terms with what they continued to perceive as his social error in electing a career in occupational practice instead of becoming a "real doctor."

World War I moved the technology of medicine in directions particularly applicable to industrial practice, but technique alone would not be the key to open the doors to respectability. In addition to the new toxicological awareness observed by Hamilton, a catalogue of the major medical advances during the war would include improvements in the treatment of wounds, defense against poisonous gas, the creation of aviation medicine, the investigation of trench fever, preventive inoculation against tetanus in gunshot wounds, inoculation against typhoid fever, rehabilitation of the wounded, fatigue studies, and researches in

---

2. This is evident in the membership of the AAIP&S, more than half of whom continued to show the word "surgeon" in their titles through the early 1930s (Selleck and Whittaker 1962:263). Official statistics are useless for tracking these trends but do indicate the dominance of surgery by subsuming "occupational medicine" under "surgery" in official tallies of physician distribution up through 1949 (Stevens 1971: table I, 162).

efficiency. Legge argues that these wartime developments materially strengthened the postwar practice of industrial medicine (Legge 1952).

The real legacy of the war, and the wellspring for the profession's gradual growth, was a moral or political victory, not a technical one. The war created a climate in which industrial medicine could be appreciated. Physical examinations of employees, a cornerstone of industrial medicine, had been suspect on grounds that they protect the employer, not the employee. In the context of war, however, they could be recast as part of the national defense effort designed to reduce absenteeism and to increase production of urgently needed supplies. For the first time since the eighteenth-century public-health reforms, industrial medicine found itself aligned with the broad public interest. Selleck and Whittaker portray this period as "momentous" for the profession, a "turning of the tide in favor of in-plant medical services, physical examinations as a criterion in job placement, and the rehabilitation of disabled and handicapped veterans" (Selleck and Whittaker 1962:86).

The full effects of this "momentous" period were only gradually if ever to be widely felt; the end of World War I—and even the onset of World War II—found industrial medicine still in a state of limbo. This situation did improve slightly during the "open shop era" of labor unrest during the prosperous mid- to late 1920s. Whereas during the war the fortunes of organized labor had seemed to parallel those of industrial medicine, the close of hostilities brought the divergent interests of the two groups into sharp relief.

To capitalize on the momentum created by the war emergency, the profession needed a peacetime rationale that would paper over the cracks between interests of employers and employees. That rationale was articulated by Clarence D. Selby, M.D., an industrial surgeon and former health commissioner for the city of Toledo, Ohio, who had spent a portion of the war in Washington conducting a Public Health Service survey of medical programs in industry.

Selby reported his findings in a document known as "Bulletin 99." In it he took industry to task for supporting physical examinations of job candidates, ostensibly to aid in intelligent assignment but so superficially conducted as to amount to little more than crude screening for the most obvious defects. If medical examination were genuinely intended to improve job placement, then the rational employer faced with labor shortage would intensify these efforts so that each worker's productive potential could be deployed most effectively. But some firms were abandoning the practice of preemployment medical examinations because the war-imposed labor scarcity forced them to accept most applicants. Selby had to infer that these abandoned programs must have been motivated by a desire to screen out defectives. This was, in his view, a perversion of the goals of industrial medicine.

Bulletin 99 built a strong case for the employment of industrial physicians, well versed in the demands of specific jobs, to assist management in assigning applicants of varying physical abilities to work they could perform well and in supervising and supporting those employees in the performance of their tasks. Selby commended the few companies with fine medical programs in place, not, he said, as "a gift to labor, but purely a function of good business." He enumerated ways in which he found management well served by a competent medical program, first as "an acknowledgment of their obligation toward the workers who sustain injuries during employment and an economical means of procuring expert attention for them." Also, such a program "is deemed capable of removing or minimizing certain causes of lost time." Further, a medical program "is one of several activities that have been found to be of use in removing certain unstabilizing influences from employment and as such can be expected to assist in holding down the labor turnover." Such a program "enables the workers to produce more . . . prevents litigation and reduces compensation expenses . . . contributes to a sense of security among employees and promotes a feeling of good will toward the management." Finally, it is "imperative in isolated industrial establishments" (Selby 1919:106).

Recognizing the challenge of balancing these complex and not wholly concordant ends, Selby paid particular attention to the physician's unusual position in an industrial setting. "Although fundamentally the science of medicine," he said, industrial medicine occupies a position "similar to that of employment, safety, and compensation. All are specialties in the science of management." He granted that "medical training does not necessarily contribute to an understanding of this relationship" and observed that physicians lacking such an understanding "have reluctance in accepting the materialistic viewpoint of employers and, conversely, have difficulty in persuading employers to accept their professional points of view." Physicians must understand industrial medicine as, "in a measure, a compromise between the ideals of medicine and the necessities of business," and that the way to approach this compromise is to recognize "that medical service in industries, to be of the greatest possible usefulness, must benefit primarily the working people. The benefit to industry naturally follows" (Selby 1919:5).

Between the two world wars, the specialty strove to make the transition from the limited technical functions of the industrial surgeon to Selby's broader medical role in the service of the organization. Selby's credo—that the physician can concern himself with the good of the individual, confident that the good of the employer will naturally follow—

was central to this process because it seemed to resolve the potential conflict between a clinician's duty to his patient and an employee's to his boss. Otto Geier, another spokesman for the field during this transitional period, stretched Selby's thinking and argued that the industrial physician could serve as a kind of impartial mediator between the employer and the employee, "an essential middleman between management and labor, representative of both, biased toward neither . . . a role for which he is ideally fitted by the training and discipline of a profession that places health above all partisan consideration" (Selleck and Whittaker 1962:127).

The resolutely nonpartisan role harks back to Justice Brandeis's notion of lawyering for the situation; again it is structured for heroism because it removes the "rules of role." The industrial physician was to use "health" as the criterion variable that would protect him from biasing his actions toward either management or labor. But health is too relative, elastic, and value-laden a concept to stabilize the industrial physician in the heavy partisan winds blowing between management and labor.[3]

The interwar period saw tremendous expansion of manufacturing output, after a brief (but serious) postwar economic slump from the summer of 1920 until the spring of 1922. Although, as Chandler documents in his history of the modern business enterprise, "the broad patterns of growth . . . were clear" before World War I, it was the postwar period that saw the rapid and wide diffusion of innovative management techniques developed by the pioneering firms—"the visible hand of management . . . coordinating the flow of goods through the economy" (Chandler 1977:339). Management became professionalized and increasingly systematic and self-conscious in "coordinating, monitoring and planning for the activities of a large number of operating units" engaged in marketing and production (Chandler 1977:464).

This was a period when unions should in theory have been growing with the expanding economy but instead were losing ground, in part because employers were sponsoring "welfare work" and other managerial techniques deliberately intended to preempt union activities and sap the strength of the labor movement. The welfare proponents may have been sincere in their desire to foster cooperation and trust between labor and management. Their goal, nonetheless, was to mold employee attitudes and behavior in order to cultivate stable attachments. It was a reassertion of managerial authority in the face of the unions' attack (Perrow 1977:

---

3. This bedrock observation in the sociology of knowledge has often fruitfully been applied in analyses of aspects of the medical enterprise that bear indirectly on the role of the company doctor. For examples, see Conrad and Schneider (1980), Conrad and Kern (1986), Zola (1978, 1983), Navarro (1976), and Navarro and Berman (1983).

63). In this context, nothing—not even "the area of medical services"—could accurately be described as "a neutral zone in which plant politics had no place" (Selleck and Whittaker 1962:195).

The major alternative to "welfare work" was the "scientific management" of Fredrick Winslow Taylor (Taylor 1911). Taylorism, versions of which were fashionable well into the 1930s, conceived its mandate in terms remarkably similar to those set out for industrial physicians (Starr 1982:200). Scientific management was to be "a morally neutral method of finding the most efficient, most objective, and most rational means for solving problems, increasing profits, and for distributing wealth and services." Accomplishing this, adherents felt, would subdue labor unrest and obviate the need for unions. Taylorism was a "subtle ideological weapon" that employers would use against the expansion of unionism and "its encroachments upon managerial prerogatives" (Perrow 1977:65). It shifted the emphasis in management doctrine from the survival of the fittest—the most skilled worker showing the greatest individual initiative—envisaged in social Darwinism to a "deskilling program" (Braverman 1974) that decreased the worker's leverage, undermined his consciousness of belonging to a collective, increased the division of labor, and based the manager's authority on "science" and the need for cooperation between labor and capital. "Letting science decide" really meant letting managers control (Perrow 1977:64).

Over time Taylorism shaded into still more sophisticated doctrines that paid more attention to natural work groups and workers' psychological needs and "sought to cement the relationship between the organization's quest for rationality and the human search for happiness" (Etzioni 1964:39). But the early developments in management thinking had at least two important ramifications for the evolution of occupational medicine.

First, they set in motion the forces that would create the organizational matrix for modern occupational medical practice. The planning and control systems that according to Chandler enabled leading firms to take advantage of the possibilities for mass production and mass distribution eventually influenced personnel management and supplanted welfare work and Taylorism. General Motors, one of Chandler's polestar firms, moved in 1931 to make personnel administration a "regular responsibility at the corporation staff level," with both staff and line functions (Sloan 1963:459). As occupational medicine was integrated into this more systematic approach to the recruitment, retention, and management of personnel, medical departments began to see themselves as responsible in an ongoing way for the care of all employees. The previous mandate in most firms had been to care for the managers and either keep the workers on the job or move them off it when they became troublesome. But employee relations were gaining in importance as industry became "more bureaucratized, large, and mechanized, and employees themselves were becoming more important as capitalization increased and immigration slowed" (Perrow 1977:68). The human-capital case was beginning to hold for the business firm as it originally had for the society at large.

A second residue of Taylorism is more subtle than the first. This is the notion that "science" can be a value-free mediator between management and labor. It remains such a strong current in the writings on occupational medicine, even appearing as a premise of the profession's code of ethical conduct, that it can be considered a kind of medical Taylorism, a disembodied and hollow vestige of an abandoned managerial doctrine.

Organizing the Profession: One Step Forward, Two Steps Back

If union organizing was desultory throughout the prosperous twenties, the struggling AAIP&S was also in the doldrums. The association gained membership slowly, reaching only 257 members by 1928, and still failed to shake its involvement principally with accidents, despite repeated exhortations concerning the importance of periodic examinations in a comprehensive program of health maintenance.

Academic physicians found some new connections between health and work during this period, but such findings were slow to diffuse into industrial practice. Hamilton and others conducted important studies of lead poisoning, and attention was redirected at hazards Ramazzini knew to be associated with dust. Physiologists were making strides in academic medicine and were laying the research foundation for toxicology and the principles of industrial hygiene, based on an understanding of dose-response relationships and threshold limits for safe exposures. But all this was occurring outside of industrial medicine, whose central concerns were still methods of treating trauma and of selling industrialists on the economic and humanitarian value of a rudimentary medical program.

Medicine's center of gravity was in the teaching institutions and the hospitals, which the Flexner reforms had welded together into the intellectual hub of the health-care system. This development augured poorly for industrial medicine, a specialty largely without portfolio in the hospital setting.

But there was another beginning trend that augured poorly for workers' health but better for the specialty's future. Invisible but insidious health hazards associated with work were arousing limited public concern during the twenties, when occasional warning signals were faintly heard. Radium poisoning, for example, resulted in many illnesses and forty-one deaths among watch-dial painters in 1924, attracting some national notice.

The stock market crash of 1929 and the unemployment that followed led naturally to a temporary but "widespread curtailment of medical department activities" (Selleck and Whittaker 1962:230). But it also led to a rapid increase in the number of compensation claims for industrial diseases. These were stimulated largely by the Gauley Bridge disaster, in which hundreds of transient laborers, hired to build a hydroelectric tunnel in West Virginia, died of silicosis and other lung diseases during and shortly after the project, which lasted from 1929 to 1932. The ensuing legal complications called attention to the inadequacy of the new worker's compensation laws for cases of industrial disease. This publicity combined with the economic hardships of the Depression to create a crisis for some industries in legal liability for dust diseases not covered by the compensation laws.

As in the days leading to the original worker's compensation laws, civil courts were awarding damages at levels that alarmed employers and insurers, who sought redress in state legislatures (Trasko 1964). Most states enacted special provisions for handling dust diseases; these typically "amounted to denying workers with silicosis the same level of benefits available to other disabled employees" (Barth and Hunt 1980:3). Many states expanded their coverage of occupational diseases during the thirties, although slowly and only partially.

Significance of the War and Postwar Period

War gave industrial medicine a credo and a taste of credibility. Then the enactment and partial expansion of worker's compensation laws initiated a gradual change from concern for safety alone to concern for safety and health. Medicine took a place in some business firms as part of an interdisciplinary and interdepartmental effort aimed at conserving employees' health. Industrial processes and organizational structures assumed progressively more elaborate forms as the modern business enterprise matured in the years following the war. The health and safety enterprise experienced a parallel elaboration and drew on a variety of disciplines such as engineering, chemistry, psychology, statistics, education, nursing, medicine, and epidemiology.

Medical personnel at the corporate level were assigned corporate functions that called for interaction with other line and staff managers in labor relations, personnel, safety, benefits, and related functions, as well as with line managers and plant physicians and nurses in locations across the country. The corporate physician would have to work out a new set of relationships within the business firm, not only with the senior manager or managers who had recruited him (and whose personal physician, frequently, he had been), but also with a new stratum of technicians in middle management, with line managers, and with employees viewed not simply as patients but as a total population. The professionalization of management that Chandler (1977) documented brought pressure on industrial medicine to professionalize and standardize its role. The days were rapidly vanishing when "chairmen of the board charged into battle like General Patton—their physicians at their sides" (Ritardi 1983:54).

These changes complicated the industrial physician's life in two new ways. First they made him interdependent with staff and line managers, in a set of symmetrical relationships unusual for a physician in a professional role. An inconsistency of status was likely to be felt, and, more important, role models were lacking for the relationships he needed to forge. While a physician tended, in the outside social hierarchy, to outrank other corporate managers on his level, in the managerial realm he often found himself at a relative disadvantage, by virtue of the more extensive experience, better political connections, and easier access to information and power often possessed by "career" managers in the firm. Career managers, as Kanter (1977) has argued, derive much of their power from their upward trajectory in the organization, enabling them to cultivate a network of sponsors, peers, and subordinates, all of whom have invested in some way in their ascent. Corporate medical directors seldom have upward mobility, since their technical expertise is too specialized to have general relevance in the higher reaches of the normal business firm (Goldstein, Northwood, and Goldstein 1960).

Second, the nascent function as part of the management team challenged industrial medicine to claim a population and to demonstrate an impact. This explains the specialty's interest in periodic examinations, going back to Harry Mock at Sears, Roebuck soon after the turn of the century. A program of regular examinations provided the medical director needed access to the employee population and a means of accumulating an information base from which to derive some power. It scarcely mattered whether the examination programs could be expected to uncover enough previously unrecognized and correctable disease ultimately to be cost-effective. What did matter was that they created for the medical director the social network and the bargaining advantages he needed to hold his own in the hierarchy of the firm.

The Ongoing Drive for Professional Recognition: The 1930s

While they were working out new relationships inside their organizations, industrial physicians were also struggling for a small piece of medical "turf" controlled by their peers in the outside profession. Tensions erupted in professional journals several times in the thirties, as they had in years past. The thirties were different, though, because the interspecialty tensions were amplified during that decade by external pressures being felt by medicine as a consequence of the Depression. It was during this period that the medical profession hardened its ideological positions against what it construed as an assault on its integrity (Stevens 1971; Starr 1982). Having on earlier occasions supported national health insurance, the AMA at this time shifted permanently to the intractable opposition largely responsible for the defeat of a succession of national health insurance proposals in the thirties and forties, creating the vacuum into which private health insurance expanded (Ginzberg 1977:24).

The 1932 final report of the Committee on the Costs of Medical Care provoked a strong reaction from the AMA, excoriating "the corporate practice of medicine" and collective or institutional practice arrangements, all of which (no matter how sponsored) were branded "socialistic" or at least inspired by "outside or government intruders" (Stevens 1971:187). The corporate practice of medicine, in the AMA's lexicon, meant "contract practice" in general, any form of which could be expected to "turn doctors into hirelings and treat sick people like robots" (Davis 1932). Such forms, of course, included industrial medicine, whose practitioners responded with angry editorials in their professional newsletter, rhetorical bravado that masked a series of major steps in a process of allying themselves with the interests of organized medicine.

The implied definition of professional ethics—"keep your hands off our private patients"—was the real source of continuing problems for the industrial physician whose domain it circumscribed to exclude any responsibility for "nonoccupational health care." Industrial medicine's "ethics" were thus defined in very narrow economic terms, through the self-protectionist lens of the outside medical profession.

The larger profession was blocking innovation in the organization, financing, and delivery of personal health services, focusing on professional ethics and curriculum, not on the roles and relationships embedded in organizational structures (Stevens 1971:147–48; Starr 1982). Industrial medicine fell in line, deferred to the outside physician, would not take away his patients, and would define itself as the ideological alter ego of organized medicine.

Thus Robert Legge, a leading industrial physician, could assure the AMA at its eighty-ninth annual meeting (in 1938) that the specialty he represented "has the opportunity, with the greatest group of our population, the worker and the industrialist, to forestall a political form of medicine with which the organized profession is not in sympathy" (Legge 1938). Company-employed industrial physicians would forsake their intellectual roots in the public health movement in the remote hope of forging alliances with organized medicine.

Meanwhile the industrial physicians embarked in 1937 on a long, discouraging, and ultimately semisuccessful campaign to earn professional recognition and the capacity to self-regulate through the mechanism of an AMA-approved specialty board. Twelve such boards had been approved by the AMA between 1917 and 1936 and three more came on line in 1937, the year the AAIP&S appointed the first of many committees to study its specialty-board problem (Stevens 1971). That it would be a problem had already been telegraphed in an exploratory discussion with the AMA in 1935. The two industrial physicians who made that trip to AMA headquarters in Chicago were told that "there was no such thing as a specialty of industrial medicine and surgery . . . that this was simply one of the subtopics under general medicine" (Selleck and Whittaker 1962:419). Not until 1955 did the medical profession grant the claim to legitimacy of the specialty by then known as "occupational medicine," recognizing it only as a subdivision of preventive medicine, one of three such subdivisions, parallel and equal to public health and aviation medicine.

In this as in the other drives for specialty board designation, "questions of education, status, and restrictionism were . . . intermingled" (Stevens 1971:201). The first two questions were obviously at the heart of the industrial physicians' campaign, but the third was more peripheral. In the drive for specialty status, a pattern had been set by ophthalmology, the first of the specialty boards, whose organization was inspired by monopolistic yearnings on the part of the medically trained eye specialists who wished to exclude optometrists to prevent them from taking away business. The surgical boards likewise sought to bar physicians without specialized training from performing operations that the surgeons wanted to control. In both cases, the push toward standardization was motivated also by a desire to upgrade the quality of care and improve the social and economic standing of the specialty in question, but critics contend that these considerations were secondary to the goal of excluding pretenders (Stevens 1971; Mechanic 1979:179).

Industrial physicians faced a different sort of problem. Unlike "consulting professionals" (Freidson 1970a), such as surgeons and ophthalmologists, industrial physicians were not competing for patients in an open economic marketplace. More like the "learned professions" of the Middle Ages, industrial physicians depended for their incomes and economic survival on the patronship of an elite, in this case decisionmakers within industrial firms. Their standing with that elite, however, was colored by their stature in the eyes of the medical elite, because businessmen take their cues about what is good and bad in medicine from medical men they know socially. Industrial physicians badly needed the ability to recruit practitioners with impeccable medical credentials, and this meant that as members of an aspiring profession they needed to compete for recognition among medical students coming out of training and among respected practicing physicians.

Here they labored under several handicaps, prime among which were their identification with the despised "contract practice" and their invisibility in medical school curricula and among the role models to whom medical trainees were being exposed. The certification program could not have delivered industrial physicians instantly from this marginal status. But if they had been able to capture the certification process earlier and more completely than they did, it might have inspired them to address the fundamental issues that were consigning them to the margins of medicine: their lack of control over the structure and content of corporate medical programs, their isolation within companies from the health-care financing provided through the employee benefit package, their deferential interactions with the outside medical-care system, their tenuous or missing relationships with hospitals and medical school curricula—in short, the absence of a structured role for them to play either within the business firm or in the larger health-care system.

Lacking leverage to tackle those structural issues, industrial physicians had little defense against the charge that they were not real specialists at all. When they first requested specialty designation in 1937, they were rebuffed as simply a subspecies of general physician; when they finally won their half-victory in 1955, they had been relegated, with public health, to a branch of preventive medicine. The two rubrics were very different, and neither alone was wide enough to give them growing room. The dichotomy between the two reflected a basic tension that had long weakened them.

Significance of the Interwar Period

From the time worker's compensation laws began to solidify a role for medicine in industry, opinion had been divided on how seriously companies did or would take the health conservation mission. Industrial medicine at this time branched into two segments between which important but largely covert differences developed in mission, organization, technique, clientele, ideology, and destiny, a process of segmentation that has been characterized in other medical specialties (Bucher and Strauss 1961; Bucher 1962), and one that is symbolized in the contrasting career paths of Alice Hamilton and Alvin Schoenleber.

The public health segment continued the work of Chadwick and the other nineteenth-century reformers who had begun to document "the social relations of health and disease" (Rosen 1979:25). These scientists were animated by a concern for the welfare of the individual worker, but their methods were statistical and their orientation to populations. Normally they worked outside of industry, in academia or the government, and spent their time meticulously piecing together bits of information that might explain the etiology of occupational disease. They clearly saw their mission in the classic public health terms symbolized most elegantly by Sir John Snow's removal of the pump handle from the cholera-infected well in eighteenth-century London. The ideal interventions are organizational ones, and the frustration for this segment of the field has been the difficulty, as outsiders, of influencing the internal decisions of organizations.

The clinical segment followed in Ramazzini's tradition of ascertaining from individual patients how work was affecting their health, and health their work. Those who chose to practice in corporate settings faced a unique set of problems. If their specialty was to be a form of general practice, it would be a truncated one, foreclosed by the rules of medical etiquette from engaging in more than the most mundane of the activities comprising the general practitioner's role. But if the distinctive feature of their specialty lay outside general practice, in the public health tradition as a kind of private-sector analogue to the sanitary reform movement, then they faced other equally serious constraints. Here they would meet bureaucratic pressures to define their roles and pursue their causal chains just short of any clear clash with the profit-oriented ends of the business enterprises in whose employ they served. Professional ideologies and self-interests on the one side, bureaucratic imperatives on the other, channeled them into a narrow path. A gradual erosion would be needed in the constraining power of those two realms—medicine and management—to widen the potential path of the industrial physician. World War II set the process in motion.

An Expanding Mandate for Occupational Health: 1940s and 1950s

The Second World War, even more than the First, radically altered the labor market. The Depression had provided employers a wide pool from which to select employees. The draft changed that by systematically removing from the pool a large cohort of able-bodied men. Manpower conservation and productivity again became patriotic duties for the nation President Roosevelt had declared the "arsenal of democracy."

Absenteeism rates nevertheless increased and, when analyzed, were found to reflect illnesses unassociated with occupational exposures in much greater preponderance than those linked directly with work. Mental health was also discovered at this time to be an important determinant of an employee's attendance record. These discoveries could in theory have given the industrial physicians involved in the defense effort license to begin calling for measures to close the gap between occupational and nonoccupational medicine.

One way would have been to enlist the aid of the private practitioner in the campaign to reduce absence, as was done in the Soviet Union shortly after the war (Field 1957). Alternatively, the industrial physician could have begun following the progress of the industrial patient through an episode of illness from the day he left the plant through his hospitalization and convalescence and his gradual and medically supervised resumption of full job responsibilities. This approach would have meant encroaching upon the terrain of the considerably depleted cadre of private practitioners—those who had stayed home from the war.

The appreciation that developed during the war of the influence on productivity of "nonoccupational" health factors might have greatly expanded the scope of occupational medical practice. Such an impact, however, was relatively minor and slow to be felt. As late as 1971, a survey of industrial health programs found skepticism on the part of corporate executives about the wisdom of increasing their firms' involvement in nonoccupational health care. The primary reason cited was "deference to what many management executives, and many occupational physicians as well, regard as the economic or marketing rights of private physicians" (Lusterman 1974:15–16).

The real influence of the war on the practice of industrial medicine was more indirect. First, it accelerated the movement of the federal government toward a more central role in the oversight of workplace conditions. The process was already in motion well before the outbreak of war. In 1933, President Roosevelt had named Frances Perkins his secretary of labor; from her work in New York state she brought experience in and a commitment to the safety and health of workers. A year after her appointment, she created the Bureau of Labor Standards "as a rallying point for those interested in job safety and health" and "the first permanent federal agency established primarily to promote safety and health for the entire work force," chiefly by helping the states improve their programs (MacLaury 1981).

The initiative for protecting workers had rested principally with the states, only five of which had organized occupational health programs by 1935. The Social Security Act, passed that year, earmarked funds for public health programs, including industrial hygiene. Congress passed its first specific industrial health legislation in the Walsh-Healey Public Contracts Act of 1936: it imposed safety standards on employers holding sizable government contracts. In 1939, when the U.S. Public Health Service was moved organizationally to the Federal Security Administration (from the Treasury Department) and geographically to Bethesda, Maryland (from Washington, D.C.), a Division of Industrial Hygiene was established in the National Institute of Health. By 1943, the Public Health Service was collaborating with industrial hygiene units in thirty-eight states and six cities and, in response to the war emergency, had assigned nearly every state health department a physician specializing in industrial hygiene. The Public Health Service's own annual budget for industrial health swelled during the war years to $4.5 million, only to shrink back again after the war (the total 1955 budget was $544,000) (Goldsmith and Kerr 1982:34). In retrospect, these early programs were far from adequate to the task (Page and O'Brien 1973), but they did begin to set a precedent for federal initiative in occupational safety and health even though it took until the late 1960s for pressure to be felt.[4]

A second indirect but significant influence the war had on industrial medicine was greatly to accelerate industrial growth and development in the decades immediately following the war's end. This period of prosperity had important subsidiary effects. Full employment had been demonstrated feasible during the war, and an expanding postwar economy held unemployment rates relatively low. Employers tended as a result to develop a longer-term perspective on the health and productive potential of their employees, more of whom were expected to spend an entire career with a single corporation. The drive immediately following the war to rehabilitate and reemploy disabled veterans provided the "high road" that Selby had mapped in 1919 in his Bulletin 99. Using medical examinations simply to discriminate against job applicants or employees with physical limitations was one thing; using them as part of a program of therapeutic treatment and job adjustment, quite another. The economic and social pressures that gradually came to bear on corporations created new incentives for this positive role for industrial medicine.

But the overriding difference between the two world wars in their impact on the evolution of industrial medicine was that the momentum generated by the first was shorter-lived. Following the second, the momentum continued and even built, as can be seen in the dynamics of membership in AAIP&S. From the armistice in 1918, when there were 340 members, through 1938, when the rolls reached the 545 mark, the association's membership averaged just over 300 physicians per year. Starting in 1939 (the year World War II began), the association had 894 members and its membership began to climb. In 1945, the year just after the war ended, it reached 1,637 and continued to increase, to 2,184 members by 1950 and by 1959 to 4,000 only then to drop again just below 4,000 for the next twenty years for reasons which are obscure (see table 3.1).

In 1951 the American Association of Industrial Physicians and Sur-

4. These trends are discussed by Goldsmith and Kerr (1982), Ashford (1976), and Mintz (1984), among others. Somers and Somers (1954:210–14) and Ashford (1976: 141–207) discuss the emergence of a federal role in occupational safety and health. Selleck and Whittaker (1962) make frequent, scattered references to it as well.

Table 3.1
Membership Rates in the Principal Professional Association of Occupational Physicians, 1915–1986

Year	Members	Year	Members
1916	150	1951	2281
1917	220	1952	2432
1918	275	1953	2800
1919	340	1954	2816
1920	400	1955	2997
1921	499	1956	3258
1922	493	1957	3361
1923	364	1958	3516
1924	203	1959	4000
1925	230	1960	3825
1926	216	1961	3765
1927	252	1962	3638
1928	257	1963	3707
1929	227	1964	3709
1930	315	1965	3720
1931	338	1966	3749
1932	330	1967	3832
1933	325	1968	3867
1934	327	1969	3963
1935	257	1970	3625
1936	320	1971	3644
1937	410	1972	3592
1938	545	1973	3620
1939	894	1974	3748
1940	1023	1975	3684
1941	1200	1976	3706
1942	1352	1977	3796
1943	1505	1978	3956
1944	1574	1979	4043
1945	1637	1980	4128
1946	1630	1981	4401
1947	1671	1982	4401
1948	1915	1983	4373
1949	2101	1984	4449
1950	2184	1985	4356
		1986	4574

Note: The association has progressed through several changes of name, from the American Association of Physicians and Surgeons in Industry, to the Industrial Medical Association, and finally the American Occupational Medical Association (AOMA).

Sources: 1916–1958 from Selleck and Whittaker (1962:442); 1960–1986 from the AOMA.

geons voted to condense its name to the Industrial Medical Association, changed again a few years later to the American Occupational Medical Association (AOMA), the organization's current name. Meanwhile, a smaller group, limited to physicians engaged in the full-time practice of occupational medicine (in one or more settings), had been organized in 1946 as the American Academy of Occupational Medicine (AAOM), the name it still uses.

World War II was a watershed also for the development of health insurance, fundamentally altering the socioeconomic context for the practice of all kinds of medicine, including that in corporations. The story has been told elsewhere (Somers and Somers 1967; Law 1976; Krizay and Wilson 1974, Starr 1982). It involved a gradual awakening to the way employment-based financing of health services was both a cause and an effect of rising health-care costs, driving them upward in a vicious circle. Private industry, as payer for care, had become intimately involved in the financing of health services because fringe benefits were deductible as corporate business expenses and were pretax income for employees. Throughout the postwar period employers, willy-nilly, assumed or had thrust upon them a growing share of the costs of health insurance as those costs rose. There would eventually be important ramifications for the practice of occupational medicine as companies became actively involved in efforts to moderate the escalation of costs.

Profound alterations in industrial processes, also of significance to company physicians, occurred during this postwar period. Rapid technological change, stimulated by the war economy, drove refinements in production techniques, creating new, more complex, and less well-understood hazards against which the American worker would need protection. Furnishing employment free from recognized hazards became doubly complex, involving both a moving target (advances in industrial processes bringing new substances into the workplace almost daily) and a changing and unpredictable arsenal (instability in scientific knowledge and in measurement techniques, altering benchmark definitions of the nature and scope of the problem). Increasingly sensitive measurements would place a growing burden on employers to anticipate exposures that though not immediately detectable, could harbor future liability on a very large scale.

Significance of the Years Just Before and After World War II

The conceptual distinction between "occupational" and "nonoccupational" health was challenged during World War II by evidence that a worker's job performance could be as tied to life outside the plant as to life within. This had little direct impact on the practice of occupational medicine, however, except in the precedent it obliquely set. Other precedent-setting trends were also appearing during this period. A federal presence in occupational health was just beginning to develop in the New Deal, and industrial health specialists gained some visibility when the war created an imperative to conserve the nation's productive capacity and to rehabilitate the injured. Labor's surge of postwar collective bargaining brought corporations into the health-care equation as a substantial and growing source of financing for care, although at this stage as passive conduits, not active participants. Explosive technological growth in the decades following the war filled the working environment with unstudied and potentially serious invisible, microchemical risks. All of these trends began to coalesce in the turbulent 1960s behind a grassroots struggle for the enactment of federal legislation designed to protect industrial workers and to empower them with the information and legal tools they would need to continue protecting themselves.

Origins and Impact of OSHA: 1960-1986

Many published accounts describe the conditions and events that inspired Congress to enact the landmark Occupational Safety and Health Act of 1970.[5] Effective labor agitation was a decisive factor, spearheaded by the United Mine Workers' campaign to win compensation for black-lung disease, which came to fruition in 1969 when Congress passed the Coal Mine Safety and Health Act (Smith 1986). Other driving forces included a rising injury rate (partly reflecting several widely publicized mining disasters that helped galvanize public opinion), a new awareness of the problem of occupational disease, associated with a growing environmental protection movement, and fundamental changes in the demographics and the expectations of the American labor force (Ashford 1976).

Difficulties OSHA encountered in its first half-decade are equally well documented: the absence of support in a strongly probusiness political climate, the ill-considered enactment of 450 "consensus standards" that exposed the agency to ridicule, and abject failure in both setting and enforcing meaningful standards. After the election of a Democratic administration in 1976, OSHA shifted its allegiances from industry to labor, made headway on its regulatory agenda, and came under intensified attack from the business sector, in public hearings, legislatures, polling booths, courts, and the mass media (Bingham 1982; Coye, Smith, and Mazzocchi 1984).

---

5. See, e.g., Ashford (1976), Donnelly (1982), Foulkes (1973), Page and O'Brien (1973), Mintz (1984), Goldsmith and Kerr (1982), Kelman (1981), Mendeloff (1980), Nichols and Zeckhauser (1977), and Coye, Smith, and Mazzocchi (1984).

Throughout this period, employers and their representatives opposed and resented the law, which curtailed management discretion in labor relations and the organization of work (Coye, Smith, and Mazzocchi 1984), while it seemed to portend substantial new costs for the abatement and surveillance of hazards. Labor pushed hard for a broad interpretation of the law's mandate, but management blocked its implementation at every possible turn. OSHA cast government and industry in starkly adversarial roles, and corporate physicians took up the cudgels as representatives of management. They resisted government intrusion into a formerly private domain of employer-employee relations and felt the sting of barbed criticism from officials in the new health and safety bureaucracies (Yodaikin and Robbins 1980; U.S. Department of Labor 1980b;35242–43). The irony is that they could not fail to perceive that their status as professionals inside the firm could be enhanced by new pressure the government was bringing to bear from the outside. It would force companies to expend nonproductive resources in support of the activities of occupational health practitioners, in effect converting employee health conservation—the profession's long-standing manifest goal—into a legitimate product of the industrial firm (Freedman 1981). Some in-house health professionals joked that the law's acronym—OSHA—stood for "our savior has arrived" (Kelman 1981:90), but corporate medical directors who went on public record preached the company gospel. Their ideological commitment, espoused since the close of World War I, was to "occupational medicine as a function of private enterprise" (Selleck and Whittaker 1962:87). Government regulation was therefore perceived as a threat, however much it might strengthen their hand.

That these external pressures should have enhanced the corporate physician's stature finds support in the reduction of pressure as the Reagan administration was dismantling the government regulatory apparatus. A Washington-based newsletter reported that many occupational health professionals were "laid off" in this period (Fishbein 1982:1). Because there are no meaningful data on employers' investment in health and safety programs or on the numbers and distribution of professionals to staff them, it is impossible to fully reconcile contradictory impressions of what the future may hold for the profession of occupational medicine.

If the past is prologue, external pressures and political rather than technical developments will be the stimuli to whatever progress the profession can make. With or without a strong government presence, the social and political forces unleashed in the past several decades seem unlikely to go away. Progress for company physicians, if it does come, will be measured in enhanced influence in corporate decisionmaking, a higher titer of trust, and a larger dividend of job satisfaction. Throughout the profession's emergence, these three interrelated issues have remained the central themes; influence, trust, and satisfaction are the commodities that physicians in corporations have struggled over the years to eke out as best they could. A closer look at what they do and at roles they play will bring these themes into sharper focus.

4 ■ The Corporate Medical Director

A physician, Ramazzini, was "the father of occupational medicine," but contemporary corporate medical directors are as likely to be heard quoting Peter Drucker or other writers popular in management circles as citing medical references. More than other questions, the issue of their cardinal identity—whether they are managers or physicians first—bifurcates the field. Some view themselves as doctors *in* corporations, family or community physicians whose family happens to be a community of workers. Others are more properly viewed as doctors *of* corporations, part of the management team, to which they bring medical expertise, just as the corporate counsel contributes a legal perspective.

Every corporate medical department has its own peculiar history, fits in a culture, and faces contingencies that differentiate it from others in other companies. However, data profiling the distribution of physicians among American corporations are sketchy at best. The few researchers who have thought to ask the questions have glossed over important details, such as whether the physicians employed by corporations are full- or part-time and, in the latter case, how their professional time is allocated and compensated.

In seeking to understand what the roles and role pressures of corporate physicians are and what the future may hold for them, answers to at least the following questions would be instructive. First, how many occupational physicians practice in American corporations? Of those, how many (a) practice full-time in a single company? (b) practice at corporate headquarters versus at plant or other operating installations? (c) spend full time delivering occupational medical services to employees but split their time among several employers? (d) spend only part of their professional time delivering occupational medical services, and among those, what proportion do they spend, and what activities take up the balance of their time?

Second, how many American corporations employ one or more full-time physicians? Among those, how many have corporate medical directors or chief medical officers at the corporate level? What is the distribution of plant physicians and of physician-to-employee ratios both company-wide and plant by plant?

Third, what characteristics of companies (their industries and technologies, their workforces and locations, their philosophies and management styles, the level of their "commitment" to employee health conservation, and so on) are associated with the employment of one or more physicians? What kinds of companies have the highest ratios of physicians to employees? Is there any evidence that they are delivering a higher quality health program?

Fourth (as a possibly expanding alternative to the salaried in-house model), are there noteworthy changes in the balance between in-house occupational medical services and those secured from clinics or consulting groups outside of corporations through contracts or fee-for-service arrangements?

Finally, can important trends be discerned in the answers to any of these questions? What hypotheses are suggested and is there evidence that a larger role is opening for occupational physicians or that a "new breed" of physician is being attracted to the field?

Unfortunately, available data permit only the most tentative and impressionistic answers to these basic questions.[1] Fragmentary information is available from membership rosters of relevant professional organizations including the American Occupational Medical Association, the American Academy of Occupational Medicine, the American Medical Association, the American Public Health Association, and the American College of Preventive Medicine. Each provides a piece of a large and complex mosaic.

A few special studies have been done, but none recently. In New York, a business-supported private research organization called the Conference Board conducts periodic studies of company personnel practices,

1. The Graduate Medical Education National Advisory Committee to the Secretary of Health and Human Services issued a report in 1980 projecting the need for physicians in all specialties. Known as the GEMENAC report, it commented on how difficult it is to measure manpower needs for preventive medical specialties, including occupational health, and pointed to a need for improvements in methodology and data. In most medical specialties the committee found surpluses, but for occupational medicine it projected a "target" need for 3,900 practitioners in 1990, a level that it expected would be "unreachable," based on current supplies and the capacity of the training system (GEMENAC 1980:231). Meanwhile, the supply of physicians in general is growing rapidly in relation to the population available to be served.

including the employment of health personnel. The National Institute for Occupational Safety and Health (NIOSH) published a report in 1978, seeking to estimate the need for occupational health manpower, including physicians. NIOSH has twice conducted large-scale national surveys of occupational health hazards in the workplace and has included a series of fourteen questions on the availability of medical services on- and off-site. The first, called the National Occupational Hazards Survey, was in the field from 1972 to 1974 and the second, called the National Occupational Exposure Survey, from 1981 to 1983. Other than in a preliminary paper presented at an international symposium (Pederson, Seiber, and Sundin 1986), those data have not yet been published, but they will be valuable when available. Also, the American College of Preventive Medicine has been surveying the need for practitioners of this specialty, which includes occupational medicine. Officials of the federal government's Bureau of Health Professions reported in April 1986 that they have been trying for over a year to secure clearance from the Office of Management and Budget to conduct a survey of manpower in the public health fields, including occupational medicine.

In 1986 the American Occupational Medical Association had 4,574 members, all physicians. Comparable numbers from previous years appear in table 3.1. Available demographic and practice information, summarized in figure 4.1 and table 4.1, indicate that 70 percent of respondents say they practice full time, although how many are salaried employees of a single company cannot be ascertained from the data. According to the NIOSH manpower survey, 62 percent of the jobs for occupational physicians in 1977 were rated by employers as "full-time," but the identity of those employers is unclear, making it difficult to know how to interpret the assessment of needs.

The American College of Preventive Medicine is the organization charged with examining occupational physicians for "board certification" in their specialty. About 400 occupational physicians belong to the college and as board-certified practitioners probably practice their specialty full time, although again not necessarily in a single organization. The American Public Health Association's section in occupational health, founded with about 11 members in 1914, had reached 1,278 members as of the last official count, in 1986. Of these, 381 were physicians, very few in corporate settings.

On the 1983 AMA master file a total of 2,648 physicians listed their primary specialty as occupational medicine, comprising 0.5 percent of active physicians. (Historical trends in these data appear in table 1.1.) Of these AMA-registered occupational physicians, 1,775 said they were involved in patient care, and of those, 1,672 were office-based, 103 hospital-based, 710 medical administrators, 52 researchers, 23 medical edu-

Table 4.1
Selected Characteristics of Members of the
American Occupational Medical Association, 1984[1]

	No. of respondents	Percentage of respondents
Gender		
Male	1977	93
Female	157	7
Years of experience		
less than 6	413	20
6-12	593	28
more than 12	1080	52
Medical department staff size		
less than 5	759	36
5-14	771	37
14-24	198	9
more than 24	361	17
Academic appointment		
No	1351	64
Yes	744	36
Work status		
Full-time	1459	70
Part-time	627	30
Practice location		
Industry	1208	59
Solo or clinical group practice	532	26
Military/government	143	7
Hospital[2]	82	4
Academia	82	4
Number of patients		
1-100	136	7
101-200	32	2
201-500	105	5
more than 500	1752	87
Annual teaching hours		
less than 5	1263	60
5-25	410	20
26-50	152	5
more than 50	263	12
Other professional societies		
to which respondents belong		
American Medical Association	1369 (64%)	
American Academy of Occupational Medicine	134	
American Academy of Family Physicians	104	
American College of Preventive Medicine	82	
American College of Physicians	80	
American College of Surgeons	42	
American Society of Internal Medicine	33	
American College of Emergency Physicians	29	
American Thoracic Society	18	
American College of Chest Physicians	15	
Plus 29 other medical subspecialty societies		

Table 4.1 (*continued*)

States where licensed
100–400: NY, CA, PA, OH, TX, IL, NJ, MI, MD, IN, FL
 70–99: VA, CO, MO, CT, NC, MA, MN, LA, WA, WI, TN
 30–69: KY, GA, AZ, OK, IA, KS, AL, DE, SC, OR, NB, DC, WV
  0–29: NM, ME, AR, UT, MS, ID, WY, VT, AK, HI, NH, NV, ND, RI, MT, SD, PR

---

1. Data supplied by the American Occupational Medical Association from membership survey in 1984. Total membership at that time was thirty-nine hundred; response rate to the survey was approximately fifty percent. Data should therefore be considered with caution, owing to the likelihood of response bias. Not all who responded to the survey answered every question.

2. Hospital practice has been growing rapidly since the time of the survey (personal communication, Donald Hoops, executive director of AOMA, 24 February 1987).

cators, and 88 in "other" activities. Whether they practice in business firms seems to be a question the AMA neglects to ask.

Among 1986 AOMA members, half (57 percent) of the 2,113 respondents indicating place of employment appear to be in the industrial sector: corporations (34 percent), companies (9 percent), plants (14 percent). The balance work in group (8 percent) and solo (10 percent) practices, clinics (14 percent), hospitals (4 percent), academia (3 percent), government (4 percent), the military (2 percent), and "other" (3 percent). Table 1.3 listed corporations employing more than five physicians (full-time or part-time) based on the 1986 membership roster of AOMA and informal telephone surveys.

The most extensive special studies of the employment of physicians in industry have been conducted by the Conference Board. Lusterman's 1974 report of a 1971 survey, though dated and limited, remains the most informative source of data on the corporate employment of health professionals. His sample comprised 800 companies, each with 500 or more employees. Of the 800, 12 percent employed one or more full-time physicians, but among the largest (firms with 50,000 or more employees), 81 percent had at least one full-time physician on the payroll. Lusterman's data also showed that the likelihood of a firm's employing at least one occupational physician varies by industry type (manufacturing and financial institutions were most likely to employ full-time physicians, wholesale and retail firms least so); varies directly with company earnings per employee and urbanization of the workforce; and varies inversely with the percentage of the workforce that is female. Extrapolating from his findings, Lusterman estimated that throughout American industry in 1971, some 3,200 physicians were employed full-time in about 850 companies. The modal corporate employer of one or more

Figure 4.1.
The Elements of Corporate Health Programs

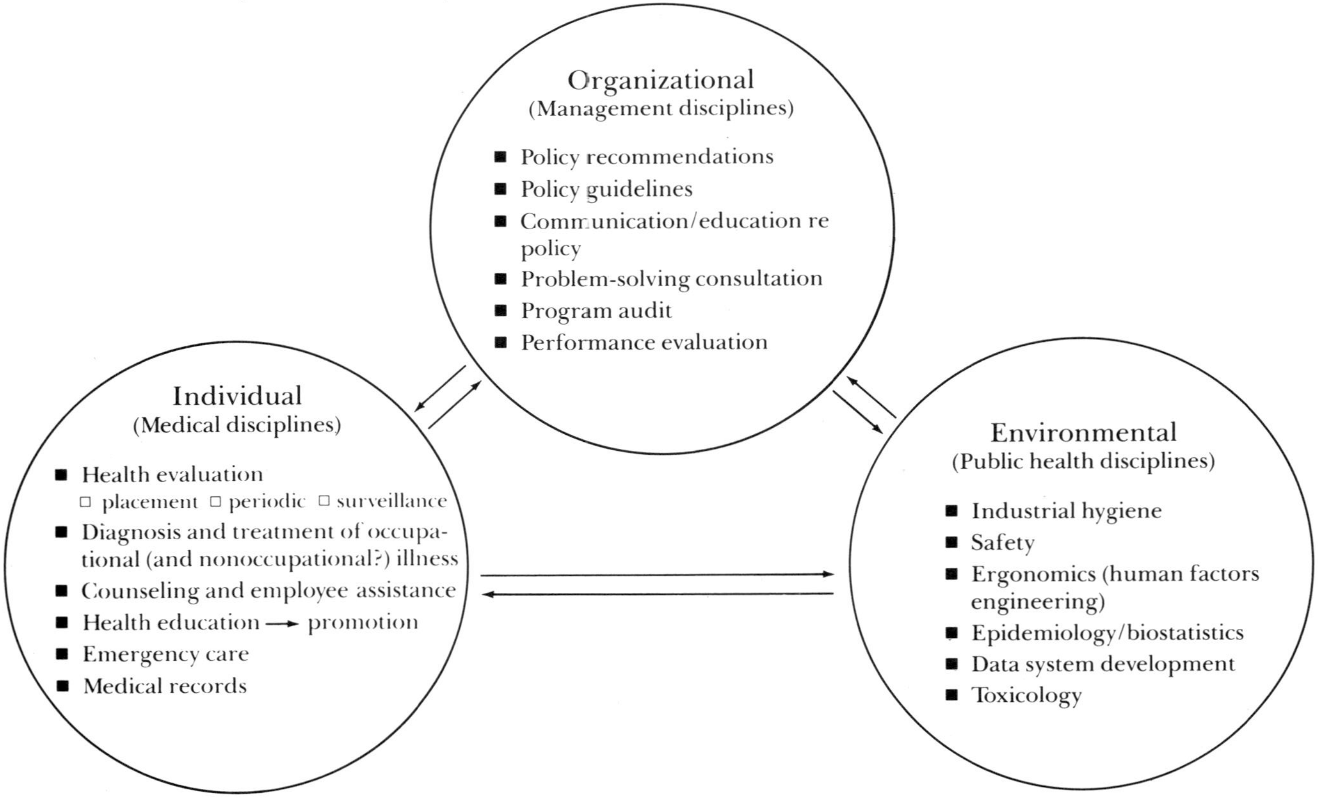

Organizational
(Management disciplines)

- Policy recommendations
- Policy guidelines
- Communication/education re policy
- Problem-solving consultation
- Program audit
- Performance evaluation

Environmental
(Public health disciplines)

- Industrial hygiene
- Safety
- Ergonomics (human factors engineering)
- Epidemiology/biostatistics
- Data system development
- Toxicology

Individual
(Medical disciplines)

- Health evaluation
  ☐ placement ☐ periodic ☐ surveillance
- Diagnosis and treatment of occupational (and nonoccupational?) illness
- Counseling and employee assistance
- Health education ⟶ promotion
- Emergency care
- Medical records

occupational physicians can be characterized, in sum, as a very large, highly profitable manufacturing or financial institution in the male-dominated heart of American industry (Lusterman 1974). Lusterman stopped at this rather limited descriptive analysis of his sizable data set and presented it at such a high level of aggregation that inferences cannot be drawn about factors that covary with the employment of physicians.

A more recent Conference Board survey of the status of a miscellany of "personnel practices" (Gorlin 1981) found patterns in the distribution of occupational physicians that seemed consonant with Lusterman's earlier and more detailed examination of health programs. Gorlin elicited responses on the employment of medical personnel from only one quarter, 573 corporations, of her total sample. Of those, 108 reported that they employ one or more "general" physicians full-time. Part-time physicians were reported on the payrolls of 111 of the responding firms. To what degree the two categories overlap (reflecting companies that employ both full- and part-time physicians) cannot be ascertained from the study. Neither Gorlin nor Lusterman asked companies that employ full-time physicians how many they actually employ. These statistics, remarkably, are entirely unavailable.

Without rudimentary accounting data on the distribution of physicians in industry, one can only speculate about differences among corporations in the numbers of physicians they employ and why. Nor can valid conclusions be drawn except on the most superficial level about historical trends in the corporate employment of physicians. Moreover, one must question what this statistic would actually measure. Analogous companies with similar levels of commitment and concern, for example (and similar records of performance, if they could be gauged), might face similar health challenges and yet develop equally defensible administrative mechanisms for deploying medical personnel in vastly different ways. Companies can arrange for high-quality occupational health services with few or no physicians on their payroll, through a managed system of contracts with external providers of care. The number of full-time physicians a company employs conveys descriptive information about the way its medical program operates and the roles its physicians play (the primary focus of this book) but serves rather poorly as a credible proxy for performance.

This observation underlines a problem for corporate physicians that was evident in the historical material in chapters 2 and 3. Defining the in-house physician's mission and contribution and measuring his performance remains a challenge still largely unresolved. Satisfactory measures of performance have to be more dynamic than the structural foundations inferred from numbers of providers employed and dollars spent, but even these fundamental measures are unavailable to physicians in corporations. More dynamic measures of performance would assess processes or, even better, outcomes. That these are difficult to define and defend has long been occupational medicine's Achilles' heel (Follman 1978; Bond, Buchwalter, and Perkin 1968; Fielding 1982a, 1982b).

Questions about the contribution of a corporate physician or his ability to point to and quantify a convincing impact emerge glancingly from these data on where physicians are employed. In addition, questions arise about the profiles of the physicians themselves. Members of AOMA range in age from under 40 (17 percent) to over 80 (1 percent), with half in the 51-to-70 age range. In "years of experience" they range from less than 5 (20 percent) to more than 12 (52 percent). That nearly half of this relatively old population reports fewer than 13 years of experience may be related to the tendency to enter occupational medicine in mid-career. The size of staff of which they are a part (whether they are heads or not is unclear) ranges from less than 5 (36 percent) to over 25 (17 percent); the number of patients ranges from 100 or fewer (7 percent) to over 500 (87 percent) (table 4.1). To assess whether and how the field is changing would require longitudinal data or a much more thorough survey than anyone has been able to conduct.

Anecdotally, there is a sense that younger physicians are being attracted to the field and that a public health orientation is becoming more pronounced. Interviews with incumbent medical directors reveal that wide diversity persists in what they do and the concerns they express. A few vignettes illustrate just how striking this diversity is. One corporate physician with a toxicological background (Dr. Thomas Maxwell)[2] had been orchestrating the work of a panel of distinguished scientists commissioned by his health-care products firm to interpret some perplexing data showing a statistically significant increase in chromosome anomalies among a small cohort of the company's 40,000 U.S. employees working at a single plant where a possible carcinogen was being used. "Toxicology is where the action is for occupational medicine" as far as Dr. Maxwell was concerned. Dr. Justin Poulter, the only full-time physician employed by a much smaller firm (a public utility of about 4,000 employees), wanted to obtain some formal training in toxicology and epidemiology but never had the opportunity. He ruefully observed that the closest he comes to handling public health problems is fielding complaints about "conditions in the washrooms" on the floor below his office.

2. Pseudonyms are used throughout the book to identify corporate physicians quoted or described from material obtained in interviews. The appendix provides brief summary descriptions (but not identifications) of the interviewees.

Two corporate medical directors of Boston-headquartered firms in the 35,000-employee range see each other occasionally at professional meetings but find little common ground. Their self-conceptions and taxonomic preferences are so discordant that one—Dr. Ralph Bradford—comfortably referred to himself as a "company doctor" and then went on to describe how he aligned himself with employees against overzealous personnel administrators, while the other—Dr. Russell Wyman—insisted that the one essential insight into his role was that he is "not a company doctor," because a company doctor is "four square against the employee." But he went on to explain how he deals with the "malingering" employee—the one "who has too much 'con' mixed in with his personality."

Some corporate physicians see the necessity of demonstrating a positive return on investment, but others denigrate "the cost-benefit stuff" as "pseudo-science." Some see the escalation in costs of employee health benefits as an opportunity to expand their own turf, while others skirt it as the turf of someone else. A few are consulted by senior executives for advice on sensitive and weighty matters, but many others struggle vainly to attract the attention of managers who seem to feel that physicians have what Thorstein Veblen called a "trained incapacity" to manage effectively. This strong diversity of opinion on basic roles and definitions is a persistent undercurrent of writings from and on the field of occupational medicine.[3]

What Corporate Medical Directors Do

Efforts to resolve ambiguity and standardize practice for the field have been initiated from time to time by the American Occupational Medical Association, through periodic consensus documents, including one on the scope of corporate medical departments (American Occupational Medical Association 1979) and another on careers in occupational medicine (American Occupational Medical Association 1981). These documents, together with textbooks by academicians and practitioners, describe essential and discretionary elements of occupational medical programs, as do the policy and procedure manuals many companies distribute to their staff or contract physicians.

The major building blocks of company health and safety programs are thus relatively easy to identify. But there are obvious differences in

---

3. For example, exhortative articles on why and how corporate physicians should become better managers are appearing with increasing regularity in the profession's specialty journal. Many are published versions of papers presented at recent annual meetings of the American Occupational Medical Association. See McDonagh (1982), Collings (1982), Stearns and Roberts (1982), Ritardi (1983), and McCahan (1983).

emphasis between firms or industries whose employees are distributed differently—demographically, geographically, and in the health requirements of their work. While such factors affect the types of health hazards to which employees are exposed, variations from company to company reflect more than hazards alone. If a bank faces different challenges than do chemical manufacturers, construction firms, or airlines of similar size, the differences can be ascribed to technological aspects of the work, educational and cultural characteristics of the workforces and their expectations, economic and regulatory pressures on the industries, the way employees are distributed across the country, styles of human resource management and labor market competition, the structure of the benefit package, and a welter of other variables.

Some screening and protection activities are mandated by statute and regulation (not only those of OSHA, but federal and state requirements that certain classes of employee—like pilots and drivers—be examined periodically) (Rothstein 1984). Beyond these requirements, though, the health services a company offers its employees are largely a matter of discretion, albeit discretion bounded often by uncontrollable circumstances—the real or perceived severity of health hazards in the production process or the salience of health issues in the corporate culture. Allied Corporation's trials with kepone, those of Manville Corporation with asbestos, and of Union Carbide with plant safety epitomize disquieting experiences many corporations have had in the last decade. That is one kind of salience. Another is evident at a company such as Johnson and Johnson, which sells health care products; PepsiCo, which sells a youth culture (the "Pepsi Generation"); or Xerox, with an advertising campaign ("Team Xerox") and product line (Marathon copiers) consciously linked to the company's health programs for employees. All three have high-visibility programs to assist their employees in the pursuit of vitality and physical fitness, as does Campbell Soup, now that the "Campbell Soup kids" have slimmed down, so that the company's product will continue to be perceived as wholesome. Product lines have a fundamental influence on the health culture of a firm.

Collective bargaining has also become a factor in the design of health and safety programs. Unions as a group were criticized for being slow to take up the cause of their members' safety (and especially their health) on the job (Page and O'Brien 1973), although there have been notable exceptions, including the United Mine Workers of America and the Oil, Chemical, and Atomic Workers Union. Even now, labor activists debate whether health and safety are of great enough concern to workers to be an effective organizing tool (Coye, Smith, and Mazzocchi 1984). Still, the consciousness of workers has been raised (Nelkin and Brown 1984), health and safety have been recognized (as of 1966) by the National Labor Relations Board as mandatory subjects for collective bargaining and, as of 1974, fully 93 percent of large labor contracts (covering 1,000 or more workers) contained safety and health provisions of various types (Coye, Smith, and Mazzocchi 1984: 96). Although less than 20 percent of the workforce is unionized and the proportion is falling, many companies feel the pressure, directly or indirectly, of a grassroots health and safety movement that has been building momentum over the past two decades.

With so many external factors influencing their ultimate scope and shape, the behavior of company-sponsored health programs seems almost to defy meaningful generalization. Nevertheless, their functions can be better understood by classifying them into three broad and enduring conceptual categories, corresponding roughly to control mechanisms available to protect a worker's health. Those mechanisms are generally classified into three distinct levels of control (Office of Technology Assessment 1985).

Controls on the first level depend on "personal protection," using devices such as respirators or ear plugs, which augment the individual's defenses against harmful agents. The second level of control uses engineering strategies to restructure the workplace and minimize exposure, by either removing hazardous materials or building barriers around them. On the third level, controls employ administrative mechanisms, such as the scheduling of work, which limits the amount or intensity of an individual's exposure or excludes certain classes of workers from certain types of jobs. Although a comprehensive health and safety program often sees its mission in broader terms than protecting workers against the overt hazards of their jobs, the three-part taxonomy provides basic concepts that can be stretched to inform the broader set of activities as well. It can be said of any corporate health or safety initiative that it is oriented principally toward one of the three levels of control: the individual, the working environment, or the organizational arrangements that fix relationships between individuals and working environments. This suggests that any corporate medical department will have three essential functions.

A Medical Function

The first group of activities, oriented toward individuals, sometimes serves the organization's needs (fitting workers to jobs, keeping them fit to work, and assessing "the work-relatedness of disease") (Kusnetz and Hutchinson 1979), and sometimes the individual's (providing health care or counseling services or offering voluntary health examinations). But all activities in this category involve assessments of the health of individuals or imply actions directed more at individuals than at the physical environment or the organizational structure. This does not mean that they are always left to the individual's discretion. Many corporate health policies begin with the statement that healthy employees are essential to the company's successful conduct of its business, that health maintenance is primarily an individual responsibility, and that the company provides a health conservation program to help individuals achieve that goal. However, the implicit rationale for many of the activities in this category is that the organization needs information on the health of individuals in order to assign workers to jobs, administer benefit programs, and protect the corporation from legal liability. When in possession of pertinent information on individuals, corporations generally reserve the discretion to act on it, even without the individual's concurrence. As we shall see, this puts company physicians in an awkward position.

The individually oriented category of effort draws on the health disciplines and is staffed predominantly by physicians, nurses, and allied health professionals. In this sense, it is the central core of occupational medicine. It includes evaluations of employees' health at various critical junctures in their careers, in particular before they are hired or assigned (or reassigned) to a specific job, after an episode of illness or injury, and periodically at intervals determined by both the hazards with which they work and the company's policy governing the scope of the medical program (Rothstein 1984). Referrals are made to outside resources for definitive treatment when the examinations uncover conditions beyond the department's purview. Maintaining relations with outside providers thus becomes central to the in-house physician's concerns.

The individually focused activities also include diagnosis and treatment of occupational injuries or illnesses and whatever amount of care for nonoccupational illness company policy and departmental resources permit. True primary health care goes well beyond corporate medicine's traditional involvement in diagnosis, treatment, and early referral of anything but the most routine cases (Walsh and Tell 1984). Out of deference to private practitioners, company policies often state that liaison with the employee's personal physician enables the medical department to integrate its services into the employee's total health-care needs in a way that complements and does not undermine or threaten the relationship between employees and their personal physicians.

Emergency care and maintenance of medical records are basic activities in the individual realm, the complexity of which varies with the setting and circumstances. In large chemical plants, elaborate emergency protocols are commonplace. Some headquarters medical staffs in high-profile firms (for example, those with South African investments or operations) participate in planning the company's response in the event of a terrorist threat or attack.

Also in the individually oriented activities, most large corporations include some health education among the services they provide; elaborate "health promotion" or "wellness" programs are being developed in a number of companies, and these extend the traditional health education mission. Counseling or employee assistance programs (especially those that deal with substance abuse) are becoming extremely widespread, often but not always under the aegis of corporate medical departments (Walsh 1982).

An Environmental Function

The public health paradigm defines the disease process as the confluence of a susceptible host with an infectious, toxic, or otherwise harmful agent, in a facilitating environment. The chain of causality can be broken by making decisive changes in any one of those three variables. The individually oriented activities in a health and safety program focus on the host—that is, on individual employees and their susceptibility to various kinds of harm. The environmentally oriented ones focus on both the agent and the environment, as well as on the circumstances that may bring them together with a susceptible host. For this reason they draw on disciplines related to public health.

The activities in this category involve medical personnel but also (depending largely on the mix of products and productive processes) safety experts, industrial hygienists, epidemiologists or biostatisticians, and human factors engineers. It is a "health protection" effort, encompassing programs to monitor exposures in the workplace, both immediate hazards (the traditional safety task) and longer-term, lower-level toxic risks (the concern of industrial hygiene). Monitoring is done through direct inspection of the workplace and indirectly through biological tests and clinical evaluations of potentially exposed employees. But the second kind of monitoring is individually oriented and therefore categorized more logically with health services activities.

Physicians in medical departments with narrowly defined domains (a structural question addressed below) may themselves participate only in this biological monitoring aspect of environmental health. But if they are in companies with serious health hazards, they normally spend much of their time interacting and conferring with the company's public health personnel. Companies with few health hazards have little or no involvement in this sphere. That may change—for two reasons. First, chemicals are becoming more prevalent in all kinds of production processes, and questions are arising about the long-term health effects of a growing number of substances and commercial operations.

The second imperative that may eventually drive all kinds of companies into the environmental sphere is the problem of occupational stress, which is complicated by the automation of white-collar jobs. When visual display terminals—the screens used with computers—first appeared as a potential occupational health hazard, the initial concern emphasized physiological harm. Later, emotional or adjustment issues (for example, fears about being displaced by machines) were thought to be principally involved, and finally the problem was defined as ergonomic, having to do with the design of furniture and of keyboards and screens (National Research Council 1983). The concern therefore shifted from the original individually oriented medical focus to a more conventional environmental health concern, broadly construed. Automation of office work is likely to exhibit this general pattern.

The environmental category involves hazard-abatement procedures, with the necessary educational and communication efforts involved in implementing such controls. Keeping abreast of changing government regulations is a particular challenge here too. The conduct of epidemiological, ergonomic, and toxicological studies and the development of integrated data systems for passive epidemiological surveillance of the workforce also belong under the environmental rubric; such activities are in various stages of development, although for the most part only in large companies deeply involved in the production or use of chemicals, petrochemicals, and other very hazardous materials. Some companies also look to their health and safety programs for direct or indirect stewardship for the health effects on anyone (not just the company's employees) of all products and byproducts entering or leaving the workplace. These are product-safety functions, which can also be found in a wide range of other departments—some quite far removed from the medical program—units such as quality assurance, engineering, marketing, insurance, risk management, research and development, legal, and administration (McGuire 1979:19).

The activities discussed so far—whether individually or environmentally oriented—establish the line responsibilities of a corporate medical department, the programs it carries out. These may vary widely from one firm to another in scope (how many issues it addresses), implementation (how much it invests in addressing each issue), and availability (how many divisions, locations, employees, dependents, retirees, and others it attempts to serve).

In surveys of large employers, for example, most respondents say they do sponsor "health education programs" (Gorlin 1981), an ambiguous finding because many activities can legitimately support an affirmative response to such a question. "Programs" range from an occasional admonition in the company house organ against smoking, the heavy use of salt, or a sedentary lifestyle to the multifaceted interventions a few companies (IBM, Johnson and Johnson, Kimberly-Clark, PepsiCo, Xerox) have developed to educate and motivate their employees (and sometimes dependents and retirees as well) and to change the corporate culture in hopes of reinforcing behavioral change toward more healthful living (Parkinson et al. 1982).

The same vagaries of definition confound the interpretation of data showing the distribution of other corporate health programs, such as "medical examinations" (how often, for what conditions, using what technology, providing what feedback and follow-up?), or "employee assistance" (with what range of emotional and substance-abuse problems, with what degree of pressure to improve job performance, using what treatment modalities for what period of time and with what provisions for follow-up?) (Walsh 1985a).

On top of this variation in the content of different programs called by the same names sits wide variation in policies (for example, defining eligibility to participate in a program), as well as frequent disjunctions between the formal policy describing a program and the actual level and manner of its implementation throughout what is often a highly decentralized and widely dispersed organization. These policy issues are the focus of the third broad category of corporate medical activities.

An Organizational Function

The third category includes policy and planning activities, such as recommending new and revised corporate health policies and guidelines for implementation, auditing the company-wide occupational health program against established policies and procedures, and providing for training and continuing education opportunities for health professionals on the staff. These take place principally on the corporate level, although decentralized medical programs in operating divisions sometimes replicate at the plant or division level much of the organizational function at corporate headquarters.

Other integrating activities in this category include liaison and communication within the department and into the field medical offices, as well as with other corporate-level departments whose jurisdictions overlap that of the medical department, giving the two entities "shared accountability" for aspects of the health program. Important among these overlapping areas is the benefits staff, with whom some corporate medical departments interact with increasing regularity, providing input into the design of the employee health-benefit package and participating in the routine administration of certain benefit programs, most commonly long-term disability insurance, where medical judgment may be needed. Liaison with the engineering or research and development staff is important if health and human-performance concerns are to be reflected in the early design of new production processes—not only physical aspects of the organization of work, but social arrangements as well. Again, these interactions may take place not only at the corporate office but also between corporate and operating personnel and within the operating entities, among the various health-related disciplines there.

As in the other two realms, companies vary here in the amount of corporate energy they devote to these activities. They use a variety of mechanisms (policy statements, task forces and committees, statements of accountability, briefing sessions, incentive systems) to shape and implement health policy within the corporation. The choice of integrating and communicating mechanisms reflects in part the circumstances and prevailing practices of a particular firm. Also it reflects the location of the boundaries around the medical department—the question of structure, or how the company organizes to undertake its health programs.

The three categories of activity are summarized in figure 4.2. Any appearance of standardization is misleading owing to wide disparities from company to company and, within a given company, from site to site in the degree to which various programs are actually being implemented. In health evaluation, or rehabilitation, or hazard-abatement programs, or in data-system development, such disparities are reflected in questions like: how long has the activity been conducted; is it governed by a formal written policy, and how fully is the policy being carried out in practice; what proportion of the workforce is eligible and by what criteria; how frequently is it conducted, how is it staffed, who participates, is it evaluated, what is its cost, and so on.

The Structures of Corporate Health Programs

Closely related to these functional questions but conceptually distinct are questions of the structures of health and safety programs in American firms. The structures partially militate the functions. Structures define task environments and working relationships, both within the organization and beyond. Many corporate medical directors describe as an important function the interaction with other company departments and disciplines involved in environmental surveillance and control. Some corporate structures, however, place those environmental disciplines *within* the overall health and safety apparatus. In such cases, environmental surveillance becomes a direct function of the health and safety department, so that liaison outside the department is no longer necessary.

Structures reflect the different ways companies choose to allocate responsibility for meeting objectives in occupational safety and health. A series of interlocking questions uncovers the structural consequences of those implicit policy choices:

1. Which of the functions are conducted anywhere in the company and which are not? Of those carried out somewhere in the firm,
2. which are centralized at the corporate level and which are not? Of those centralized at the corporate level,
3. which are conducted directly by the corporate medical department and which are not? And with respect to those functions not under its direction,
4. what consultative and supportive roles is the corporate medical department in a position to play?

Figure 4.2 abstracts the essential elements of six common corporate structures for health and safety programs. The six structures, in turn, create at least sixteen distinct structural locations in which full-time corporate physicians can find themselves. Six of those locations commonly carry the title "corporate medical director." Roles of corporate physicians vary markedly in these different structural situations, although levels in the hierarchy can be misleading as an emblem of influence or authority in the firm.

A few large companies with elaborate health and safety programs have integrated them horizontally, as depicted by type I in figure 4.2. Examples are Johnson and Johnson, IBM, and Alcoa, all of which have developed these structures only within the past decade, and in some cases within the past three to five years. More common than the first, the second structure (type II) appears to be similar from the corporate medical director's perspective except that he (or she) reports in the first instance to a physician, in the second to a lay manager. This one difference, however, can markedly affect the roles those two physicians play. Where he reports to another physician, the corporate medical director will less often be the company's spokesman on medical concerns—resolving an issue with organized labor, presenting testimony in a government forum, or conveying sensitive information to employees or the press. The corporate medical director whose physician-boss handles these public appearances probably enjoys less prestige in the corporation than does his counterpart in an otherwise comparable role, who is the most senior physician in the firm. On the other hand, he, unlike that counterpart, has a professional peer who can run interference for him in the corporate boardroom. That simplifies his life. Meanwhile, if he performs well, his future prospects may differ from those of his counterpart in the second structure, who probably cannot look forward in the future to a significant job promotion in his own company.

Corporate physicians have seldom climbed the management ladder to jobs that extend their purview beyond health and safety affairs. Very few have traded corporate medical directorships for higher-level positions

Type I

```
                    director (or VP)
                    health & safety (M.D.)          ← Ia
     ┌──────┬──────────┬─────────┬──────────┬──────────────┐
industrial  etc.   corporate    etc.     safety      environmental
hygiene            medical               director    medicine
director           director                          director
                   (M.D.)             ← Ib
                      │
                   corporate          ← Ic
                   physicians
                      │
                location physicians   ← Id
                and nurses
```

Type II

```
    ┌ ─ ─ ─ ─ ─ ─ ─ ─ ─ ─ ─ ─ ┐
   etc.      safety       corporate
                          medical director
    IIa ──────────────→
                          corporate
    IIb ──────────────→   physicians
                              │
                          location physicians
    IIc ──────────────→   (and nurses)
```

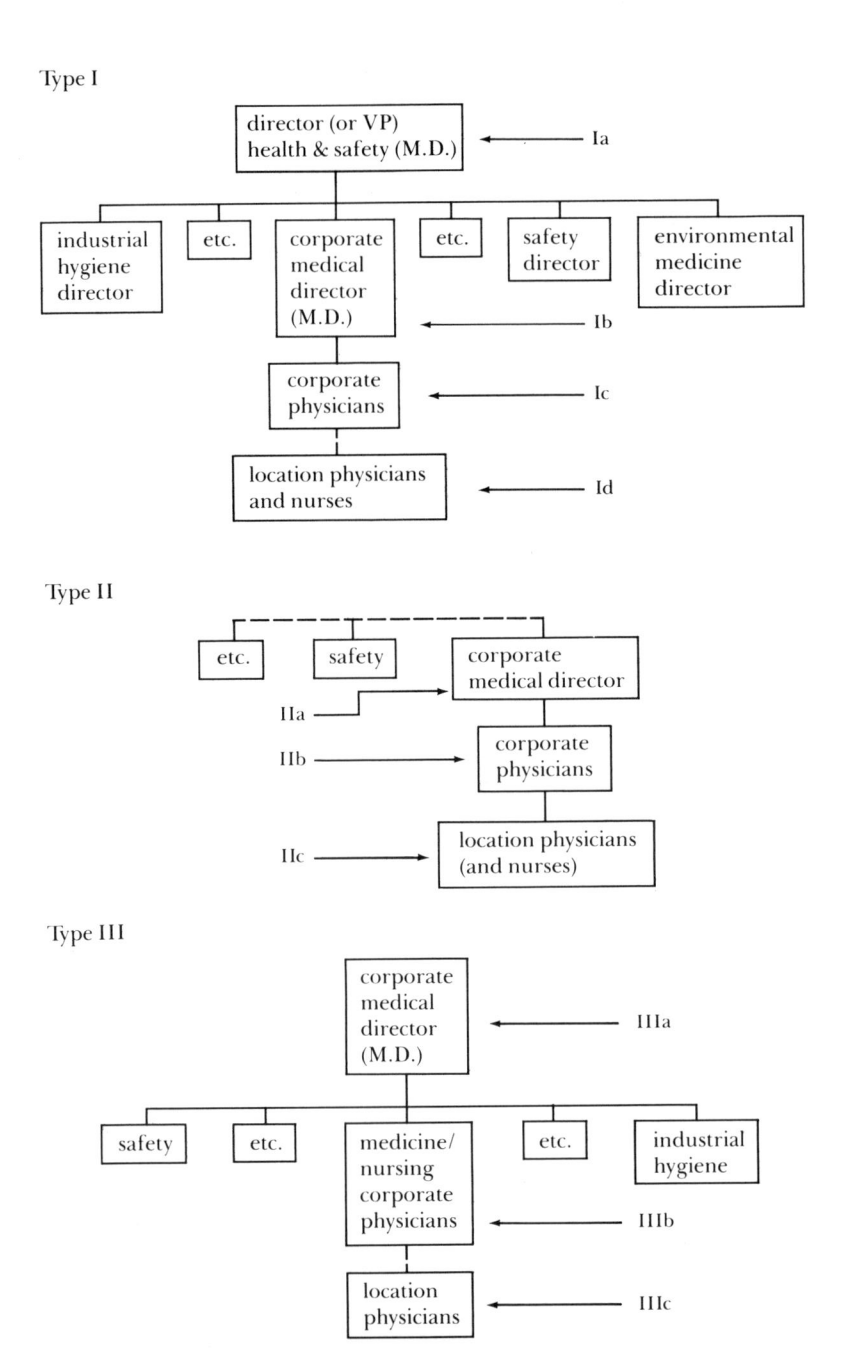

Type III

```
                 corporate
                 medical
                 director            ← IIIa
                 (M.D.)
     ┌───────┬──────────┬──────────┬──────────┐
   safety  etc.     medicine/    etc.    industrial
                    nursing               hygiene
                    corporate
                    physicians    ← IIIb
                        │
                    location      ← IIIc
                    physicians
```

Figure 4.2.
Some Common Structures of Corporate Health and Safety Programs

Type IV

(no safety, industrial hygiene, etc.)

corporate medical director ← IVa

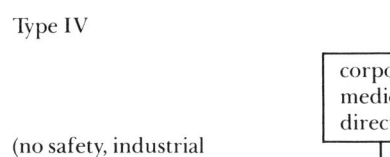

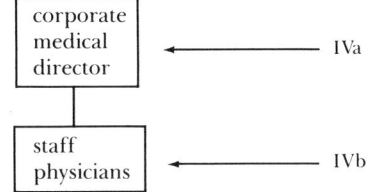

staff physicians ← IVb

Type V

conglomerate corporate headquarters (no medical department)

corporate medical directors (operating companies) ← Va

location physicians (and nurses) ← Vb

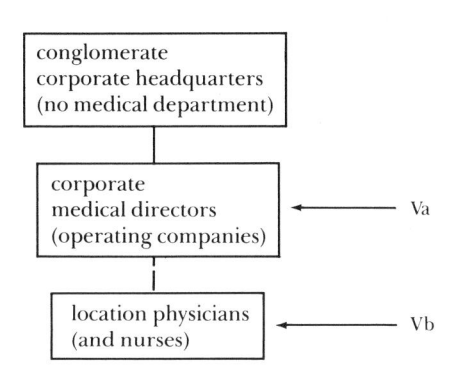

Type VI

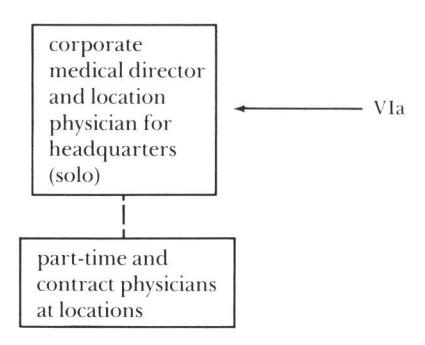

corporate medical director and location physician for headquarters (solo) ← VIa

part-time and contract physicians at locations

16 different structural locations for full-time corporate physicians

Figure 4.2 (*continued*)

managing an entire personnel or human-resources department, or one charged with environmental-quality engineering and product integrity. As a result, the corporate medical director's job has had a built-in ceiling except in the first structure, where there is a "physician's role" to be aspired to in the slot above. These factors create restraints on the influence, trust, and satisfaction available to corporate physicians in their organizational niche.

In the third structure, the corporate medical director's role resembles that of the director or vice president of health and safety in the first. Both have responsibility for many or all of the occupational health disciplines, not only occupational medicine and nursing but also industrial hygiene, safety, and whichever of the other environmentally oriented disciplines (for example, biostatistics, epidemiology, or ergonomics) the company supports. How many additional disciplines come under this expanded health and safety department (whatever its director's title) varies from company to company and from time to time. When a medium-sized chemical company recruited as corporate medical director a physician with strong toxicology credentials, industrial hygiene was moved under his directorship, but safety, "which had always been a big deal" in the firm, was left alone. One electric utility recently moved safety under the corporate medical director, after years of separation, because a management consulting firm advised the company that its divisions tended to be broken down into units too small for maximal efficiency.

The fourth structure in figure 4.2 is that found in financial institutions and other large corporations without serious enough physical health hazards to warrant safety and industrial hygiene operations. Their labor forces are mostly white-collar and their jobs mostly safe. By that criterion, insurance companies qualify as well, but they are a special case because of the central roles physicians play at that industry's technical core—in underwriting, claims analysis, and physical examination, either of applicants for life and health insurance policies or of policyholders who have filed claims. The corporate medical director of a large insurance company tends to play a hybrid role, in part as an occupational physician managing a traditional employee health service, in part as an insurance physician, overseeing or at least interacting with a whole department of other physicians engaged in work related directly to the company's essential product. In the larger companies, these various functions are usually housed in different areas or departments of the firm (Warshaw 1977). But even if totally separate, the physicians engaged in the delivery of employee health services in an insurance firm have a different status and outlook from those of physicians in firms whose product has little if anything to do with health and health-care delivery and whose operating units employ no physicians. Physicians for pharmaceutical firms also play unique roles in product development and testing and in marketing to other physicians (Barber 1967; Fox 1961). These set them apart from corporate medical directors exclusively charged with employee health conservation or management.

The Medical Director's "Role"

Such diversity as we have seen in the functions and structures of corporate medical programs, and such dissonance as we have heard among corporate medical directors on fundamental definitions and directions, seem to undermine the very notion that these physicians occupy a distinguishable or coherent "role." But the heuristic value of a concept like "social role" is that it can capture common features in phenomena that appear diverse, and in so doing can provide insights that would otherwise be lost.

Role theory has been challenged and advanced by the problem of heterogeneity and diversity within particular roles. Many early writings were uncritical in accepting "the postulate of role consensus" and defined a role as a fairly immutable and consistent set of expectations (or rights and obligations) that society attaches to a given status or social position. The articulation of these roles was seen as a central mechanism through which a social system enables its members to realize individual and collective goals. Doubtful that social roles actually win the broad consensus that early analysts apparently took for granted, Gross, Mason, and McEachern (1958) noted a more recent trend in social science to view role consensus as a variable requiring investigation, not as a given. The distinction is important. If consensus is assumed, differences in role behavior tend to be explained by differences in the attitudes, values, and personalities of the role incumbents. But if one assumes that *expectations* may vary—that people whose opinions matter will differ in their views of the obligations that attach to a particular position—then questions about role behavior give way to questions about how expectations are shaped and by whom: what Merton (1968:422–38) calls a "role set." These refinements in role theory led next to the observation that competing expectations reflect subdivisions of a given role into various "role sectors," each oriented to a different "counterposition" within the total role set. This conceptual framework provides a tool for sifting through the complexities and inconsistencies in the corporate medical director's role in search of a few essential elements. It also begins to hint at subtler questions of influence and status.

Sources of Authority

The organizational structures described in figure 4.2 interact in intricate ways with two other structural issues—titles and reporting relationships—that strongly affect status. Both are symbols that have animated or annoyed corporate physicians since the specialty first emerged. Some corporate medical directors hold the title vice president, including those at Citibank, Kimberly-Clark, General Mills, General Foods, General Electric, several of the large insurance firms (and, no doubt, several others). That the title is relatively rare is confirmed in 1986 statistics provided by the American Occupational Medical Association. Only 69 (or 3.5 percent) of over 2,000 members who responded to the survey reported that their titles were president or vice president. Of these, an indeterminate number practice in hospitals, clinics, consulting firms, and other such organizations where the title signifies something quite different than it does in a large corporation. Titles vary across and within industries. Although banks and insurance firms have more vice presidents for corporate medicine than do other companies, they tend to be less sparing with that title than are companies in other industries. Reading too much into titles, without understanding what they signify in a particular corporate context, can be misleading.

Reporting relationships should be less variable and less purely symbolic than titles and therefore more significant. The essential idea behind a monocratic bureaucracy is that power resides at the top, and the closer an office is to that pinnacle, the more power it confers. Occupational physicians consider their rank a serious if thorny issue (Roberts 1978b). During his thirty-year tenure at Exxon, Norbert Roberts said he watched one after another of his company's operating divisions, acting independently, upgrade the reporting status of their medical directors, whereupon, in his view, the quality of the medical programs and their ability to recruit physicians improved perceptibly. These were the "empirical" impressions that he believed justified his recommendation to his "thinking" colleagues that they consider avoiding associations with companies in which their proposals would have to be communicated through a hierarchy of lay managers before reaching the top.

But union physicians disagree. Loren Kerr, of the United Mine Workers of America, expressed an opinion shared by many in organized labor when he implied that corporations assign their medical directors lofty titles and positions in order to coopt them into a management mindset inconsistent with the interests of the workers who are their patients. Problems in industrial physicians' relationships with workers have "been accentuated," he said, "by the elevation of physicians in the corporate structure to positions of technical advisors sharing management viewpoints" (Kerr 1977:6).

The contradiction in these two views of the optimal placement of a corporate physician gives one indication that this is not a simple issue. Questions of how highly in the corporate structure the top physician is placed, how broad is his or her domain, and how dark is the "dotted line" linking the medical departments in the operating units to the corporate-level department are fundamental to an understanding of the roles corporate physicians play. These relate to the "elusive" questions of corporate philosophy and mission, the underlying rationale for the medical effort, and the ways in which medical personnel interpret their mandate from top management. All have to do fundamentally with issues of authority.

Moving from the concrete level of describing how specific programs look and behave to a more abstract plane of seeking to understand why they exist introduces a common dilemma for social science. There is an inherent tension between concepts that are idiographic (or particularizing) and those that are nomothetic (or generalizing). Corporate physicians' stature, status, and roles are sufficiently complex that an adequate description of them must be so rooted in a particular time and place as to provide little or no basis for comparison with related phenomena. Idiographic concepts seem called for here. And any concepts that can be used in a nomothetic way to synthesize and generalize from specific cases and to facilitate comparison will have to be so general that they will fail to capture what is unique and distinctive to any given case. Max Weber, who explicitly identified this tension, also developed an analytic construct for dealing with it: the ideal type, "a measuring rod that enables investigators to discern similarities and differences in concrete cases" (Coser 1971:227). Weber's ideal type is a heuristic device, an aid to analysis. It oversimplifies and deliberately distorts reality by distilling out distinguishing characteristics and core elements. Weber emphasizes that the construct is "ideal" in the sense of being a pure or idealized form of a phenomenon, not in an evaluative sense: "The idea of an ethical imperative, or a 'model' of what 'ought' to exist, is to be carefully distinguished from the analytical construct, which is 'ideal' in the strictly logical sense of the term" (Miller 1963:29). Weber's virtuoso uses of this analytic device were in his explication of the way the Protestant ethic (an ideal type) fostered the spirit of modern capitalism (Green 1959) and in his seminal work on the nature of "bureaucracy," an organizational form that he described in detail as an ideal type (Weber 1947:324–41).

The Weberian analysis of bureaucracy (Weber 1947) provides not only the analytic tool but also the generic concepts needed to characterize corporate medical departments in ideal typic terms. The theoretical problem that drew Weber into that analysis resembles the practical problem corporate medical directors face. In both cases, the underlying issue is legitimacy of authority. Chapter 1 stated the problem for corporate physicians as essentially an issue of social control and medical work, juxtaposed professionally rooted standards of conduct against organizationally imposed rules of role, and wondered which prevails when a physician enters the full-time employ of a corporation with a mission that is entirely nonmedical. The importance of rules of role in a modern bureaucracy was among Weber's central insights. Those rules, he said, rest on legal-rational authority, one type of authority used to legitimate control of others' behavior. Legitimacy enables authority to be claimed by those who exercise it and to be accepted by those over whom it is exercised. Another important way legitimacy can be achieved in modern societies is through what Weber called charismatic authority, which attaches to an individual by virtue of his ability to kindle allegiance and inspire followers to break with the past and join him in his mission.

Two ideal types of corporate medical departments can be postulated from this. The first is an "institutional" program. Firmly entrenched in corporate policy and structure, it derives its legitimacy from this formal status. As an inherent part of the bureaucracy, the institutional program exercises an authority based on rules and procedures, job descriptions, and clearly established lines of accountability. This authority transcends the influence of any one individual. The "organizational" functions outlined in figure 4.1 are elaborately developed in the institutional programs because it is from them that the department's legitimacy flows. Managers in these corporations judge the performance of their medical personnel according to the contribution they make to the smooth operation of the organization, their willingness and ability to help solve problems that the organization defines as worthy of attention.

Contrary to the institutional program, the second ideal type, like Weber's charismatic authority, draws for its legitimacy within the organization on qualities that attach to an individual. It is antibureaucratic or "idiosyncratic." In this case, however, the authority requires not so much the charismatic force of an individual's personality or an ability to inspire followers. Instead, the authority this physician enjoys within the corporation derives from the external, professional role that senior management has imported into the organization in part for its symbolic value. The charisma of social role, or the role mystique of physicians in modern society, sustains an otherwise ambiguous corporate role and enables the firm's other managers to perceive it as legitimate. As one medical director answered in response to the question whether he is held to account for the results of his programs, "No. The front office likes to feel good about the medical department."

Because it is shaped and defined more by an individual than by an organization, this type of corporate medical department tends to be idiosyncratic, emphasizing those aspects of occupational medicine that the particular incumbent feels most comfortable practicing. The idiosyncratic nature of the program is reinforced by the inevitable insecurity of individually based authority. Those seeking to maintain charismatic authority cannot afford to take risks or to surround themselves with people possessing expertise they lack. Any deputies they have will tend to be acolytes who can be counted on not to undermine their fragile authority. In the case of the idiosyncratic corporate medical programs, this instability will limit the scope of the program to the areas in which the incumbent medical director has expertise. Programs resting on this type of authority tend to be found in companies where paternalism has been a strong factor. They tend to have first-generation medical directors who came to the firm through a personal relationship with its chief executive. The influence that physicians in this situation can exercise often derives from the external mobility they are believed to have. They can stand up to management from time to time because management knows—and they know—that they can go back to their private practices or their academic posts. They have the authority of "exit" but not necessarily of "voice" (Hirschman 1970).

For Weber, ideal types need only be "plausible and objectively possible"; they need not exist in reality. Like Weber's ideal types, the "institutional" versus the "idiosyncratic" corporate medical programs are oversimplifications. Yet they do speak to a reality in occupational medicine, where the man-makes-the-job theme has become a truism.

Some corporate health programs do appear more tightly woven into the institution's fabric than others. The institutional programs are seen by management as a means to an end. The end is defined by the organization; it may be a perception that chemicals need to be understood and controlled more effectively than they have been, as at Allied Corporation, or that absenteeism needs to be managed, or that government regulations need to be anticipated or satisfied. The idiosyncratic programs are seen by management as an end in themselves. The physician is brought into the corporation as a symbol of management concern for the health and welfare of employees. He is given wide latitude and little in the way of a specific organizational mandate. He may develop one over time, in which case his program may gradually evolve toward the institutional type. Otherwise, his retirement creates a succession crisis because the company's senior managers so closely identify the medical program with one individual physician that they fear he may be irreplaceable. Weber identified this as a generic problem for charismatic authority, which, he said, has to be somehow "routinized" if it is to weather the succession crisis.

The two ideal types circle back to the underlying theme identified in chapter 1—the problem of how some physicians are able to adapt to a practice situation that others consider difficult at the very least. From the standpoint of the physician, according to one line of thought, the program based on institutional authority should offer the preferable solution. If ambiguous and conflicting expectations in a role are as stressful as role theory indicates (Gross, Mason, and McEachern 1958; Kahn et al. 1964), then the institutional program's clearer articulation of accountabilities should relieve some of the pressures of the corporate physician's job.

On the other hand, theories of professionalism would favor the idiosyncratic program as the one that would provide the physician the latitude he would need to adapt most comfortably. This interpretation holds if professions as occupations are universalistic and oriented toward an outside reference group that values specialized expertise. Professionals, according to Gouldner (1957), are "cosmopolitans" who in contrast to "locals" are less loyal to the organizations where they work, more committed to the skills they possess, and more oriented for approbation and intellectual stimulation outwardly to their professional peers than inwardly to the organization. Advanced degrees, publishing, and the opportunity to do their own research are important to cosmopolitans, who tend to know fewer of the organization's managers and, within the organization, to commit themselves more exclusively to a department in which they share professional interests than to the wider entity. They may be in an organization, but they are not of it. The organization employs them because it needs their expertise, but it loses some loyalty in the exchange. Cosmopolitans exhibit greater willingness to leave an organization; their outward orientation makes them "itinerants" in Hughes's term (1958:136).

The institutional corporate medical program defines the physician's role in organizational terms, which must constrain his cosmopolitan tendencies. This contradiction lies at the heart of conventional theory on the conflict between professionalism and bureaucratization, and it leaves us at a loss to decide which of the ideal types is preferable from the standpoint of the physician's accommodation to the organization. Role theory yields one answer, the theory of professions, another. The question that flows from this dilemma is whether there are ways corporate physicians can reduce the ambiguity in their roles without trading away their professional autonomy. The means are not evident in the profession's formal pronouncements or in overt corporate policies governing health and safety programs. If they exist, they must be part of an iterative process of mutual accommodation that takes place in the work groups and daily routines to which we now turn our attention.

■ *PART THREE*
Inside the Corporation

5 ■ Clinicians in Corporations

However varied and unpredictable the activities of corporate medical departments, all can be said to involve corporate medical directors in two essential roles. These physicians are both managers, oriented toward their employers (in activities focused on the organization and the work environment), and physicians, oriented toward employees (in activities directed at individual workers and their health). Further, it is possible to arrange both managers and physicians along two continuua or axes. For physicians one pole is occupied by those who relate strictly to individual patients one-on-one, the other by those who concern themselves exclusively with large populations.

Managers, as a rule, can be differentiated by their time horizons and arranged on a second axis whose two extremes are an operational, reactive, day-to-day orientation at one pole and a strategic,[1] anticipatory, futuristic one at the other. Combining these axes creates a model that defines four major sectors of a corporate medical director's role: (1) clinical and (2) population medicine; (3) operational and (4) strategic management (see figure 5.1). Although individual medical directors emphasize different sectors of that total role, all have to concern themselves to some degree with issues in each quadrant. Each sector gives rise to its own complex amalgam of expectations from various role sets (other

---

1. The distinction being drawn here between operational and strategic management has principally to do with the dimension of time. In most definitions of corporate strategy a long-range perspective is stated or implied. Chandler, for example, defines strategy as "the determination of the basic long-term goals and objectives of an enterprise and the adoption of courses of action and allocation of resources necessary for carrying out those goals" (Chandler 1962:13). The other important dimension implied in the term "strategic" is that of purposeful planning.

94 ■ INSIDE THE CORPORATION

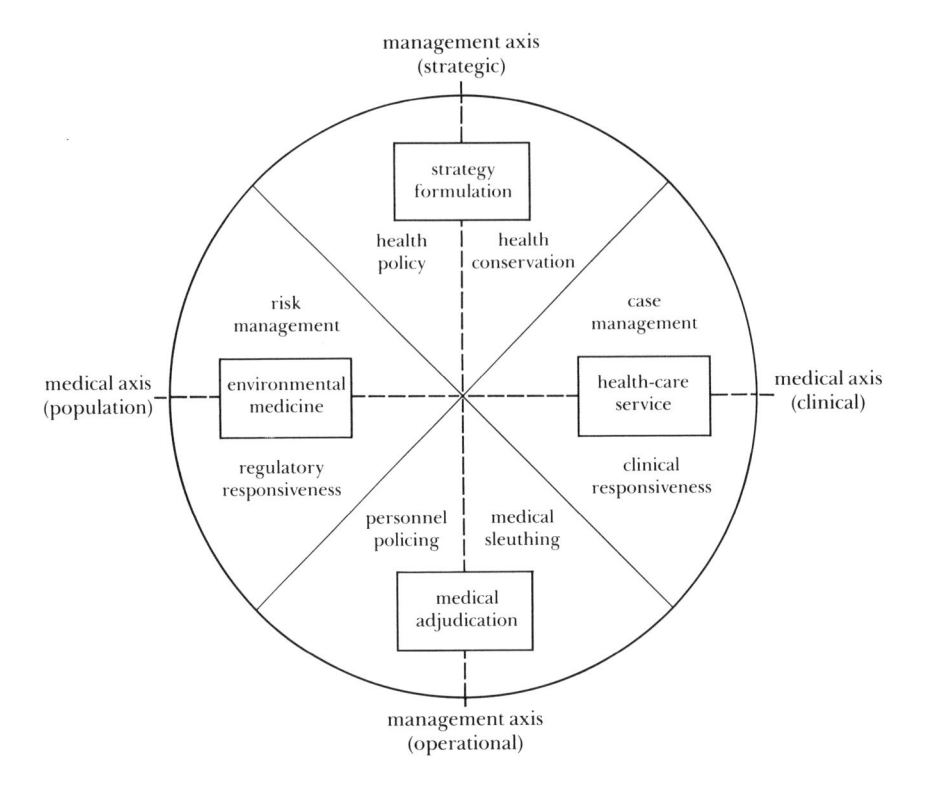

[Figure: Circular diagram showing sectors of corporate physician's role. Vertical axis: management axis (strategic) at top, management axis (operational) at bottom. Horizontal axis: medical axis (population) on left, medical axis (clinical) on right. Four boxed sectors around the center: strategy formulation (top), environmental medicine (left), health-care service (right), medical adjudication (bottom). Eight labeled wedge sectors: health policy, health conservation, case management, clinical responsiveness, medical sleuthing, personnel policing, regulatory responsiveness, risk management.]

Source: Reprinted from Walsh (1982).

Figure 5.1.
Sectors of Corporate Physician's Role

managers, rank-and-file employees, other physicians, and so on). The four shade into one another and subdivide further where the shadings meet, and the strategic sector represents, at present, a largely inchoate and composite role: some corporate physicians are developing certain aspects of it, some certain others. This becomes clearer as the three established sectors are characterized more fully, and the fourth is adumbrated.

The Clinical Pole of The Medical Axis

The extent to which an individual corporate medical director personally becomes involved in clinical medicine is closely tied to the policy question, long an issue for occupational medicine, of how far a given company goes toward providing extensive treatment for a wide range of acute and chronic health problems, whatever their etiology.

The early genesis of corporate occupational medicine, described in chapter 2, was a form of vertical integration, in which firms with remote operations brought within their organizational boundaries basic medical care functions they were unable to purchase. Eligible workers, in this conceptual scheme, were treated as a capital asset, and preventive health maintenance was a cost of doing business. Some contemporary economists foresee renewed interest in this strategy as prices continue to escalate for health care purchased on the outside, with health insurance financed predominantly through the employment relationship (Sahin and Taylor 1979).

Part II traced the origins of the sharp line—drawn by the American Medical Association, adhered to by industrial physicians, and deferred to by corporate executives—which excluded from the proper scope of occupational medicine treatment of any illness or injury unrelated to work. The distinction between occupational and nonoccupational illness has always been elusive, and the traditional lines are now blurring. In a 1971 amendment to earlier policy statements, the AMA loosened its original strictures against nonoccupational involvement of occupational physicians.

Some corporations offer their employees a wide range of primary health-care services, and these expanded in-house programs typically evolve along predictable lines. The company brings in part-time specialists, for example in internal medicine, dermatology, orthopedics, psychiatry. Some then establish formal links with the outside health-care system, and a very few have brought the benefit package into a closed system of financing and services, in the form of a corporate-sponsored health maintenance organization (Walsh and Tell 1984).

The Pros and Cons of Corporate-Sponsored Medicine

Opinion is divided on the merits of this approach. Advocates believe it makes sense both economically and medically. They feel that the corporate medical department is capable of performing a variety of routine tests and procedures more efficiently and as effectively as employees can obtain elsewhere. Most large companies conduct some periodic screening and preventive services as well as government-mandated medical surveillance. Having made this initial investment, it is argued, a company choosing not to deliver more extensive primary care from its medical department is in effect paying twice for the same health care—once in the capital investment already sunk in the medical operation, again through the experience-rated premiums for the employee benefit plan. The convenience of the medical department should save time away from work, and a high-quality comprehensive health program is good for morale and for the department's overall credibility with employees. Done well, it is also good medicine, the argument continues, probably superior to outside practitioners' care in its integration of work histories and the company's screening data into a comprehensive and continuous system of primary care. It allows corporate physicians to practice their clinical skills and therefore enables the corporation to recruit first-quality practitioners and permits the profession to attract new talent. Advocates of the approach consider it the surest way to upgrade occupational medicine and bring it into the mainstream of good primary care. Critics challenge both the economic and the medical premises. They assert that companies expanding their primary-care services are likely to be the ones who pay twice since there is no way of knowing whether the employee's visit to the "expanded medical department" is an adjunct or an alternative to his use of outside medical services. One corporate medical director who expressed such reservations was Dr. Edward Bower, corporate medical director of a socially conscious nonunion company in the chemical-products industry (Walsh 1985b). He said he started out with the "thesis" that "it is silly to have a medical presence in a community—any community, including a corporate one—and not to provide real medical care." Several years later he had 22 people reporting to him in six medical facilities, two with physician staffing, to serve his firm's 13,000 employees based in its principal state. At the headquarters location, where 3,000 employees worked, the central facility was covered by Bower, spending about 60 percent of his time in clinical care, and five part-time specialists: two orthopedic surgeons, another internist, a dermatologist, and a psychiatrist. Radiological services were available there through an arrangement with a neighboring hospital. The company's other large medical site, about ten miles away, served 4,000 employees twenty-four hours a day in a three-shift operation staffed by nurses whose work was overseen by the second of the firm's two full-time physicians. In addition, a physicians' assistant and a nurse practitioner "rode the circuit" among the six locations within a twenty-mile radius. The six facilities logged 92,000 patient visits in 1980. The question haunting Bower was "what is the return?"

> We could get by with a lot less and still meet OSHA standards. Other than employee satisfaction, which wears thin after a while, where's the quid pro quo; what's the rationale? How do you know we're not just adding more intensity to an already saturated system? How many of these visits are truly cost-avoidance visits in the sense that they would have taken place and been paid for through the benefit if we hadn't been right here for free? How much preemptive care are we providing or are we just creating Parkinson's Law?

In the name of "intellectual honesty," he felt these questions needed to be faced.

Companies offering extensive primary-care services have not been able to demonstrate a measurable impact on their overall premiums or to substantiate the claim that the convenience factor saves time away from work. The advocates, parenthetically, feel strongly that the lack of a measurable impact reflects deficiencies and insensitivities in the insurance industry's accounting procedures rather than a real absence of effect. The critics argue, further, that most large corporations are too widely dispersed geographically for the approach to be practical in more than one or two highly concentrated locations. Neither dependents, who account for at least two-thirds of a company's health-care costs, nor retirees are normally included in the population an in-house medical program endeavors to serve. Those who argue against a strong corporate presence in primary health care believe companies should allocate their finite health resources to preventive occupational programs, directed either to environmental monitoring and control or to lifestyle-oriented "wellness" programs. They see occupational health in the vanguard of the new national strategy of health promotion and disease prevention and consider it inappropriate for corporations to duplicate and undercut the existing community medical infrastructure, including hospitals and voluntary health agencies.

A middle ground of sorts stands between the two extremes. In this view the corporate medical department can serve a brokering function, maintaining collegial ties with a far-flung outside medical network, screening employees and referring them for needed care, following up afterward, and informally monitoring quality by keeping an eye on the forms that come through from outside practitioners for disability and other insurance claims. A certain amount of primary health care seems virtually unavoidable. In England, there is a strong ideological bias against company sponsorship of comprehensive medical services as inimical to the spirit and vitality of the National Health Service.[2] Even there it was estimated by a national committee of inquiry that about one-third of the time of industrial health practitioners is taken up by "casualty work and treatment . . . the sort of work undertaken by general practitioners in the NHS"—work the committee explicitly excluded from its definition of occupational medicine (Robens 1972:118). Ameri-

---

2. It would be instructive to conduct a systematic comparison of occupational medicine in the United States and in the United Kingdom. Available British documents seem much clearer on the multiplicity of roles played by corporate physicians and the need to give cognizance to the conflicts that ensue (see, e.g., Royal College of Physicians 1980; British Medical Association 1980). The need for a clear separation of in-house from community medicine is strongly articulated in an important report to Parliament (Robens 1972:122).

can occupational physicians frequently make the same observation; whether or not they ought to be delivering primary care, the reality of the situation is that they typically do (Culpepper, quoted in Egdahl and Walsh 1983:36).

In its official capacity, occupational medicine in the United States even now consistently eschews more than a passing and largely passive responsibility for the delivery of personal health services—the one-on-one primary care at the clinical end of the medical axis that separates a few companies such as Gillette (Greer, Kantrowitz, and White 1977), Kaiser Industries (Somers 1971), Gates Rubber Company (Lusterman 1974), R. J. Reynolds (Tudor 1977), and Exxon Corporation (Roberts 1974) from most other American firms. Convention has confined the delivery of personal health services by corporate medical programs to situations in which the injury or illness is causally linked to conditions at work or can be treated quickly so the employee can return to his work station. This convention, as we have seen, arose principally out of deference to the economic interests of organized medicine and shaped a medical specialty without clear title to any clinical problems beyond the most mundane and with responsibility for only a fragment of the care needed by a patient for any given episode of illness.

These same economic forces in medicine built a third-party payment system on the bedrock principle that patients must have freedom to select their physicians. This has meant that the services provided through a company-sponsored medical program have tended to supplement but not necessarily replace services available to employees on the outside, through the health insurance coverage they receive as a fringe benefit. As a result, the in-house programs face a dual challenge: first, they need a way to entice employees to use their services, but then they need to make a case that what they are doing is cost effective. The corporate medical director at a large public utility was grappling with this problem:

> We became attracted to the notion of directing more attention to the front end of the health care system—of trying to intervene earlier. In 1968 we went to the Bronx to do primary care: not necessarily to do it ourselves but to get it done right, to manage the system. The question was, how would we do it, where would we get the forces? We couldn't get the state to set us up in business. The medical society wasn't about to give us a mandate. I woke up one morning to the realization that the key was the individual employee. If we could get him or her to give us the authority, then we could begin to manage. We could shorten hospital stays and direct people to competent doctors—anything was possible with that authorization from the employee—that would be our lever.

While this medical director was seeking to capitalize on the escalation in health-care costs to forge a new mission for his medical department, other corporate physicians worried about potential threats from the crisis in health-care costs. One, Dr. Sydney Allen, muttered that occupational medicine was becoming "extinct like the dodo bird." Allen was on the national staff of a professional society, capping a corporate medical career that had included the corporate medical directorships at two large firms, including a telephone operating company. His specialty, he believed, would have to define a compelling case for companies to support their own programs of primary care and preventive medicine. Otherwise, rising health-care costs would lead corporations to conclude "that they are paying twice for health care and that in-house programs are superfluous." Ever since state laws began to give workers free choice of physicians in worker's compensation cases, he said, this scenario had been discussed from time to time at the annual meetings of the Ramazzini Society and the Medical Directors' Forum.[3] It bothered him, though, that few of his colleagues seemed genuinely concerned about these trends. They seemed resigned to occupational medicine's circumscribed clinical role and blind to the danger that forces in medicine might shrink it to the vanishing point.

The Realities of Corporate-Sponsored Medicine

As influenced by the expectations of organized medicine, then, occupational medicine can be said to have defined its service-delivery role very narrowly. But definitions flowing out of corporate medical directors' day-to-day orientations to other reference groups are actually less straightforward than official positions seem to imply. Circumstances often arise in which corporate medical directors elect or are called upon to perform functions that are essentially clinical or that draw on skills, expertise, or "credibility" unique to a clinician.

The expectation that a corporate medical director will function as a

---

3. The Medical Directors' Forum is an informal association, started in the 1950s by the medical directors of Ford and AT&T. It comprises thirty-five corporate medical directors of American firms, each with responsibility for multiplant operations in a broad geographical area. The membership is said to include representation of service and manufacturing industries. The Ramazzini Society is an older and more prestigious overlapping organization. It was founded in 1942 at the instigation of Clarence D. Selby (the author of Bulletin 99, described in chapter 2) and Carey P. McCord (of Chrysler). Members are "specialists in Ramazzini as well as in medicine" (Selleck and Whittaker 1962:illustration no. 75, following p. 230). Selleck and Whittaker placed the membership at "seldom more than a score," but another source (an anonymous personal communication) said there are thirty-one "Rams" now, increased from thirty the year the person who was supposed to be counting "had a little too much to drink." The Ramazzini Society is resolutely informal and unofficial, "with no officers, no directors, no charge, no by-laws, no dues, and no official positions about anything." Neither organization releases its membership list, although one member of the Rams goes public each year with an annual "oration," subsequently published in the *Journal of Occupational Medicine*, and some others list their membership on their curriculum vitae.

clinician permeates those few companies (Gillette, Gates Rubber, Kaiser Industries) that define the department's mission as the delivery of personal health services. But other companies also regard patient care as a central aspect of the department's contribution, and those that do typically like to be able to look upon their physicians—including the corporate medical director—as first-rate clinicians. Consider Dr. Julius Whitesides, corporate medical director of a large petroleum producer, whose management, he said, had a strong "philosophical" commitment to preventive medicine. Whitesides saw this commitment manifested in what he termed a "utopian medical world"—a full-scale multispecialty group practice operating out of the company's headquarters in a large metropolitan area, where only about 200 of its employees were based.

The company had over 100,000 employees worldwide, served by a medical program of close to 400 health professionals including about 125 physicians and 180 nurses, plus industrial hygienists, toxicologists, epidemiologists, and medical support staff. Just over 40 of those professionals worked in the headquarters office, comprising two divisions. In the "operations division," which dated back to about 1920, when the company first established a medical department, 8 full-time physicians shared the clinical consultation responsibilities in the headquarters medical department and also served in a medical advisory capacity to the company's domestic and international outposts. The "research and environmental health division," established around 1950, was staffed by industrial hygienists, epidemiologists, toxicologists, and other disciplines related to public health and chemical or sanitary engineering.

Outstanding clinical capabilities were the signal criterion by which this firm judged physicians being considered for staff positions with the medical facility. All of the corporate physicians were board-certified internists, and all worked at local medical schools or hospitals, "without compensation from those institutions, to maintain their contact with the mainstream of medicine outside industry." Whitesides looked for clinical credentials: "We don't hire M.D.-Ph.D.s from [schools of public health]. I don't doubt that they're well trained, but not for the kind of preventive medicine we're trying to deliver. We hire clinicians who learn occupational medicine after they come here."

He considered it virtually impossible to maintain the respect and trust of management and of the unions unless he stayed current medically. Accordingly, it was company policy for all its occupational physicians, no matter how heavy their administrative duties, still to bear some responsibility for direct patient care. The policy formerly required that no physician spend more than half-time away from clinical duties, but the three most senior physicians had become so deeply involved in management and so highly paid that, Whitesides said, allocating half their time to patients could no longer be justified:

We can hire a young internist who is close enough to his training that he provides much better care than I can now at half the cost to the company. My clinical time is justified in terms of the extent to which my effectiveness would be diminished by a loss of clinical competence. I know what my limits are and when I need help, there are first-rate specialists down the hall to whom I have no qualms about 'losing' my patients.

Some firms draw different conclusions from similar realities and partition off their highly paid physicians from any administration, which they feel can be performed more efficiently by a lower-cost lay manager. Edward Bower's boss called him "a good manager who can absorb some new responsibilities without having to give up his clinical role" but added that "we try not to tie up a lot of his time by asking him to run things." But Whitesides's company had enough depth in its physician staff that it could elevate some to senior managerial roles and delegate the bulk of the patient care to the more junior ones, whose training was fresher. The depth reflected a pioneering history in occupational health, going back to the 1920s, when, according to the 1982 chairman: "Long before government regulation existed as we know it today, our medical department participated in the corporation's decisionmaking at the highest level. . . . By the late 1940s a more comprehensive program of occupational medicine was in operation with a growing professional staff."

Having served for about six years as director of the firm's entire medical effort, including the research and environmental health division, Whitesides was nearing retirement at the time of the interview and felt, in retrospect, that external pressures were making it increasingly difficult for corporate physicians to focus as singlemindedly on preventive medical care as was possible more than thirty years earlier when he first joined the firm. After 1975 a "great expansion" in "knowledge and awareness" had caused his company to treble its staff for "environmental concerns and toxicological testing," while the size of the operations division concerned with preventive medicine "has changed very little over the past several decades."

> The most significant change I've seen over the years is in this sense of priorities. When I came, the industrial hygiene people were the ones concerned with preventing the company from exposing employees to conditions that might be harmful. The rest of us were practicing preventive clinical medicine. Now the medical department's very first priority is to anticipate and prevent the harm that can arise out of work. It was the unique opportunity I saw here to practice an idyllic form of preventive medicine that attracted me some thirty years ago. I'm not sure I would have come to [this company] or indeed to occupational medical practice if the priorities then had been as now.

A younger physician who joined his much newer and smaller company (a chemical company founded after World War II, with fewer than

15,000 employees worldwide) in 1975 as its first corporate medical director, Dr. Harold Monroe, was *attracted* by the contemporary emphasis on environmental health. In terms of a clinical role, his circumstances and his company's expectations were markedly different from those in Whitesides's firm, and yet there were evocative similarities in what the two physicians said about their own clinical limitations. Monroe said this:

> I don't get a particular charge out of thumping some vice president's back, knowing that he'd get a much better exam from one of these fully trained former residents I've just hired. My feeling is that we ought to use our most sensitive detector, whatever it is we're trying to measure. The most sensitive detector I've got for doing a physical exam is someone whose clinical skills are more current than mine.

Monroe was extolling the socially progressive history and management style at his own company but added, lest he convey the impression that "it's all perfection here," that he "faulted" himself for the fact that "I'm not a good clinician any more." The clinical burden at this chemical company was carried entirely by part-time physicians, four serving the headquarters location and four more at each of four other plant sites. The company employed about 10,000 people in the United States, 3,500 within range of corporate headquarters. The company believed it did not have a large enough concentration of employees to justify an expensive on-site program.

Using part-time physicians was Monroe's deliberate choice, on quality grounds: "I want smart guys, good doctors. If I tried to fill these slots full-time, I wouldn't get the quality people that I want. Usually I hire someone just out of his residency. His clinical skills are sharp. In other communities where I don't hire my own people, I find a good local internist to hook into."

His company did not see itself in the preventive medicine business to the degree Whitesides's did, but, he said, was "not doctrinaire" about the distinction between occupational and nonoccupational health problems. Account was taken of logistics and the time employees would have to spend off the job. The medical department willingly did any testing or follow-up an outside physician ordered for a patient, stored medicine for this purpose in the clinic's refrigerator, but left the initiative with the individual employee and his private physician. If an employee came to the medical department with a simple problem clearly unrelated to the job, the company's physicians would treat it. They dispensed ointments, cough drops, penicillin, and other common medications; conducted premarital serology and "that kind of thing"; but drew the line at treatment likely to involve a number of repeat visits—for example, diabetes or digitalis regulation. "We are comfortable with ourselves on this score, even though it isn't formal policy," Monroe said. There were approximately twenty-five to thirty clinic visits a day, and the volume of use was "not an issue in our performance." In contrast, other corporate medical directors cited numbers of clinic visits in a way that made them seem the pre-eminent justification for the company's investment in in-house health programs.

For all their modesty about their own clinical skills, both Whitesides and Monroe had been recognized formally, in national offices held and awards won, as well as informally by their peers, as among the half-dozen or so top practitioners in their field. They could afford to admit to some loss of technical expertise in the clinical realm because they had so obviously gained both expertise and recognition in the professional and managerial ones. And if they deferred to other physicians on puzzling clinical problems, it still remained true that both carried ultimate responsibility for the quality of the employee health service—in one case concentrated in a large in-house multispecialty group practice, in the other dispersed through a network of contracts and connections with local practitioners.

Both men played a role as first among equals in an organized medical service, a role in which credibility with one's professional peers is important. That credibility can be won in various ways but a current store of clinical knowledge probably helps—or its absence hurts. It may be more important in the context of an on-site group practice, where breaches of clinical judgment are more likely to be visible, as pointed out by Dr. Arthur Lawrence, who had moved back and forth from hospital-based academic medicine to plant-based occupational medicine:

> In a small situation—an occupational clinic or even something like [a hospital ambulatory care service]—if you make a mistake it's more visible. If you say it's a cold and it turns out three days later to have been infectious mononucleosis, even though there is no way you could have known three days before which it was, the word gets around that mistakes were made. It's a closed goldfish bowl.

An anecdote that illustrates this point was recounted by Dr. Whitesides, whose in-house program was of the group-practice type. When he was still a staff physician, he was rushing to finish his morning's clinical cases so that he could accompany the corporate medical director to an important meeting. That corporate medical director—his predecessor—was no longer clinically active but to expedite the departure offered to see one of Dr. Whitesides's patients. As it happened the patient was a known diabetic, on whom this corporate medical director ordered a glucose tolerance test—a grievous error in the younger man's eyes and one that shook his respect for his mentor and made him resolve never to become that remote from clinical practice.

When occupational health programs are arranged in this group-practice fashion, it stands to reason that clinical credentials will be valued for all the physicians, however episodic their involvement in patient care. The medical director of an active university health service, Dr. James Childress, summarized the situation well:

> You're right that the clinical work is part of my essence. I'm not sure the top person necessarily has to be a clinician. But there has to be an open gate back and forth to the clinical expertise, whether it's the guy on the top or one below him. I myself would find it pretty hard to sit in this chair and keep the confidence of the physicians on the staff without playing that clinical role.

Programs arranged in a network fashion are likely to make fewer immediate demands on the corporate medical director's current clinical knowledge, although the issue for occupational medicine of how its practitioners can maintain clinical competence remains a vexing one, even if only as a problem in recruiting and managing other physicians.

On the recruiting question, the lack of clinical stimulation has long been viewed as occupational medicine's albatross. Discussing the manpower deficit in occupational medicine, one radical critic encapsulated her findings in the sardonic subtitle, "Suppose They Gave a Profession and Nobody Came" (Mazzocchi 1977). The critics find no surprise in the shortage of physicians willing to embark on careers in a low-prestige specialty, neglected in medical school curricula and postgraduate training programs, isolated in an out-of-the-way niche of medicine concerned with routine treatment of job-related illness and disability—"finger-wrapping," as some refer to the work. Testimony to the tedium was provided by Ernest Hemingway's son, an industrial physician in New York City, said in a 1976 *New York Times* article to have left the field because "the work was necessary but dull" (quoted in Follman 1978). "Lack of intellectual challenge" was one factor cited in a (not recent) survey of medical students, who discounted public health or preventive medicine as attractive career options. Other considerations they cited were "an uncongenial subject matter," "little personal contact with patients," and "slow or uncertain benefits to patients" (Cahalan, Colette, and Hilmar 1957). In an effort to raise the profile of occupational medicine, Dr. Ralph Bradford occasionally had local medical students rotate through his department, but the way he described his work in this connection made one wonder if the medical students would be attracted or driven away: "When I was in medical school there was nothing. The work here isn't terribly intriguing but we try to create a positive impression, even if it is delayed." The delay he considered inevitable because of compelling reasons he saw for physicians not to choose occupational medicine at the beginning of a career, because "there is just not enough diversity. They are not ready without having been in private practice first." Again he conveyed a lack of enthusiasm about the nature of his work, as he described himself coming to terms with it:

> Most physicians like to see patients from start to finish and don't like to relinquish control over patient care. If I had gone directly into occupational medicine right out of medical school, I would have been dissatisfied. Any physician who has not done some private practice would be disappointed with this job: you have to look on this sort of job for what it is—examining healthy people, doing routine physicals. After only a short time in private practice, I sort of got a kick—not in a perverse sense—out of finding something wrong with someone who thought he was healthy.

Having overcome the initial recruiting problem, corporate medical directors, whether or not they themselves are active clinically, still face the problem of how to protect the clinical skills of the doctors the company employs. For example, Dr. Arnold Bennett, who had just been appointed health and safety director of a large firm in the information business, was personally playing no clinical role but was overseeing the quality of the clinical services provided by nearly fifty full-time physicians company-wide. He felt responsible for nurturing the clinical skills of the staff physicians involved in patient care. They were being asked to trade clinical skills for administrative involvement, and he worried about whether they were receiving enough personal benefits to compensate for that loss:

> My primary allegiance should be to see that medicine is represented properly throughout the corporation, that an atmosphere exists where the people who have these skills and want to continue practicing them can do that. We have to focus on the young people coming behind us. To ask them to lose their clinical skills right away scares the hell out of them. We have to give them something in the offset and say, "Hey, look at the corporate guys who are up here and the opportunity for maturation and for doing bigger things with a wider scope." They're scared as they begin to feel that they are losing their skills, and it's very important that programs have visible room for growth.

A further aspect of the clinical dilemma confronting corporate physicians has been implied or explicitly stated in some of the preceding comments about the risk of losing clinical intuition. That risk reflects the shortage of challenging clinical material in a corporate physician's job. The difficult and interesting cases either elude the company facility, because truly sick people stay home from work, or are referred out quickly, as beyond the department's legitimate purview. The risk reflects also the structural fact that most occupational clinics serve populations too small to justify staffing by more than one or perhaps two physicians, who therefore lack the stimulation of working with their peers.

A corollary to the shortage of interesting clinical tasks is the surfeit of uninteresting ones—the routine examinations of basically healthy people mentioned by Dr. Bradford, who said he derives some satisfaction as a medical detective of this sort. Others do too, but few would argue with Schilling's view that "the routine superficial examination of large numbers of potentially healthy people can be intensely boring and can lead to a lowering of professional standards. As a result, much occupational health practice can still be limited in its range and fail to attract and retain able doctors" (Schilling, 1981:43).

Creative use of nurses and mid-level health professionals such as nurse practitioners and physician's assistants is seen by many as part of the solution to this problem, and most corporate medical directors struggle with the question of how best to use and develop the nursing staff. The problem can be mitigated also by "using examinations more selectively" (Schilling 1981:42)—for example, by involving the physician only when an initial screen of some kind has eliminated individuals least likely to have unrecognized health conditions. But many corporations use periodic examinations as perquisites for employees in the executive and managerial ranks and want physicians to perform them, as part of the ritual.

Edward Bower had become disillusioned and resigned his post of eleven years. As he described his disaffection, these rituals seemed central to it:

> The medical department is nothing more than a high-visibility benefit. We're viewed by employees almost like vending machines. This is tough for the big egos in health care, who aren't used to being thought of in this way. I always tell people who come to work here from nonindustrial settings that they must be prepared for something very different, because, like it or not, we are an industrial relations function. The nurses on the front lines are getting no ego gratification at all—and they need some.

The morale of the nursing staff had become a particular article of contention when economic reversals in 1979 impelled Bower's company to look for places to cut expenses. The entire personnel budget, including the medical department's $1 million annual operating figure, was subjected to "zero-based budgeting." In this austerity climate, Bower recommended reducing the nursing staff by three or four and was disgusted to see the proposal dismissed out of hand:

> I'm the only guy who's trying to *de*crease his empire, and they won't let me do it. Now they've decided to cross-charge the nurses to the operating divisions. That solves the budget problems of the personnel department. But it

leaves me with administrative headaches and a tremendous morale problem among underemployed nurses with only part of a job. Management puts the nurses in a class with fire extinguishers—as something that ought to be seen there. It's said that they're needed for emergency coverage, but it's well known that without a physician back-up, a nurse is no better in an emergency than a good first-aider. Again we're fighting conventional wisdom. Add to that the quasi-counseling role that the nurses get into, and they're relatively untouchable. It's just optics, just hypocrisy.

Also, using nonphysicians to perform medical care exacerbates the problem many company doctors have with isolation from medical peers. In fact, Bower's successor, Dr. Lawrence, believed that Bower's real mistake had been to paint himself into an isolated corner:

> Ed fought for more physical sites, better equipment, and the physiology of the medical department and not for doctors. He bought into the physician's assistant/nurse-practitioner as a substitute for the physician. Six or seven years ago, this was the in thing. It was argued on grounds of cost benefit and efficiency and so on. It may be true that physician's assistants can do much of what physicians do, but the general public still relates to physicians, and physicians still relate to outside physicians.

What happened, in this view, was that the emphasis on "physiology" of the medical department—the physical plant and the administrative mechanisms to make it an efficient operation—was a kind of administrative rationality that clashed with professional rationality. In rationalizing and streamlining the department, Lawrence argued, Bower set up a structure where he had to lose his clinical acuity.

> It is an unbelievable chore to stay at the razor's edge, particularly if you're the only physician in a small company. That is what happened to Ed. After ten years of sore throats and sprained ankles, he began to feel that he was losing his skills. Discussing cases with nurses just isn't the same as discussing them with physicians. You are not linked to the hospitals, you don't see interns and residents. You don't have medical and academic stimulation and you can't keep up. The advances in medicine pass you by, it's easy to become rusty, and you become insecure. That's Ed's problem. He knows intellectually how to administer lydocaine for tachycardia but doesn't feel he could do it if he were working in an emergency room and had to. He's lost his self-confidence. So even if you don't start out in a corporate setting as one of the lazy people who wants to work only from nine to five, it's easy to become one of those types. I believe that Ed felt that he was becoming one and that that's the reason why he chose to leave.

For corporate medical directors who themselves carry heavy clinical duties, the balance struck between medicine and administration affects their own daily routines. For those whose clinical involvement centers around managing the work of other physicians, staffing an in-house medical facility has policy implications rather than personal ones. In their case, an occasional examination of a senior manager may serve the latent function of providing a unique type of access to the highest echelons of the firm. This function is frequently mentioned by practitioners in the field; its importance was described by the president of a consulting firm that sells health-promotion programs. For marketing purposes, he had to be alert to whether a given corporate medical director was in a position to commit the company to invest in his product. His "gut feeling" about corporate medical directors:

> There are only a few who have autonomy and the ability to spend money and try things that may be far out. And this has a lot to do with personality and personal relationships. [One who does have such power] spends about 10 percent of his time in clinical activities and he sees only the top people in the company. He does business during those clinical consultations and uses them to sell a point. He might trade a fitness site for an occupational physician. He's a great poker player, a gamesman.[4]

Jet-Set Medicine and the Expatriate Employee

Another kind of personal health service that brings some corporate medical directors into contact with powerful executives is a form of jet-set or telecommunications medicine practiced by many in multinational firms. They bring a medical presence to meetings of the board of directors, visit remote outposts to reassure expatriate managers that the company has not forgotten them, consult with managers and local physicians in foreign countries when an employee, a dependent, or even a valued customer needs advice on how to handle a nascent medical emergency. Dr. Frank Lee, corporate medical director of a rapidly expanding 40,000-employee defense contractor and computer-parts manufacturer, described this aspect of his job with palpable zest:

> There are a lot of problems in dealing with medical resources in foreign countries. You have to be able to evaluate local resources and sort through complex cross-cultural differences. If my guy or his wife gets sick, I may have to check out the surgeon at King Hussein Hospital—who is he, where did he train, that sort of thing. Or I'm on the phone to a doctor in Buenos Aires trying to assess whether the wife of one of our executives is too sick to be flown home. Or our chief marketing person in Quito suffers a massive

---

4. This is a reference to Michael Maccoby's popular book *The Gamesman* (1976), which categorizes corporate managers as (1) gamesmen, (2) craftsmen, (3) jungle fighters, or (4) company men. There are parallels between those categories and the four sectors of the corporate physician's role. Medical adjudication is work for company men, clinical medicine for craftsmen, population medicine for jungle fighters, and strategy formulation for gamesmen.

coronary and I get on the Lear jet and fly down there. This foreign thing makes the job very interesting.

The issue of the expatriate employee is addressed prospectively by a metals manufacturer with mines all over the world. Dr. Stanley Morrison had been corporate medical director and began the tradition of employing a consulting psychiatrist part-time to interview employees destined for foreign assignments. Morrison died but the tradition continued. Dr. Gerald Cohen, the psychiatrist occupying that role, asks prospective expatriates to bring their spouses to the session, the purpose of which, he emphasizes, is less to screen out unlikely candidates than to prepare them all:

> My role is to help them understand the emotional obstacles the family as a unit is likely to face overseas. Before I came, they had cast the psychiatrist in the role of a gatekeeper, but I see my role differently. Here's an example: a recently married couple, both previously married, and the woman had just won a tough court fight for custody of her children. Now [the company] was transferring her husband overseas. She was afraid, with reason, that going abroad might jeopardize her custody, but she also didn't want to hold her new husband back in his career. The classic bind. I could play the heavy in that situation and say that in my professional judgment, although you are fully capable of handling the job and the adjustment, the timing is not right for the transfer.

For those he did think were ready to go overseas, he also gave advice on how to make the transition as painless as possible, encouraging the family as a group to talk over their feelings about the move and to allow the children to give vent to their anxiety and sadness at leaving their friends.

Serendipitous Second Opinion

This specific consulting task can be delegated to a part-time psychiatrist, but many corporate medical directors make themselves available for confidential consultations with managers of high rank, who would be reluctant to discuss medical or personal concerns with anyone below the most senior physician. Although many companies have structured "employee assistance" or staff counseling programs for the rank-and-file, the corporate medical director, if he is highly placed and respected, is more often the social and organizational peer to whom senior management turns with problems. Dr. Norman Schultz, a vice president in a large midwestern consumer products firm, articulated this need:

> People at the top level have problems just the same as people down the line, and their decisions are very critical in the sense of the welfare of the enterprise. Now if they're bothered because of alcoholism or problems with their kids or other serious medical problems that aren't being dealt with or man-

aged properly, this can have a great impact on the company. And if you have no medical person who's involved at a high level, to be of help and service to these people, I think it's a serious mistake.

At various levels in the hierarchy, the counseling role is a function many corporate physicians perform informally, providing second opinions or initial referrals for managers seeking advice on how to handle a health-related problem of their own or someone close to them. It tends to evolve serendipitously, as the physician interacts with individual managers in official situations—whether clinical (perhaps in a periodic examination) or mangerial (perhaps puzzling over a work-site health problem)—and gradually wins their trust. After fourteen years in a field location as a division medical director, Dr. Fred Tyler was moved to headquarters to become corporate medical director. He noticed that he was no longer being called upon for informal medical consultations of this sort and attributed it not to the official change in jobs but to the change in venue and the loss of "personal identification" managers in his previous site had established with him over the years.

Corporate medical directors who are themselves involved in the delivery of personal health services tend to take this second-opinion function quite seriously. Dr. Lee, for example, had left his private practice only three years earlier for the full-time corporate job and felt that his clinical background distinguished his role from that of more traditional occupational physicians:

> At one time the industrial physician was a retiree or someone who was sick and wanted to work in a sheltered environment and to practice first aid. Now the younger man is interested in coming into the field. He sees industrial medicine differently and wants more from it. . . . I do take care of the executives; I am their second-opinion type of guy. That is very much my job.

Dr. Charles Sinsky, who had been vice president and corporate medical director at a large metropolitan bank for about eighteen years, placed even more emphasis on his oversight responsibility for the quality of the care received by the bank's employees: "One of my most valuable services [to this company] is getting people to the right doctors. Every family needs a doctor and [this bank] is just an extended family. They need a representative overlooking their care. From where I sit, it looks to me like 30 percent of our people are getting substandard care."

The evidence Sinsky saw of care he considered substandard appeared mostly on insurance claims or disability forms from attending physicians —evidence of unnecessary procedures (too many hernia repairs and hysterectomies)[5] or inept handling of disabilities (cardiac arrhythmias, lower back pain, and the like). The frustration of seeing most of this evidence after the fact led him to propose to management that the bank set up its own prepaid health plan and run it out of the medical department. As a member of the quality assurance committee of a large teaching hospital in town, he felt he had "a pretty good handle on the problems of assuring quality from the hospital's perspective." The prepaid plan would give him a vehicle for conducting "triage and preliminary evaluation" at the bank's medical facility and making appropriate referrals to outside practitioners he could trust. The bank's benefits specialists doubted the financial feasibility of the plan, which Sinsky continued to discuss four years later, without kindling much enthusiasm.

This awareness of the lapses of quality in general medical practice and the opportunity they present for a corporate physician to play a "watchdog" role was a persistent theme in the interviews, is explored on occasion in the literature,[6] but rarely seems to be an important spring to action. Corporate medical directors may brood in private conversations with outsiders or other managers about the particular window their positions provide onto widely recognized defects of the health-care system—overutilization, underexplanation, and general fragmentation of services and expertise—but in their interactions with patients, most tend to be circumspect. Dr. Lawrence pointed out that they adhere to the professional code against undermining a colleague:

> You can't go around bad-mouthing an employee's doctor. We're always careful to say "You're in very good hands. Is it all right with you if I just call your doctor and chat with him about your condition?" or words to that effect. The object is to make the employee see that we care. This overrides all the negativity attached to having sometimes to play a policing role. That's the art of medicine; they don't teach it in medical school.

Doc, Do You Take Private Patients?

The sensibilities of patients may be part of the reason for circumspection, but the delicate matter of a company physician's relations with out-

---

5. In all cases, these were little more than the crudest of impressions, picking up on a theme in the literature that there is an excess of surgery and providing the company doctors with an opportunity to criticize outside physicians (from whom, over the years, they have received so much calumny) and to claim license to perform a special watchdog function curbing these putative excesses among practicing physicians.

6. See, e.g., the quotation attributed to Dr. Otto Geier, speaking to the American Society of Mechanical Engineers' 1917 annual meeting: "The average worker receives his first complete physical examination in the industrial clinic. He is too often the victim of blind gunshot prescriptions. The industrial clinic is teaching him to seek a better type of physician for himself and his family, and in that sense the industrial physician is tending to raise the standard of private practice on the outside" (McKiever 1965:12).

side practitioners is the overriding factor. Like other clinical issues, this can surface as a policy matter for a corporate medical director managing other physicians or as a personal one to the extent that he himself is involved in the delivery of medical care. On the policy level, Dr. Monroe, who hired part-time physicians just out of their residency as a deliberate strategy to get "first-rate" clinicians, advised them at the outset on how to handle potential conflicts of interest between their corporate and private practices:

> The internists I hire are senior residents, just starting out in practice. I talk to them and tell them something along these lines: "You will see people needing further care, and you will know that you would be the best possible person to give them that care because you've just been trained and you know what you're doing." But I admonish them against offering themselves, unless pressed. If the employee says, flat out, "Doc, do you take private patients?" I tell my guy, then he can in good conscience say yes. But the employee must take the initiative. Of course we must strike a balance here because if we bend too far in the other direction, we can make these young physicians starve to death, and that's not good either, for them or for our employees.

The process of evolving a personal modus operandi was described by several other corporate physicians in the study. Dr. Sarah Farmer, for example, was the associate medical director of a large New York firm with a group-practice style in-house service. She had been in that job for eight years and at the firm, initially as a consulting obstetrician-gynecologist on duty a half-day per week, for another seven and a half years. Leafing through a sheaf of telephone messages that had accumulated during the morning, she commented on how "different occupational medicine is from what people think." There was a message from a woman employee with a colostomy, Gloria Smith, long ago transferred to another part of the state, who nonetheless still called Farmer regularly for advice and support. Another call had come from a district manager with whom Farmer said she used to argue over policy matters; now he was seeking her advice on what to do about his wife's back problem. Another of the messages was from a woman in Brooklyn who as a young trainee ten years earlier had begun looking to Farmer "to sanction her health care and guide her through it." Subsequently a successful executive with a fine internist in Brooklyn Heights, she continued to check in for advice when a problem arose. There were several other such messages, and Farmer took obvious pride and pleasure in the personal relationships they bespoke. "You can become as involved with your patients as you choose," she said. "I've always had a prescription pad in my purse. Some of my patients live in Harlem and can't afford a doctor. Or they live in the Bronx and can't find one. In such cases I'll gently inquire whether they'd like me to write a prescription. These people are smart. The average working man and woman—the Gloria Smiths—are smart. We don't have to patronize them."

Equally comfortable in his white clinician's coat, Dr. William Neeley, a plant physician in Tennessee, had started with his company on a part-time basis (ten hours a week) while maintaining an established private practice. Over a two-year period, he increased his hours at the plant until he was putting in eight-hour days there but still seeing private patients at his office in the evenings. It was Dr. Stanley Morrison who had recruited him. Morrison was at the time an eminent figure in occupational medicine, himself formerly a busy private practitioner, and corporate medical director at headquarters in western Pennsylvania. Neeley recalled how Morrison "used to preach to me" about the need to tread lightly on the private practitioner's turf:

> He'd tell me that I was going to get into trouble practicing private medicine in the plant. I was giving my private patients who worked for [the company] an open invitation to see me at the plant clinic if that was more convenient for them. I'm not all that mercenary and it seemed a more sensible use of their time and mine. I'd tell them that I could see their families at my private office in the evenings. By inference, of course, this could have been construed as an enticement to other workers in the plant who were not my patients, and this was the aspect of it that worried Stan.

This arrangement continued for about a decade, until Neely closed down the private practice. "I didn't like billing," he said, "and had to do it all myself because the practice was small. And I didn't like treating geriatric and pediatric patients." A year later, the company moved him to one of its largest plants in a different city. He had no ties there with private practice but knew how to build bridges. He joined the staff of the hospital and accepted committee assignments. He made it a point to visit the company's employees when they were hospitalized. Also, he recognized that "if we're technically not in competition with the family physician, as a practical matter we are. We all know the issues are purely economic." So, gradually, he evolved working relationships with the practitioners in this new community, one at a time:

> I call the personal physician and say "Your patient, Mr. X, has a strep throat. Shall I send him over?" The physician says, "I'm awfully busy right now, how do you know he has strep throat?" And I say, "Because I examined him." Then the physician more often than not will say, "Will you do me a favor and treat it for me?" And I say, "Fine," and that's the last time I call that doctor. They look upon it as a favor if we relieve them of that stuff. They already have a full load of patients.

Relieving the community physicians of routine episodic care seemed for the most part not to threaten them, but only if the company physician was careful to recognize and respect the community physicians' claim on long-term relationships with their patients.

> Where we do draw the line is on chronic disease. And on that we are a major referral source to them. What we take away in the simple stuff we give back two- or three-fold in diseases that otherwise would have gone undetected. And they know that. But it has to be a process of evolution, the way I did it in [my first corporate job]. You have to evolve to that. You can't just come in and slap the guy in the face. The supervisors used to contact the outside physicians sometimes when I first came here and I put an end to that. They're just as glad too; they don't enjoy checking up on employees that way.

The Clinical Pole in Summary—Clinicians versus Scientists

In sum, it can be said that when corporate medical directors are asked whether and in what ways their clinical skills are important—how much actual "laying on of hands" they feel they need to do to preserve their authenticity—their answers vary but collectively convey the impression that they separate on this issue into two basic types: the clinicians and the scientists.

The clinicians come from private-practice backgrounds and define their professional essence in terms of patient care. They are internists by training, or former family physicians, for whom some clinical involvement is requisite to sustaining personal feelings of competence and the respect of their professional colleagues, both in the company and outside. An occasional clinical duty legitimates these physicians in their own eyes and warrants their claim to expertise. They regret the crowding out of clinical involvement by mounting administrative duties. One, for example, expressed the wish that his son, who was applying to medical school, would become the real clinician that he himself had inadvertently failed to be. Another, Dr. Lee, regretted that his hope of maintaining a small private practice on the side had not materialized. "I'm kind of surprised," he said. "I thought a few referrals and consultations would keep my edge sharp. But I guess once you're out of the cloakroom, you're no longer needed."

Some of these clinicians argue, further, that clinical credibility facilitates their relations with management and labor. This case is weakened by the lack of obvious mechanisms through which managers or union representatives—mostly nonphysicians—judge whether a corporate physician still has his "clinical touch." The technical competence of professionals is generally considered opaque to the laity; indeed, this is the chief rationale for the autonomy professionals enjoy. When pressed for clear operational definitions of what they mean when they say that their physicians are "good clinicians," business managers generally fall back on external credentials, reputation, and professional contacts—indices which must be insensitive to the gradual atrophy of clinical skills that seems to be the main fear. But there is a sense, as one textbook points out, in which the medical mystique attaches peculiarly to the physician *qua* clinician:

> Whatever occupational physicians consider their main function should be, it is in the therapeutic role that they are most often judged by both employers and employees. . . . There are many who believe that, except in emergencies, "treatment" should not be included amongst the functions of an occupational health service. On the other hand, society usually expects a doctor to be a clinician, and it is as a clinician that he can most readily establish his reputation. Few actions of a doctor win the confidence and support of workers and management more than prompt and expert treatment of a serious illness or injury occurring in the factory (Taylor and Raffle 1981:148).

It should be noted that this comment comes from a British textbook in occupational medicine. In England, with its National Health Service, there is a clearer consensus than in the United States that health-care resources are finite. The British understand occupational medicine's unique position in an integrated system of health services. They feel it should be consciously organized in such a way as to complement and not duplicate or undermine the treatment services available through the NHS.

Physicians of the second type on this clinical dimension—the scientists—are more in tune with the British philosophy. They come from backgrounds in preventive medicine, toxicology, or occupational health, where the one-on-one interaction has never been their chief pleasure. They describe a process at some stage in their training or early career where they began gravitating away from this aspect of medicine and began thinking more in terms of populations or scientific problems. Monroe referred to himself as an "odd duck" in that he followed a "formal pathway" into occupational medicine, through a master's degree and doctorate in public health and a residency at one of the companies with an extensive occupational medical unit. He said he was even then spending more time with the toxicologists than with the clinicians. He did a government stint (at a high level) and later joined his corporation, but he said that even before he went off to the government, his practice was largely consultative, with perfunctory clinical observations of patients "because that was part of the ritual." For him and for others of this type, joining a corporation full time seldom means giving up the centerpiece of their professional lives in quite the way it often does for a true clinician.

116 ■ INSIDE THE CORPORATION

Robert Ingersoll also belonged in this category of scientists. With both legal and medical degrees, he had been a White House Fellow and a candidate for the United States Senate before accepting a corporate post. He expressed these feelings about a clinical role:

> I get my clinical jollies elsewhere, working on hospital staffs and with PSROs. I end up being a doctor's doctor. I try not to admit patients to the hospital. I try to hook them up with a good internist and to follow over his shoulder if it's a tough case. You can't allow yourself to get immersed in clinical issues. If that's your bag, then a corporate medical director for a larger company is the wrong way to go.

Dr. Bennett too was more scientist than clinician. He had been appointed by the governor to his state's OSHA review board and had organized a consulting business in occupational health before assuming full-time responsibilities for the medical program of a giant corporation. Clinically he had been doing only fairly exotic consultations related to toxic exposures, along with some hypnosis for stress reduction. Dr. Thomas Maxwell did basic toxicological research associated with the space program before taking over as health and safety director of a large health-care products firm. He and others stressed that they had no aversion to direct patient care but saw it as a diversion from the more challenging business of occupational medicine. "I'm not hands-on at all now, though not by desire, but by time, effort, and energy. When you're involved in clinical medicine, you can't walk away from it. You are consumed by it. In a few years, I may go back to it, though—that is, do a little clinical work here so I don't begin to feel out of touch."

The balanced view, in summary, accords "treatment" or clinical services a proper place in occupational medicine and in the role of the corporate medical director to the extent that they support or at least do not jeopardize the discipline's more important responsibility to prevent illness (Schilling 1981:43–44).

Involvement in the delivery of clinical services, in the majority view, makes sense for corporate medical directors chiefly as a means to a more important end—the prevention of occupational illness and injury in an employee population. The "laying on of hands" by the corporate medical director or other staff physicians in an in-house dispensary may be a way for the company to achieve some minor efficiencies. But from the medical director's standpoint, its real justification is symbolic. It meets the expectations and helps inspire the confidence of management and of employees, and it provides access to information on potential problems in the workplace. Seeing patients one at a time gives the corporate medical director a glimpse of what ought to be his real interest—the larger population.

6 ■ The Population as Patient

The gap in occupational medicine separating clinicians from scientists mirrors a division in the medical profession generally. Again, the English originally advanced the debate: Cochrane arguing for systematic assessment of the effectiveness of medical interventions (Cochrane 1971), McKeown questioning the contribution of medical measures to the modern transformation in the health of the populace (McKeown 1976). Granting that until the 1950s most knowledge about disease came through the study of clinical material available to physicians in their private practices, Cochrane, McKeown, and others in medicine's loyal opposition insist that the time has come to apply more rigorous, critical, and statistical forms of reasoning in formulating and addressing major problems of health and illness (Bunker, Barnes, and Mosteller 1977). In this, they share a kinship with the segment of occupational medicine we have been calling, for want of a better term, the scientific.

Prevention as Unrealized Potential

A leading American proponent of a more statistically grounded approach to health is Milton Terris. He contends that epidemiology must play "a more major role in the formulation of health policy" if the potential of prevention is to receive more than the considerable "lip service" now being paid by the health professions and the wider society. For major obstacles to this desired redirection of resources, he blames clinical medicine: "Among the significant obstacles to epidemiology as a guide to health policy are the views of clinicians who are unwilling to accept the validity of epidemiologic discoveries" (Terris 1980: 329).

Resistance of this kind comes from clinicians Terris terms "scientific," in their disdain for epidemiologic evidence as "merely statistical" and their willingness to accept only "confirmation by so-called real science" in animal studies. Dr. Alice Hamilton, who years earlier experienced first-hand the clinical obstructionism of which Terris writes, would not have been so charitable as to attribute it to "science." She saw an ideological functionality in the managers' blind spot. Employers "quieted [their] consciences" by asserting that "alcohol, not lead exposure, was making their workers sick." From her own profession she could generate little help. She "used to suggest gently to . . . medical colleagues that it would be useful to have actual figures showing how alcoholism favored plumbism, but none of them seemed to be interested in collecting such proof, although they held to the theory firmly" (Hamilton 1943:6).

The overlap that Hamilton observed between the industrialist's vested interest in overlooking the harm in workplace exposure and the clinician's indifference to the problem is also central to Terris's concern. The "scientific" obstacles, he says, have been buttressed by "private interests attempting to prevent acceptance of epidemiologic facts." For Terris the most "blatant example" is in tobacco research, but he and others recognize that "the history of occupational medicine is replete with such instances." He proposes public policies to change the private incentives but also looks to occupational medicine to shoulder much of the burden of the "second public health revolution" he is trying to rally. A "basic component" of his overall preventive program is "screening of well persons for early identification and treatment of disease," and because "treatment following screening presents special problems" of compliance, the workplace becomes an important setting for conducting the necessary follow-up (Terris 1980:337).

Terris's core thesis is that "if epidemiology is used as a guide to health policy, the latter will be based on the primacy of prevention" (Terris 1980:334). Occupational medicine has long seen prevention as its primary mission, a logical end for a medical specialty whose clientele is working and mostly healthy. The specialty's responsibility for a defined population (a particular workforce) has supported its claim to an identity distinct from most other branches of medicine. Ostensibly it stands at the crossroad between clinical and population medicine, whose inputs, Stallones points out, good epidemiology combines, not only as a matter of methodological strategy, but also for epistemological reasons, because while "disease in an individual may be expected to have biologically understandable causes, . . . a community is a social organization; thus, the distribution of disease in communities is a social phenomenon, and as such may be expected to have social causes" (Stallones 1980:73).

Here, then, is the basis for a rebuttal of "the doctrine of specific etiology" (Dubos 1959:177), which, chapter 2 showed, diverted public health early in its evolution from including within its central mission responsibility for aggressive social intervention. Studying the patterns of illness broadens notions of causation to include social factors, not only physical ones. How else are we to explain, for example, the persistent observation that members of lower classes have higher rates of mortality, morbidity, and disability from virtually all causes of illness (Syme and Berkman 1986)? Such findings demand social explanations side by side with clinical ones. And where explanations are partly social, interventions must be too, or they will fail.

Asking a corporate physician to think in these terms is to imply that he should move, in our model, along the medical axis from the clinical toward the population pole. Clinical inputs remain relevant; indeed, epidemiological studies more often than not originate in an observation by one or more alert clinicians. And even the best studies leave clinical and biomedical questions unanswered; invariably room remains for competing interpretations. Terris's conservative "scientists" reserve their judgment for the results of definitive animal and molecular-level studies, a luxury seldom available to a corporate physician whose employer needs an earlier judgment, however tentative it must be. While the clinical activities in a corporate medical director's role involve diagnosing illness, approaching the population pole introduces the diagnosis of risk based on probabilities, patterns among groups, and inductive reasoning from the cellular and molecular level to individuals and populations. Inherently difficult as such extrapolation has always been, two sets of recent forces have greatly multiplied the complexities of the task.

First, the risks themselves have become more profound and pervasive with the steady proliferation of chemicals in commerce since World War II and other, often related, technological changes associated with the revolutions in microelectronics, computer technology, artificial intelligence (resulting in factory automation and robotics, among other effects on work), biotechnology, laser and materials science technologies, and so on. The rate of technological change has been outpacing the nation's capability to respond with adequate assessment of the safety of new materials and processes and with appropriate regulation. Assessment of environmental risk—of the effects of a job on health—is therefore much more challenging in the 1980s than ever before.

Second, a new kind of risk assessment using data from newly available large-scale, longitudinal epidemiological research such as the Framingham heart study is beginning to spread in industry. Focusing as much on the way health may affect a worker's long-term ability to perform his job as on the obverse, it emphasizes lifestyle factors associated with increased risk of illness and premature death. Lifestyle-oriented health-risk appraisal and risk reduction at the worksite have been gaining increasing attention in professional journals and in the public media, the latter proclaiming the advent of a "wellness revolution."[1] On the utility and importance of wellness interventions, American managers polarize between believers and skeptics. The polarity is evident among corporate physicians, too, only some of whom are embracing the new wellness movement. All will need to define what role they can and should play in shaping their companies' missions and strategies with respect to lifestyle risks and health promotion. Moving toward the population pole begins to raise broader questions and to call on managerial skills, related, for example, to assessing, procuring, and managing outside vendors and to formulating an overarching strategy. It used to be much simpler.

Some clinicians in the field express nostalgia, as Julius Whitesides did, for the days when preventive medicine could maintain an individual focus. He happily consigned issues of environmental control to the engineers and wanted no part of the accountants' cost-benefit questions. At the same time, he recognized the futility of preventive medicine without adequate measures to anticipate, minimize, and detect early evidence of potentially harmful exposures and granted that the larger population must be of concern to a contemporary occupational physician. Dr. Manfred Blumgarten, a corporate medical director who had been with a very large European-based international chemical firm for nearly thirty years, echoed and amplified Whitesides's sentiments:

> Today it is more and more difficult to be a doctor in industry. Sometimes I feel shivering in my skin when someone new comes into the office and confides his troubles to me. I want to say, "My dear, thank you for your confidence in me." I feel we should change places across the table. When I started, all we needed was a stethoscope, a finger on the pulse, and a blood-pressure reading. Now all this risk-benefit evaluation makes it so difficult. We must keep the black spots off our white coats. We must keep our coats very clean.

Keeping Black Spots off White Coats

The new preoccupation with risk-benefit evaluation complicates the corporate physician's life because it is, as Dinman (1980) has described it, "an eternal dilemma of tragic choices."

As physicians with stewardship for populations, corporate medical di-

---

1. There is a growing literature, much of it in an advocacy vein, on worksite health promotion. Articles appear regularly in professional and trade publications including the *Journal of Occupational Medicine, Business and Health, Corporate Commentary, Occupational Health and Safety*, and *Business Insurance*. Several monographs and texts are now available, including Parkinson et al (1982) and O'Donnell and Ainsworth (1984). Review articles include those by Fielding (1984b), Herzlinger and Calkins (1986), and Kiefhaber and Goldbeck (1984). Rapid commercialization in the field is creating a situation where the lines are blurring between science and salesmanship. Good evaluation studies are still exceedingly rare.

rectors have to worry about both the availability and quality of empirical data and its interpretation by managers in the firm, employees, unions, government, the press, and others involved in the second step. In the role-theory language of Gross and his colleagues (1958), this one sector of the "focal role" implies several "counterpositions." The frustrations that corporate medical directors often express about their involvements here reflect this cacophony of competing expectations.

On one hand, their comments frequently convey the belief that government and the public are overemotional about the hazards of work and that the press is often ill-informed or irresponsibly alarmist. On the other, they often perceive that their companies must respond to these public concerns or face increasingly onerous regulation and damaging publicity. Blumgarten's perspective is illustrative and, because his frame of reference was Europe rather than the United States, indicates a perspective that may be generic in more or less extreme form to industrial physicians in the capitalist nations of the industrialized world.

Blumgarten's corporation employed about 125,000 people in sixty countries and 320 operating companies. He was titular head of a medical staff comprising 173 physicians worldwide. In the headquarters location, where 53,000 employees worked in a vast complex that spanned four square miles and produced 18,000 chemicals of which 6,000 were final products, Blumgarten directly oversaw the work of a 130-member "occupational medicine and health protection" staff, including 17 plant physicians, 2 epidemiologists, a geneticist, and 2 specialists in electronic data processing. His department interacted with separate units responsible for toxicological research, safety, and the equivalent of industrial hygiene (although not called that), none of which was within his direct domain. He taught one afternoon a week at a major university and published frequently on subjects ranging from basic toxicology to management of industrial medicine. He seemed particularly to value these academic credentials and was addressed by everyone in the plant as Herr Professor Blumgarten.

As technically demanding as this multifaceted job must have been, Blumgarten kept coming back to the problem of how to assuage fears he considered unreasonable and bring some balance to the debate about the chemicals in modern society. In this connection, he spoke with enthusiasm of the "open days" he held on ten occasions the previous year, when union representatives, politicians, "socialists," teachers, and other local opinion leaders were invited to visit the plant and hear about the health protection program: "Everyone was super-satisfied. Now they are better informed—other than through the mass media. The people who write the articles for the newspapers don't even know how to pronounce bischloromethylether. And they write press articles on us nearly every day."

He described an incident with the press over chromosome studies the company had been conducting for nearly a decade. These were not, he said emphatically, for the purpose of screening out employees with genetic defects but were part of the company's total program of research on the health effects of chemicals: "We hold meetings with employees to explain what this is about and everything is fine. Then, suddenly, the press gets exercised. I am called, then the union is called. I call the union people in and explain and everyone is reassured for now—I hope. But you never know."

The uncertainty comes from the volatility of the issues and the interest they therefore stimulate among press people and politicians. A carefully qualified scientific observation, he believed, would be amplified and distorted in the hands of the news media: "In which journal should we publish? That is a real problem. We publish a scientific paper and it gets picked up in the press. The politicians start receiving blows and they then turn to our executives and want to know, 'Why haven't you been informing us?' That makes our executives less willing next time to have us identify problems."

An example was a paper Blumgarten published in a professional journal on occupational health. A distillation of his thoughts on policy issues facing the field, it began with the imperative that "the workplace will be safe" and ended with eighteen recommendations for achieving this goal. Toward the end of the list he made the suggestion that one way to handle toxic chemicals with long latency periods would be to reserve for older workers those few jobs where it is impossible to reduce exposure to zero. The press picked up on that one recommendation and, in Blumgarten's view, blew it out of proportion.

At the same time that he resented the alarmism he felt was fostered by the news media, Blumgarten, like many of his peers in the United States, found in this turbulent environment ammunition he could use to advance some of his ideas with senior managers in the firm. Walking over to lunch in the executive dining room, he spoke to several executives who he said were all his patients: "The head of the company is my patient and my friend. So is the union head." Stopping to introduce his American guests to a group of senior executives standing just outside the dining hall, he exchanged words with them about his worry that regulations around the world would more and more be patterned after the restrictive approach in the United States. Gravely, he suggested that this would "stifle innovation" and proposed an international conference of chemical firms: "We must develop a mechanism for industry involvement. Only industry has the resources to perform these investigations—academics cannot do the longitudinal studies. We need a consensus in private industry on the priorities for some unique studies—'you do benzene; I'll do something else.' Uniform data are needed for these studies. Only then can we hope to erect a barrier to regulation."

Barriers to Regulation and Regulatory Barriers

Blumgarten's American colleagues, who live with the regulations he feared would influence lawmakers in other nations, share his feelings that there are regulatory excesses. Part of the reason is that they have been acculturated into management thinking. There is an ongoing debate in the field over whether physicians higher in the management hierarchy are less likely to express dissenting views—because they share a managerial orientation and have been coopted into management thinking—or more likely to do so because of the external credentials and mobility they presumably have. The cooptation thesis was lent support in this study by the finding that nearly all the company physicians interviewed expressed the perspective that regulations are excessive. This was true even among physicians in the most senior positions, who said they felt independent of management control and who almost certainly would have had external mobility had they wanted or needed to change jobs. Dr. Monroe was a good example. He talked of regulatory excesses while he projected himself and his company as highly responsible in their handling of chemicals. He considered himself fortunate in this respect: "I don't have to be a front man. [The CEO] would rather see his company fold than would he knowingly do harm to his employees or the general public."

He said he "sleeps well at night" because he "calls it like [he sees] it." He also suggested (and this was later confirmed) that some of organized labor's outspoken critics of corporate physicians "would regard Whitesides, me, and Gottlieb as decent fellows." Monroe and Gottlieb held offices in the federal government (not in OSHA or NIOSH) and were, perhaps for that reason, particularly offended by the "regulatory stupidity" they believed they had seen in occupational health and safety during OSHA's first decade.

The lead standard promulgated by OSHA was cited as an example of regulatory excess by several corporate medical directors. It required that employees with blood-lead levels above a particular threshold be sent to an outside hematologist for an independent evaluation. "The sensible thing," as far as Monroe was concerned, "would be to take another reading the next week. Even the hematologists, who stand to gain, find this regulation a joke." Another "stupidity" he saw was the requirement in the benzene standard that examinations be conducted every other month. "What are you looking for with that frequency—hemorrhages?" Monroe asked. "If so, we might as well just line up the hearses outside the plant gates."

In a similar vein, Dr. Trevor Gottlieb, vice president and corporate medical director of a large company with very serious health hazards, complained that OSHA had been "inept." He cited the "high-titer of self-delusion" on the benzene issue and the failure of the U.S. Supreme Court even to "challenge the slogans OSHA was using": "A commitment to ideology on the part of the regulators has colored their judgment. It's a new thing—having your social commitment color your scientific interpretation of the facts. In the old days, if you were a scientist, you *under*stated your case."

Having himself been in government in those halcyon days, Gottlieb thought the generation of regulators he was dealing with in 1980 was "feeling powerful, trying to indict things, doing sloppy work." If he were in charge now, he said, he would "go to the periodic table, look at the structures," and ask some searching questions about where future problems are likely to arise in industrial processes: "That's where real progress can be made, although I'm a traitor to industry to say it. There's so much we already know that's not being used because no one's integrating it. They should be developing rubrics for separating obvious disease entities and for defining what constitutes adequate evidence of cause and effect."

The tongue-in-cheek confession of treason conveyed more about Gottlieb's conversion than anything else he said. It clearly implied the stance that a corporate physician has no business even thinking about ways that society can make meaningful progress toward holding companies to account for the protection of workers' health. The government, from which he had come, was now the adversary, and Gottlieb was seeing the world through the "meaning system" (Berger 1963) of corporate management, placing himself squarely in the management camp.

For all their private disapproval of regulatory mistakes, these same corporate medical directors tempered their criticisms when they spoke for the record. Just as the clinical elements of their role made them wary of offending private physicians, so their responsibility for populations required that they work with regulators. Gottlieb was irritated when a senior executive in his firm made a public statement raking the regulators over the coals: "I told him, 'We're both grandparents, don't you know about the dirty-diaper syndrome? You've had your fun, and now I'm left to clean up the mess.'"

In Gottlieb's view and that of some of his professional peers, overstatement by government regulators and other workers' advocates complicates the corporate physician's task of stimulating appropriate concern among corporate managers when worrisome evidence does come to light. He faulted the "so-called workers' advocates" for "doing their own cause more harm than good" when they "overstate their case and imply that all or most disease originates in the workplace": "People wonder how something like asbestos or vinyl chloride could have happened—how management could have been so evil. Yes, there were villains and rogues. But more often there is ignorance, self-delusion, and naiveté." When early evidence of trouble begins to appear, he argued, managers want it not to be true and therefore tend to deny it, demanding better proof. This denial process is abetted, Gottlieb said, by management's accurate perception that the environmentalists, regulators, and workers' advocates are inclined to exaggerate and "cry wolf."

Labor representatives, on the other side, insist that in this field time has all too often shown the situation to be even more serious than the "alarmists'" worst fears. They ascribe management's delayed responses to a ruthless decision to eke as much profit as possible out of the harmful product before a public outcry forces them to curtail production. As one kind of evidence, they offer the suggestion that a company in possession of damaging information about one of its products typically will not challenge the first wave of worker's compensation cases associated with that substance but will simply pay them to keep the problem from coming to light. The majority of worker's compensation claims for occupational disease are contested (Boden 1982:319), and when they are not, labor spokesmen argue, management's reticence can often be interpreted as a desire to delay the discovery process that will eventually interfere with production and profits. The record does show, in case after case, that American industrialists have been slow to take obvious corrective steps in the face of overwhelming evidence that a substance or a process was jeopardizing their employees' health. Naturally, corporate medical directors prefer not to dwell upon this reality of industry's sins of omission and commission. They channel their emotional energy instead into barbed or sarcastic criticisms of industry's opponents—the press, government regulators, and labor and activist groups—or isolate the problem in a few egregious cases where everyone agrees a given corporation acted irresponsibly.

Gottlieb shared Blumgarten's scorn of the news media. It offended him that "physicians are getting their information about microwaves from Brodeur's writings in the popular press. They're not getting information from refereed scientific journals. That's a real danger."[2] He said someone should take a careful look at the impact the press has had on

---

2. Paul Brodeur's arresting exposés of malfeasance in the asbestos industry were serialized in the *New Yorker* and later appeared as two books (Brodeur 1974, 1985). He also studied microwave radiation exposure and made serious allegations about corporate attempts to disguise the risk to which they are willfully exposing their employees (Brodeur 1977). Brodeur writes in the best muckraking tradition, and although corporate physicians take him to task for bias and overstatement, his writings are exceedingly well documented.

public policy in occupational health and expressed the view that it has impeded progress by polarizing the debate, escalating the conflict, and driving information underground.

Am I Going to Get Cancer?

Whatever part government, labor, workers' advocates, and the press have played in promoting concern about the health hazards of work, nearly all corporate medical directors feel pressures percolating up from a generalized climate of concern. Pressures from employees troubled Samuel Perkins, the nonphysician personnel vice president to whom Dr. Bennett reported. He picked up a bottle of liquid typing correction fluid and cradled it in his hand while he reflected on how "sensitized" people are:

> Someone who works for you comes in and says, "Is this Liquid Paper safe? I've been using it for months, and inhaling it, and sometimes spilling it on my hands or clothes. You've said 'we protect our workers,' and I want to be sure that this stuff isn't harming me. What if I get pregnant, can I use it then?" So you look at the bottle, and it doesn't say what's in the stuff but you figure it must contain toluene and other solvents. So you may write the manufacturer and he may write back and say the composition of the stuff is a trade secret. Then, what do you say to that employee?

He went on to cite another example involving "chemicals customers use in routine maintenance of our products":

> We've tested our own, but the customer is free to buy anyone's chemicals. Some buy cheaper brands, and they may get it from some fly-by-night company. What about our service man who's called in to service our machine in which those cheap chemicals are being used? He comes back and asks me, "Am I going to get cancer from this infernal stuff—it gets all over my skin, it's sticky and I can't wash it off. I've been handling it for six months. Am I going to be okay?" What do you tell them?

Perkins also pointed out how separate units in the firm may have vastly different perspectives on the implications of a potential health hazard. For a time, there was concern about a chemical used in a large piece of equipment the company manufactured. During normal use, the chemical was contained and would probably have posed a hazard only, if at all, to the company's service engineers when they were working on the equipment on the customer's premises: "The product people are very nervous about this. If the medical director says, for example, that the service engineer will have to wear protective gloves when working on the machine, what on earth are the customers going to think about their own safety?"

This situation actually deteriorated, and the company felt it necessary to notify its customers of new evidence raising the possibility that the chemical in this product they had been using might be a carcinogen. An industrial hygienist on Bennett's staff was assigned the task of answering customers' questions and allaying their fears. The reactions varied, he said, from gallows humor like "Oh, you mean we can't drink the stuff at our Friday afternoon parties any more?" to genuine alarm in one customer's request for an estimate of how soon he would know whether or not he had contracted cancer from exposure to the substance.

Pressures from state and federal regulators and from his own safety department were on Dr. Lee's mind. The safety people in a separate department were the ones in his company who followed changes in regulations:

> I am spoiled by a great safety department. They wear many hats and are into sophisticated hygiene and toxicology. They are encyclopedic in their knowledge. They do the measuring for the substances in the environment, and it used to be that we had no action levels—no chemicals for which we had to do biological monitoring. But the lead standard has changed all that. Now OSHA wants physical exams as a quality control on industrial hygiene testing. That's the government's new strategy. The safety people come to me and say we have 300 people dealing with lead and we need to examine them all. The state agency is coming in and checking—"What biologicals do you have?" It catches you sitting on your hands, and we don't like that.

Unions have been criticized in the past for providing insufficient leadership on health and safety matters (Page and O'Brien 1973; Naschold 1981). But some have been vocal, adding to the pressures felt by corporate physicians. Michael Swift, a nonphysician director of health and safety for a large chemical manufacturer, mentioned several requests his firm had received from the Oil, Chemical, and Atomic Workers (a union that has fought aggressively for occupational health protection) for data and statistical analyses of particular exposures occasioning concern among union members. Some of these requests the company met, but in at least one other case: "It would have been a massive job and we thought that the payoff wouldn't be there. We said we couldn't do it, but we also told them that we were developing the capability of supplying that information in the future."

The capability Swift's company was developing, in part so that they could respond to future union requests, was a computerized health information system. Other companies working on similar projects cited different stimuli. Testifying before a Senate committee looking into health effects of vinyl chloride was for one corporate medical director, who had to admit to his company's ignorance, so "unhappy" an experience that he resolved never again to be put in that position. The consequence, according to a lawyer with the firm, was the creation of an integrated data system. Interest in developing such systems has grown rapidly in the past decade although technical progress has lagged. The competing explanations for this apparent gap between desire and accomplishment—and the issues involved in the development of sophisticated data systems—are indicative of the conflicting pressures many corporate medical directors feel.

Integrated Data Systems

The elementary idea behind an integrated data system for occupational health is that it will harness the expanding data-processing technology in systematic and cumulative monitoring of all exposures in the workplace and all evidence of biological ill effects. The information system will facilitate a kind of passive epidemiological surveillance to avoid the tragic situations in the past when "body counts" have provided the first available evidence that something has gone awry. It will encourage prospective planning of programs to conserve employees' health. Those who argue for the development of such systems point out that companies have substantially more information relevant to their employees' health than they are able to apply to the health protection effort. The fragmentation of the information accounts for its limited utility, and a sophisticated computer system is needed to marry the various components, including hospital and physician records for services covered in employee benefit plans, worker's compensation and disability claims, absenteeism records, results of periodic health examinations and screening programs, findings from industrial hygiene surveys, the content of material safety data sheets, and so on. The idea is subject to debate.

Enthusiasts, many of whom stand outside corporations and look in, conceive of integrated data systems as a *sine qua non* if companies dealing with chemicals and other invisible hazards (including job stress) are to protect their employees adequately over the long term. Some interpret the general absence of such systems as evidence of their importance—companies avoid installing them because of liabilities they fear they will incur as the systems turn up more and more evidence of the hazards of work. This Trojan-horse position is represented by Audrey Freedman of the Conference Board, whose study *Industry Response to Health Risk* left her with the uneasy feeling that "it's harikari for a private corporation in a private market system to produce this information" (Freedman 1981, 1983).

Corporate medical directors gravitate to the skeptics' camp on the issue of data systems. Here again, they see the world through management's lens, constructing elaborate arguments from the basic premise that the employees in their companies are safe. First, they challenge the Trojan-horse thesis on its terms and their own. On its terms, they accept the premise that data systems will produce new knowledge but reject the claim that there are no incentives to do so. In addition, however, many reject the enthusiasts' more fundamental premise that integrated data systems will unearth grievous new liabilities, or indeed will turn up anything new. First taking on the Trojan-horse argument, they say the incentives to learn more about the health effects of work outweigh the risks of incurring serious new liability.

Corporate physicians' faith in positive incentives for their employers to want to monitor the health effects of work rests on the belief that the government has required far more protection than the evidence will in time show was necessary—in essence, Blumgarten's belief about the need for barriers to regulation run amok. Also it rests on the premise that, as one corporate attorney said, "The goal is not to identify liability; it is to prevent it." This two-pronged position was espoused by Michael Swift, who buttressed his case with reference to a government regulation he considered excessive (the lead standard) and the apotheosis of an inadequately controlled industrial hazard that has come home to haunt industry (the asbestos tragedy): "The disincentives have existed for a long time but in some instances are becoming incentives. Look at lead. Five years of study have shown the government standard wrong. Or asbestos. If there had been data systems in the past, the situation would be very different. There is an incentive to discovery. Discovery is the company's best defense."

The weakness in this argument is the clear evidence that the hazards of asbestos were well known long before industry took effective action. What Swift seemed to imply was that the asbestos tragedy has taught top management a lesson, a sentiment echoed in comments other corporate medical directors made. "We satisfy our corporate lawyers that getting more data can help us," said the medical director of one of the nation's ten largest chemical manufacturers. Dr. Jack McCarthy, from another of the top ten, based his case on the influence the company's reputation can have in the recruitment of a medical staff. "We try," he said, "to get the best doc in town as our local plant physician. I know and my management knows that we can't get him if we have nothing more than a defensive program."

The Future Will Judge the Present

The skeptics' rejection of the Trojan-horse thesis rests on firmer ground than total faith in corporate largesse. Corporate medical directors see stronger incentives as well. One chemical firm's attorney pointed out that "evidentiary rules" are such that "issues arise case-by-case and a corporation can defend itself on grounds that the litigant was the only person in the facility who got this. That's an incentive to develop more knowledge, not less." McCarthy contended that it makes sense for companies to invest in learning more because "exposure now will produce results that will show twenty years from now. They will be judged against the norms and laws in effect then, not now." His reading of historical trends convinced McCarthy that the norms and laws of the future will be increasingly less forgiving of failures on the part of large employers to protect employees. John Blum, a medicolegal scholar, foresees a similar scenario. He tentatively suggests an analogy to malpractice law, which presumes a general community standard of practice among physicians. As some firms develop comprehensive health-surveillance systems, Blum suggests, they may create a corporate standard of practice against which others could be judged negligent if tort actions were brought against them by injured employees (Blum 1983).

Another positive impetus to learn everything possible about the hazards of the materials used in production was discussed by several corporate medical directors of companies that export their risks. "I have difficulty separating profit from safety," said the corporate medical director of one. "We produce chemicals, and if they are unsafe for our employees to work with, then they are unsafe for our customers as well." A business case for knowing more is formalized in at least some large chemical companies, where environmental data developed for employee health protection are "used by the sales force as part of their pitch."

A second line of argument is advanced by corporate medical directors skeptical of data systems. In the first instance, they argue that if passive epidemiological surveillance will unveil an epidemic before it occurs, corporations will gain more than they lose. In the second, they doubt that the systems will identify problems at all. Corporate medical directors tend to believe, and to tell their employers, that better collection and analysis of health data are unlikely to uncover hidden epidemics. Said McCarthy:

> It's not all that bad. Companies haven't been turning up a lot of liability. We sell it [the need for data systems] to business managers as an idea whose time has come. The big problems will be found anyway, with or without data systems. There was a tremendous amount of overselling of chemical carcinogenesis around 1972, but it's been ten years and we just haven't seen the evidence. It's an epidemic overdue, and the track record of companies like Kodak that have been doing surveillance for years hasn't been that bad.

Even if the workplace does harbor hidden evidence of potentially serious problems, which the corporate medical directors doubt, they also doubt that the systems being developed will provide the power to piece that evidence together. Acknowledging that the "topic is just coming on the horizon," Monroe expressed reservations about how far it would (or should) travel:

Companies are spending several millions of dollars on efforts to collect health data and exposure data and index them one to another. There is an element of pseudoscience in some of this—for example, when some of these systems attempt to divide a plant totally into geographical coordinates and map where workers are and establish an integrated dose, or others that say they're going to give their employees a little credit card and have them establish where they are at a particular time as they move around the plant by punching in and out with this plastic passport. I think that goes beyond what can reasonably be expected to yield anything useful. Also it tends to heighten the importance in total health of that which is assigned to exposure. You know, "Gee whiz, I got gall bladder disease or something else and it was because I was in a particular location." My vibrations tell me that the location of the individual is a very low order of magnitude in terms of what his total health experience will be.

A wiser investment than elaborate passive epidemiological systems, Monroe believed, are the "studies run by companies large enough to support an internal epidemiological force." He said there has been a "great profusion" of these, as well as studies by trade associations and university research groups. There has also been, he said, "a significant move toward standardization of the medical record so that collaborative studies can be done when the number of employees in an individual plant is too small to justify a study or to prove anything."

It's Been the Body Counts

Occupational medicine is divided on the question of data systems. Swift, for example, shared Monroe's view that "indexing systems" are of unproven usefulness, but he reached a different conclusion:

> I have to ask myself the question. In the past, to a great degree, with the exception of some very well-known kinds of occupational disease, it's been the body counts that have led us to what our problems are. And if the name of the game in the future is to protect employees and the liabilities of the larger corporation, one must move toward prevention and early detection to minimize those liabilities. I don't think we'll ever rid ourselves of all the risks, but I happen to believe that the more we know about what is in the workplace, the better the judgments we'll make.

Swift's point of view has wide enough currency to support, as a reasonable case, the prediction that the large companies dealing in hazardous materials will over the next ten or twenty years assume or have thrust upon them responsibility for conducting continuous and systematic monitoring of exposures in the workplace indexed to the health of exposed workers. Management will, more and more, need interpretations of ambiguous scientific data backed up by strategies to manage risk. In those firms the "population medicine" sector of the medical director's role will either become more pronounced or will be ceded to technicians with biostatistical and epidemiological experience.

Lifestyle Threats to Health: Worksite "Wellness" Programs

In smaller and/or safer firms as well, populations may come more sharply into focus, expanding the mandate of occupational medicine in rallying Terris's second public health revolution. The rapid escalation of health-care costs from the 1960s on (Walsh and Egdahl 1977), buttressed by a reconceptualization of opportunities for preventing early death and disability (Lalonde 1974; U.S. Department of Health, Education, and Welfare, 1978), has breathed new life into a "worksite wellness" movement. To capitalize on the growing interest white-collar workers are demonstrating in the active pursuit of health, some companies have developed elaborate health promotion programs in the context of employee benefits, human resource management, or in-house medical care.

Data are scarce on how widespread such programs are in American workplaces and on variability from one to the next. An adequate accounting would require a sophisticated survey, which would probably not warrant the expense, given the apparent fluidity of the situation. Media accounts and trade publications portray the wellness movement as a rapidly expanding phenomenon. Some growth seems evident too in several partial surveys that have been conducted: in a particular state (Fielding and Breslow 1983; Davis et al. 1983), among a particular sample of employers (Washington Business Group on Health 1978; Herzlinger and Calkins 1986; Hewitt Associates 1984), and so on. But generalization from these data is limited by the absence of an accepted operational definition of what a worksite health-promotion program minimally entails. For example, agreement is lacking on whether (and if so, how) to include activities traditionally done under the old rubric of occupational health and safety: hearing and eye exams, safety first campaigns, CPR training, and other kinds of orthodox health education. Many of the ostensibly new wellness programs scarcely expand things occupational health nurses have been doing for years.

Second, it is unclear what weight to give the standard preventive medicine services covered through third-party payment systems. Periodic medical examinations, prenatal and well-baby care, immunizations for children and adults, Pap smears, and myriad other screening examinations are certainly part of classic preventive services. Such services are covered to varying degrees in many but by no means all employee benefit packages. Whether they constitute worksite health promotion programs can be argued either way. Third, whatever boundaries finally are placed around the master list of included activities, consensus is lacking on how to correct for the intensity of the effort. Virtually every employer does something to encourage healthier lifestyles—hands out materials supplied free by voluntary health organizations, or runs an occasional article on health in an employee communication vehicle. At what threshold to "count" such activities as part of a genuine health promotion program is far from clear.

Despite these inadequacies in the data, there does seem to be some growth in programming and a building sense among some managers of large corporations that there will come a limit to how far they can go toward containing health-care costs by squeezing inefficiencies out of the delivery system. A longer-term option some are beginning seriously to consider is the possibility of organizing programs to help employees stay well. Still very much an open question, whether worksite health promotion ultimately will pay is currently being debated on the theoretical level (Russell 1986), while empirical data on particular interventions are just beginning to appear.

From what we already know about the difficulty of changing ingrained human behavior, it seems likely that if worksite health promotion is going to fulfill its promise, it will have to evolve multifaceted, long-term strategies that can address underlying attitudes, values and beliefs, social supports, and economic pressures, not just risk factors themselves. Thus, the promise of worksite health promotion will require the use of a broad range of strategies; indeed, its theoretical appeal is the opportunity to mobilize diverse change mechanisms, from policies and rules, to financial incentives, to social and group norms and values. As marketers, many managers are acutely aware of the secular changes taking place in social attitudes toward health. Changes are evident in the marketing strategies of companies selling many kinds of products, in growing social movements like Mothers Against Drunk Driving, in the general acceptance of policies (such as screening for drug metabolites and tough drunk-driving laws) that would have seemed intolerably invasive and coercive a decade ago. Through worksite wellness programs, some managers see the opportunity to leverage these secular changes and accelerate them. Some corporate medical directors are centrally involved in articulating this logic and mapping the development of these programs.

The Medical Axis in Perspective

Laced through the history of occupational medicine is a vision of a distinctive contribution the specialty can make: something other or broader than conventional clinical medicine. The visionaries see the breadth of their specialty in the understanding it encompasses of environmental and job-related determinants of health and in the way it extends their horizons beyond what a physician could ever hope to experience in a lifetime of clinical encounters. But they see it also as different from the practice of curative medicine.

A regular medical encounter involves a series of four generic steps: (1) the interpretation of signs and symptoms; (2) the formulation of a diagnosis; (3) the prescription of a course of treatment; and (4) the follow-up. The patient presents with a complaint and expects to go away cured or, failing cure, at least relieved of some pain and suffering. On its frontiers, occupational medicine builds from altogether different origins, as a form of preventive medicine.

In a preventive medical encounter, no patient presents with a complaint he hopes the doctor will diagnose and treat. Instead, the practitioner needs a way to identify those who can benefit from his services. For that reason, preventive medical programs often start by screening healthy populations in search of a subgroup with preventable elevated risk, whatever its cause. Screening stands in as the analogue of the patient's presentation of signs and symptoms to the curative clinician. The next steps in the preventive model involve appraising health hazards or risk factors among the individuals who have been screened out, designing an organizational, educational, or behavioral intervention, and finally, as in the curative encounter, following up.[3]

Such a model recasts the preventive medical enterprise at the heart of occupational medicine as something qualitatively different from the truncated and distorted vestige of clinical medical practice that corporate occupational medicine has often seemed to be. And when conceived in these distinctive terms, the specialty's liabilities convert to assets. The lack of diverse or interesting clinical material, inevitable with an employed and basically healthy clientele, and the tradition of referring cases out for definitive diagnosis and treatment free up time and resources to focus on the sequence of steps involved in prevention. The window occupational practice opens onto a population offers a unique opportunity to initiate the sequence of preventive steps, ground them in epidemiology, and monitor their long-term impact.

Although it is seldom set forth explicitly or fully and rarely completely realized in practice, this qualitatively different mission has long been the special promise occupational medical practice has harbored. The disappointment for its practitioners, as physicians in corporations, has been to see the promise of their discipline remain essentially unfulfilled. The reasons are complex, but one can be found in the tendency of many corporate physicians to concentrate their efforts at the clinical end of the

---

3. For the ideas in this paragraph I am indebted to Dr. Jean-Louis Gentillini of the Pasteur Institute in Lille, France.

medical axis—trying to be "real" doctors who happen to be practicing *in* corporations. And this tendency, in turn, reflects the degree to which many corporate physicians become physicians *of* corporations, aligning themselves with the interests of management, real or (often) imagined. With management, they bridle at irrationalities and overstatements in positions taken by government regulators, employee advocates, and the mass media; with management, they view the workplace as fundamentally safe and the worker as ultimately responsible for the conservation of his or her health. In this context, to look assiduously for signs of disease in basically healthy working populations—the essence of preventive medicine—is to make common cause with the adversary, to engage in a subversive activity.

Nevertheless, the special promise of occupational medicine cannot be realized without movement along the medical axis, away from orthodox clinical activities—where the focus is curing disease—toward a population-based and more probabilistic conception of preventive medicine. And this movement has been occurring. The growing role of statistics and computers in medicine is one driving force; a general cultural shift in favor of the active pursuit of health, another. But movement on the medical axis tells only half the story, because corporate medical directors also play complicated—and complicating—managerial roles.

7 ■ Doctors of Corporations

It was rumored that one vice president and corporate medical director, not universally liked, was so impressed with his dual status that he drove a car with a vanity license plate bearing the initials M.D.V.P. A colleague at another company replaced the name badge he wore at work with one identifying him as a vice president but not as an M.D. He said he came to feel that the medical identity lowered his stature in the eyes of his organizational peers and diminished his influence in decisions of consequence. Moving to the management axis of the corporate physician's role crystallizes the conflicts that have beset the field. Here the concern shifts from the expectations of individual employees or the health of employee populations to needs and exigencies of the larger corporate enterprise. The obvious question to ask is why make the transition at all. The reply many corporate physicians give is that unless they can function as managers they are severely limited in their ability to pursue objectives in preventive medicine. Dr. Bernard Tyson expressed this opinion:

> We in the profession tend to gloss over the conflicts. But they are real. The corporate physician, if he is to be effective, must be able to effect change in job design, environmental engineering, and the social arrangements of work. He hasn't got a chance if he's not part of the management structure. He's got to work from within because these changes cost money. But when he's part of management, employees may doubt his objectivity. No matter what anyone tells you, that problem is unresolved.

Ethical Dilemmas in the Managerial Realm

The profession's official attempt to confront and resolve its conflicts is embodied in a formal code of ethics adopted in 1976 (American Occupational Medical Association 1976). However, the code neglects to recognize the profession's ambivalence toward its management role. Sliding back and forth along the medical axis, the code seems, on one hand, to forsake the clinical pole by avoiding altogether the use of the word "patient" and referring to the occupational physician's client as an "employee." On the other hand, it exalts the individual relationship characteristic of a clinician by adopting, as a first principle, that practitioners should "accord highest priority to the health and safety of the individual in the workplace."

As guideposts to behavior, the twelve ethical precepts seem straightforward enough when conceived, as articulated, in the single dimension —health—implied by the medical perspective. They become considerably less helpful, however, with the introduction of a second dimension—costs—which cannot be ignored when the employer's perspective is taken into account. The code admonishes occupational physicians to "practice on a scientific basis with objectivity and integrity." Unfortunately, science lacks absolutes and serves poorly as a court of appeal. The judgments being asked of corporate physicians are often trans-scientific (Kotin 1979:560). That is, two (or more) objective, well-qualified, and ethical scientists can look at the same evidence and honestly dispute its meaning. Corporate physicians routinely face questions to which there are no objective scientific answers—an informed scientific opinion, or two or three or more, but no unique verifiable scientific solution.

If the first ethical precept were followed to the letter, corporate physicians would come down invariably on the side of overprotection when faced with scientifically unanswerable questions about harm that might attend the use of a substance or a process or even a social arrangement in the workplace. And when harm might already have been done—no matter how tenuous the evidence—the first precept would militate for full compensation. Absolute health protection and total compensation are unprofitable and perhaps even impossible, and decisions about how to ration the company's investments in health often hinge on medical definitions that corporate physicians, in their management roles, are called upon to supply.

In these decisions about allocating scarce resources for health, the ethical code provides little guidance. Yet as a routine matter, at the operational end of the management pole, they are the occasions for contention between management and labor over issues related to health. Some corporate medical directors draw very sharp lines in an effort to dissociate themselves from this contention. But to have the influence of which Dr. Tyson speaks, they have to make a contribution that the organization values. For this reason, a few of the profession's leaders are working at the strategic end of the management axis to develop what Wilensky has called "a new and more sophisticated imagery" of how "men of science" can influence "men of power" (Wilensky 1967). Together with the evolution toward population medicine, this strategic orientation to management may presage a more optimistic future for the discipline than its history would otherwise foreshadow.

Dr. Mary McDonald, a union physician who conducts epidemiological surveys in the workplace, said she reports her findings in aggregate to the involved employer, along with recommendations for action, but withholds any information that would identify a particular worker. When NIOSH set out to conduct an epidemiological study involving DuPont workers and requested that the company supply individual medical records, the company went to court rather than "break employees' confidences" by releasing such information to the government.[1]

The two situations share a focus on individual privacy but rest on divergent assumptions about the *uses* for which the information is to be gathered or to which it may be put. Dr. McDonald withheld individual identities on the assumption that obtaining information about the health status of particular workers would incline the employer to protect the company legally by taking job actions that might be contrary to workers' economic interests or to their wishes. Employees have traditionally worried that medical information gleaned in a physical exam may be used against them (Hazlett and Hummel 1957). Companies have fought government access to individually identifiable health information on the grounds that if they yield, employees will not trust companies with any sensitive health information and will cease to cooperate with their health protection programs. From one perspective the employer appears as the worker's adversary; from the other, as his ally against encroachments from outside. Corporate medical directors stand in the middle.

If they look to AOMA's ethical code they find a specific precept on the handling of information. The code stipulates that occupational physicians should "treat as confidential whatever is learned about individuals served, releasing information only when required by law or by overriding public health considerations, or to other physicians at the request of the individual according to traditional medical ethical practice; and should recognize that employers are entitled to counsel about the medi-

---

1. The literature on informing the worker about occupational health hazards is fairly well developed. Spokespersons for the profession write frequently on "right to know" and "the duty to inform" (see, e.g., Tepper 1980; Morton 1977; Karrh 1978; and Roberts 1978a). There are treatises on how to inform (see NIOSH 1977b; Committee on Public Information in the Prevention of Occupational Cancer 1977; Friedland 1978; Samways 1982). There are writings on the legal aspects of "fair information practices" (see Privacy Protection Study Commission 1977; Westin 1976; Westin and Salisbury 1980; Richter 1981; *Yale Law Journal* 1981; Lee and Rom 1982; LaDou 1981). And there is a strong muckraking literature on failures adequately to warn (see ch. 1, n. 10).

cal fitness of individuals in relation to work, but are not entitled to diagnoses or details of a specific nature" (American Occupational Medical Association 1976). This begs the central issue of the use of the information. The code's punctilio of preserving the confidentiality of diagnostic labels does protect the employee anxious to hide a stigmatizing medical condition or any that he or she considers embarrassing or compromising—a venereal disease, an abortion, substance abuse, epilepsy, diabetes, homosexuality, AIDS, infertility, a mastectomy, prostatic disease, and so on. Still, it misses the more basic point that the medical judgment or certification of fitness to work—the information on which the code places no embargo—is the real source of conflict in the management-labor field.

The Inevitability of Conflict

When problems have arisen in occupational medicine, employees have tended to worry less about whether others will find out about their health status than about whether a health finding might jeopardize their opportunities for jobs, their employment status, or their chances for career advancement (Bayer 1982). This observation is consistent with theories of the firm, ranging all the way from Marxist analysts, for whom the employment relationship is inherently rife with conflict, to someone like Chester Barnard, whose 1938 book (reissued in 1968 in an anniversary edition) stands as a *summa apologia* for the corporation (Perrow 1977:70–89), written from a distinctly managerial background and purview. Barnard's purpose in writing his book was to distill his experience as a senior manager of AT&T in how to win the cooperation of employees. One of his insights was that management-labor relationships divide into three different zones. The first he called a "zone of indifference," where workers grant management's right to call forth certain behaviors because laws or norms are strong enough to make compliance automatic. The worker is indifferent to the manager's requirement that he come to work on time, perform his job according to specification, and adhere to certain rules of conduct at work. The second of Barnard's categories was a "zone of nonacceptability," consisting of demands by the boss that management and workers agree at any given time are inappropriate, unethical, or otherwise unacceptable. The third zone was Barnard's primary concern, "a zone of neutrality," comprising behaviors for which there are no clear rules as to how legitimate it is for a manager to request them. Barnard argued that strong management works, through indoctrination and other efforts to manufacture consensus, to carve out from the zone of neutrality new ground for the zone of indifference. Labor's interest is served by moving the boundaries in the other direction in order to widen the zone of nonacceptability.

The occupational health sphere can be conceived in similar terms. Labor's side is a zone where the company is clearly accountable for the effects of the job on health; management's is a zone where the employee bears the burden for the effects of health on the ability to perform his work. The center consists of a wide band of ambiguity where the cause-and-effect relationships between health and work are poorly understood and the issue of responsibility has to be adjudicated case by case. As in Barnard's original formulation, the interests of management and labor are fundamentally at odds but the organization needs to paper over the cracks in pursuit of cooperation and harmony. The challenge for occupational medicine has been to avoid being drawn into the conflict insofar as possible, while still making a contribution that both sides value. A certain degree of involvement seems virtually unavoidable, and there is an ineffable quality to the finesse with which some practitioners of occupational medicine seem able to walk the tightrope. The reality nonetheless remains that the medical department is part of the trend toward ever more systematic personnel relations envisaged by Barnard and others. As such, the contribution it can make is to limit the scope of dissension over health to the few narrow channels that management is in a position to control.

Physicians in corporations inevitably face situations where their professional judgment of an individual's health status contradicts that of the individual himself or his personal physician. Twaddle's (1974) typology shows where such situations most often arise. From the observation that an individual's own assessment of his health status may deviate from that of other "health status definers," he constructed a four-cell diagram that highlights areas of conflict. Healthy and sick people are defined as such by themselves and other definers, but "deniers" of illness think they are well and others disagree while hypochondriacs or malingerers believe they are ill when others see them as well.

Situations implied in this formulation require the corporate medical director to function in the different roles elaborated in figure 7.1. Cell 2 calls for a medical comptroller who will verify or deny the patient's entitlement to insurance benefits, paid sick leave, or other special dispensations associated with legitimate illness. Cell 3 places the corporate physician in the position of investment analyst, evaluating whether the applicant or employee has the physical and mental health to begin or resume a specific job without endangering himself or others in whom the company has a financial interest or an exposure to legal liability.

The typology implies consensus in cells 1 and 4, where the individual and other "definers" are all of one mind. But this is misleading in the context of occupational medicine. Some of the most excruciatingly difficult issues arise in cell 4, where the *fact* of illness is uncontested. What is open to debate is the assignment of responsibility. In Parsons's (1951)

Figure 7.1
Roles of Corporate Physicians in Areas of Conflict

	Company physician's assessment of employee's health status	
Employee's self-designation (verified by his personal physician)	Well	Not Well
Well	1. (No Conflict)	3. Investment Analyst
Not well	2. Medical Comptroller	4. Expert Medical Witness

Source: Adapted from the work of Twaddle (1974).

original and seminal formulation of the sick role, illness by definition conferred on the sick person immunity from blame. Since then, many others, including Freidson (1970a, 1970b), Szasz (1970), Ryan (1972), and the Ehrenreichs (1978), have demonstrated how responsibility often remains to be negotiated when someone falls ill. Especially is this so when the illness carries a stigma, has pyschological overtones, or involves social costs, or when the social and cultural distance between patient and physician is wide and the relationship highly asymmetrical. Responsibility is most difficult to assign where causality is least well understood, and it is here that occupational medicine is most likely to encounter trouble. With these two new dimensions—assignment of responsibility and knowledge of cause and effect—cell 4 of figure 7.1 can be elaborated into figure 7.2.

Each of the four new cells harbors distinct incentives. The corporation's interests are served when individuals are held responsible and individuals' when the corporation is. Years ago, industrial accidents were blamed on the "accident-prone worker" (Ashford 1976), or companies charged injured workers with having been intoxicated (Hamilton 1943). Now workers are occasionally making their own inroads into the zone of ambiguity by winning compensation awards for heart attacks attributed to accumulations of stress on the job (Warshaw 1979)[2] or for lung can-

---

2. A review of the issue of "cumulative injury and occupational stress" notes a trend toward "expanding compensability in the workers' compensation law" (especially in California) and argues for a system to apportion disability (Mulryan, McCarthy, and LaDou 1981). I believe it still remains undeniably true, however, that workers are far more likely to be undercompensated than overcompensated for harm arising out of work (see, e.g., Barth and Hunt 1980).

Figure 7.2
When Illness Is Established. Further Occasions for Conflict

Knowledge of cause and effect relationships	Imputation of responsibility	
	Individual held responsible	Corporation held responsible
Clear	1. Alcoholism	3. On-the-job accident
Unclear	2. Heart attack Common cancers Chromosomal anomalies	4. "Occupational cancers" Reproductive anomalies

Source: Elaboration of cell 4 in fig. 7.1.

cers attributed exclusively to a possible asbestos exposure despite the synergistic effects of a heavy cigarette-smoking habit.

Ideally, corporate medical directors might elude involvement in these conflicts, and some do much of the time. But avoiding them entirely undermines whatever claim they would make to being general managers, not just specialists overseeing a narrow technical function within the company. Managers, according to Drucker (1973), share "responsibility for the performance of the enterprise." The specialist's allegiance is to his technical or professional skills; managers are preoccupied with the specific contribution they and their units can make to the whole organization. Specialists need managers whose job it is to plan, organize, integrate and measure the performance of the specialists. Medical directors in large corporations do see themselves as managers in Drucker's sense. Other managers look on them as such and expect them to share responsibility for solving the problems that arise in the three contentious cells identified in figure 7.2. Not all corporate physicians admit to the conflict in their roles, but all develop devices for distancing themselves from it. The defensive strategies themselves lend support to the claim that the conflict is real (Burchard 1954:528; Walters 1982:9–10). They provide a way to remain loyal to the organization while keeping a professional identity intact (Derber 1982). The loyalty that the organization requires of a corporate physician is evident in the categories of figure 7.1.

The Physician as Investment Analyst in the Human Capital Market

Wolfe's (1979) book about the astronauts, who behaved recklessly to convince themselves and others that they would survive danger because they had "the right stuff," illustrates a situation that falls in cell 3. The pioneering test pilot Chuck Yeager gets drunk one Sunday and falls off a horse two nights before an important flight. In real pain the next morning, he rides a dilapidated motorcycle several miles to a country doctor for primitive treatment of two broken ribs rather than submit to medical authorities on the military base, where he would receive superior treatment but be "scrubbed from the flight." Tuesday morning he climbs painfully into the cockpit and becomes the first human being to fly "through the sonic wall." It is understood that everyone, including the military physicians, would approve Yeager's behavior as a clear expression of "the righteous stuff." Still, the physicians would have had no choice but to prevent him from making the flight lest he injure himself further or damage a very expensive jet airplane. While Yeager was denying his injury to show he had the right stuff, the physicians' mandate was to protect government property—to function as investment analysts.

This function reflects a time-honored tradition of looking to the medical profession to ferret out information about health status that an individual has reason to hide. As early as 1833, when the United Kingdom passed the factory act mentioned in chapter 2, the main enforcement mechanism was the provision that all children applying for employment certificates to work in the textile mills be examined by a physician to ascertain whether they really were, as they claimed, at least nine years of age (Schilling 1981:12–13). At Ellis Island in the early 1900s, millions of new immigrants were required "to run the gauntlet of doctors in the examination hall. . . . Those who passed inspection filed on through the door that said PUSH TO NEW YORK. Those who did not were marked with a big chalk letter—'H' for heart trouble, 'F' for facial rash, 'X' for psychological problems—and shunted with the other rejects to be reexamined and possibly sent back home" (Goldman 1983:36). This was more than a public health examination to prevent the spread of disease; it was a physician's calculated appraisal of the market value of the applicants at America's doors.

The tradition persists to the present in insurance medicine, where physicians supervise the work of medical underwriters, whose job it is to assign applicants for insurance policies to an "underwriting band" or level of risk, to which is attached a specific premium charge for the policy. Warshaw observes that "the applicant, the agent, and the applicant's attending physician are prone to 'shade' the information so that the desired insurance can be obtained at the lowest possible premium rate," and he adds that in this and other situations where the applicant or claimant may be withholding relevant information "some physicians find a particularly entertaining challenge in the probing for significant information that the examinee or claimant would prefer to remain undiscovered" (Warshaw 1977:353).

The issue in Yeager's case was whether he was fit to perform a specific task, namely to undertake the historic supersonic flight. In more mundane occupational medicine, the situations that cast the physician in an analogous role are preemployment or preplacement physical examination programs, some routine fitness evaluations for specific jobs (such as piloting and driving) which may involve danger to others, and "return to work" examinations after a specified period of absence (usually a week or more) or after an absence for a particular condition (for example, a job-related injury or a heart attack). Common to all is the assessment being made of the physical and mental fitness for a particular job of an applicant for or incumbent in that job or a candidate for assignment to it. The applicant presents himself as fit; the physician probes for evidence to the contrary. The manifest function of such an examination is described in the profession's official documents: "Health . . . including . . . emotional status should be assessed prior to making recommendations to management regarding the assignment of an employee to a job to assure that the person can perform the job safely and efficiently without endangering the person's safety or health and that of others" (American Occupational Medical Association 1979).

In cataloguing these examinations among the "essential components" of an occupational health program, the profession's medical practice committee adds the strong caveat that employees should be informed of any "abnormalities or questionable abnormalities" detected in the examination and referred to another physician for "further diagnostic evaluation or treatment" (American Occupational Medical Association 1979). The significance of the caveat is its recognition that these and other "gatekeeping examinations" (Stone 1979a, 1979b), where the physician is "diagnosing for administrative purposes" (Lomas and Berman 1983), exist for reasons other than the patient's needs. This makes them inherently adversarial. The patient has not voluntarily sought out the physician's advice, and the object of the encounter is not diagnosis or treatment of a recognized problem but evaluation of the examinee at the behest of a third party. Case law has recognized this fundamental difference from the remainder of medical practice by finding as a general rule that the privileged relationship between patient and physician is suspended in examinations of this nature. Because of their adversarial undercurrents, gatekeeping examinations have posed a problem for occupational medicine.

The examinations are rationalized as protecting the individual and "others," including coworkers, customers, community members, and family extending to unborn children (Lerner 1981). Yet a latent function of the gatekeeping examination has always been to protect the employer from legal liability and other excess costs associated with hiring "high-risk" employees. Clarence Selby (as chapter 3 showed) grappled with this crypto-mission in his Bulletin 99, which pointed out an inconsistency between word and deed on the purpose of preplacement examinations. Selby reluctantly concluded that the examinations were often being conducted for the employer's narrow financial self-interest. They were used to screen out applicants who might be poor risks for stable attendance, adequate productivity, reasonable tenure, and moderate use of the employee benefit plan, as well as to identify preexisting conditions whose initial disclosure would perhaps protect the company against future compensation claims (Selby 1919).

Since Selby's day, the always inadequate coverage of occupational disease under state worker's compensation laws has expanded to some degree (Barth and Hunt 1980). Intensifying the pressure on employers to establish baseline measures as a hedge against future claims and lawsuits, this trend would be expected to encourage increased use of the preplacement examination in the negative sense that worried Selby. For this reason, perhaps, there have been legislative attempts to curtail the employer's discretion in the handling of such examinations. The federal Rehabilitation Act of 1973, seeking to prohibit discrimination against handicapped persons, requires that physical qualifications be job-related, consistent with business necessity and with safe performance of the job (U.S. Department of Labor 1974; Equal Employment Opportunity Commission 1978; Hogan and Bernacki 1981). Several state legislatures have enacted statutes that go even further in the protection of the job applicant's rights, and evolving case law was weighed on the applicant's side. Also, the Occupational Safety and Health Administration has promulgated regulations requiring baseline screening examinations as a protective measure for employees who will be exposed to certain classes of hazardous work and has stipulated fair information practices for the conduct of such examinations.[3]

These developments both simplify and complicate matters for the occupational physician. While helping to solve Selby's issue of the employer's underlying motives because they seek to define the preplacement and screening examinations as health maintenance tools, they leave a number of technical and policy issues still to be resolved on the fair and socially acceptable conduct of screening examinations (Hogan and Bernacki 1981; Walsh and Egdahl 1980).

3. For the text of the rule and the rulemaking record, see U.S. Department of Labor (1980). For a current discussion of many of the issues associated with the workers' right of access to records see Lee and Rom (1982: passim).

The Trust Issue

If these gatekeeping examinations were an unmitigated problem, the simplest solution for corporate physicians would be to prevail on management to abandon them entirely. Some have. They argue that preplacement examinations are poor predictors of future problems with employees and are not cost-effective.[4] Others accept the value of the examinations as a legitimate contribution that the medical department can make to the smooth functioning of the organization.[5] Some among this latter group draw careful lines to make the examinations as fair as they can be in the eyes of employees.

Dr. Childress, the university medical director, was particularly outspoken on this point. His opinions were echoed by a number of corporate medical directors, and Childress, who had previously practiced part-time in industry, felt that the similarities between his situation and that in a corporation were "probably more significant than the differences." He referred repeatedly to the "trust issue" and the importance of "demonstrating" to employees and students that the medical department will not betray their confidences. "It was always clear to us that if we were perceived as agents of the boss we might as well close up and go home." One of his early campaigns, when he took the job ten years earlier, was to "look carefully at the preplacement physical exam," which worried him because as "the first encounter everyone had with the medical department" he felt it made the department appear an "agent of the boss." He strove to impress on the administration the distinction that the federal government later codified into the law, "that only one category of problem matters: whether the physical capabilities of this individual match the requirements of this job." With this as an operating policy, Childress said, it was possible to hire a number of handicapped workers. He used to keep two lists, one showing the conditions that did not disqualify applicants, the other (shorter) list showing disqualifying conditions: "The game was to guess which was which, and it was hard. Dia-

---

4. Taylor and Raffle discuss the "tedious aspects," from the health professional's viewpoint, of conducting routine medical examinations. They caution that "usually the physician is quite unable to predict the person's future state of health and it is certainly true that rarely, if ever, can he predict the subsequent sickness absence of an employee from evidence usually available at this [preemployment] stage" (Taylor and Raffle 1981:188).

5. Mitchell provides a concise overview of the pros and cons of preplacement examinations, taking account of regulatory constraints. He cites relevant references and seems to come down, on balance, in favor of these examinations, if conducted appropriately (Mitchell 1982). In an earlier statement, Howe, who was director of the AMA's occupational health department, worried that "management support of occupational medicine" was diminishing because of waning enthusiasm for preplacement examinations. Not only were annual check-ups being criticized, he complained, but "even the need for the preplacement physical examination has been belittled in a few defense industries" (Howe 1964).

betes or an amputated arm would appear on the list of qualifiable disabilities, and color blindness once showed up on the list of disqualifying conditions because it happened to be a lab job requiring color discrimination." Where there was a mismatch between the applicant's capabilities and the requirements of the job, Childress instructed the staff physicians to write something noncommittal on the personnel office's form, "some gobbledegook notation, like 'the applicant's health is such that employment requires special consideration.'" At this point the staff physician (Childress or another) might also call the personnel department and indicate that the applicant was unsuited for the job but would reveal no medical information at all. He also made it a point to tell the applicant exactly what had been found and offer to contact his personal physician:

> And sometimes we'd stall the personnel office so that the applicant would have time to get back to his own physician and have the condition taken care of. I remember stalling for a couple of months while a diabetic fellow who really wanted a night watchman's job got his insulin therapy regulated. This kind of thing helped us establish through word of mouth that we were on the employee's side.

This was nearly a decade before the enactment of the Rehabilitation Act, which has had the effect of formalizing employers' policies on how to handle preplacement examinations. Some would frown upon the informal approach that Childress evolved, depending as much as it did on the discretion—and the paternalism—of the particular physician. Few contemporary occupational physicians would quarrel in principle with his policy (which is also now a precept in the American Occupational Medical Association's ethical code) of withholding specifically medical information from anyone in management. On the sharing of information with the individual involved, the field has moved slowly toward a more structured and definite policy than the one Childress described.[6]

Even with his informal protective strategies well thought out, Childress remained uneasy about the preplacement examination programs and, in the early 1970s, was able to convince the university administration to drop them:

> We finally got enough information together to make a convincing case. First of all, we never learn much from these exams—the turn-down rate is one

---

6. "The report should be discussed with the applicant and a copy given to him, along with any other findings and recommendations regarding his health. The employee should know exactly what the physician recommends to management. 'Confidential' conversations with management about the applicant's suitability for employment are not acceptable, especially if they are based on nonmedical considerations. They promote distrust of the applicant toward the doctor and the company and probably rightfully so" (Lerner 1981).

half of one percent. Second, our industrial accident rate isn't very high anyway. Third, it costs at least $20,000 a year to conduct the silly exams. And fourth, it's the wrong way for people to learn about the medical department.

When screening programs cannot be abolished[7]—and the limited evidence available suggests that they are expanding[8]—corporate physicians can sometimes find ways to keep their distance from the contentious aspects. Like many large corporations, Monroe's maintained a fleet of trucks and airplanes, along with pilots and drivers who must undergo periodic examinations to qualify for licenses from the Federal Aviation Administration (FAA) and the Federal Department of Transportation (DOT). Monroe considered himself fortunate that he was able to avoid direct involvement in those examinations: "That FAA examination is dumb, and if our pilots are going to be grounded, I don't want to be the one who has to tell them that. We don't get involved in the DOT certification either; we have community physicians do those exams for us. If one of our drivers is disqualified I want someone other than me to tell him so."

Monroe had no problem, however, playing an indirect role, as long as he could avoid appearing the villain from the employee's perspective. Indirectly he could influence the examining physician on the outside:

> I am often the guy who has to tell the doctor how tough we need him to be. If he finds something he'll either call me or the plant manager will. If it's really a public danger—a driver with a heart condition or poor eyesight who's going to be transporting hazardous cargo—we obviously don't want him smashing into a school bus. Then it may be my job to put some backbone into the local doctor. But it's all done behind the scenes. It's most unusual for one of our doctors to be involved in these examinations. Maybe we're saved from that because we're so spread out and have no choice but to contract with local doctors to perform these exams.

---

7. In April 1982, C. Craig Wright, corporate medical director of Xerox Corporation, noted in a public lecture at the American Occupational Health Conference in Toronto that he had the previous week recommended to his top management that the periodic examination program for executives be abolished "as non-cost-effective." He said he had analyzed over 4,000 results and found very few to have uncovered unknown conditions. But he also expressed doubts that his recommendation would carry the day, because the examinations were popular among employees.

8. Lusterman reported in 1974 that, "stimulated by rising costs and by the Occupational Safety and Health Act, preemployment screening is becoming ever more pervasive in industry." The proportion of employers providing such examinations had increased from 63 to 71 percent in the previous decade (Lusterman 1974:31). Gorlin's more recent findings do not show time trends, but they do suggest a robust practice, required of production or operations personnel by 83 percent of 374 respondents, of office and clerical staff by 63 percent of 543, and of lower-level exempt personnel by 63 percent of 543 firms (Gorlin 1981:41). Technological innovations may spread the practice even further in the direction Selby deplored ("Can You Pass the Job Test" 1986).

Monroe's company was still doing preplacement examinations, and he illustrated how the limitations imposed by the Rehabilitation Act and the subsequent guidelines from the Equal Employment Opportunity Commission (EEOC) still left ambiguity:

> The preemployment thing has pretty much changed now with the EEOC rulings. We can specify performance issues. We may say something like, 'We recommend this man for a job that requires good attendance.' But the debate used to be over whether you hire a diabetic or someone with another chronic disease. And the concern, of course, was to protect the insurance so that the company wouldn't have to pay and pay for treatment. Now that's not an issue any more—normally. But there are exceptions. For example, a diabetic on insulin was being considered for a job that involved rotating shifts and working alone at night. Those are the worst conditions for a diabetic, and we didn't happen to have another job so he wasn't hired and he sued us. We won that case, but you're generally in some sort of hot water or another.

Direct involvement in hiring, promotion, and firing decisions is assiduously avoided by most corporate medical directors, although not, sometimes, without a fight. Sinsky's description was fairly typical:

> Someone will call and say, 'We hear so-and-so has high blood pressure; is that so? We're looking at him for a big job.' I say I can't answer a question like that and that's the end of it. If I see a senior person with terminal cancer, I might inquire to be sure there's a back-up, but that would be rare. I did diagnose diabetes in someone who is now an executive vice president; I think that's still a well-guarded secret. At least I've told no one.

Interviews with half a dozen middle and upper managers in Sinsky's company elicited mixed reviews on how closely he guarded medical secrets. Some trusted him completely, but others had doubts, based mostly on second-hand accounts of situations in which it was felt he may have violated a confidence and spoken of an employee's medical condition to someone else in management. There was even a rumor that he had breached a confidence of the new CEO—had leaked to the committee examining this man's credentials the fact that he had not had a physical examination in four years. Stories like this were impossible to document, but it hardly mattered how accurate they actually were since the stories themselves convinced many ambitious managers that they would be foolish to let the medical department learn anything about their physical or mental fitness that could ever be used against them in the intensely competitive climb up the corporate ladder.

One division director at Sinsky's firm said he waged an unsuccessful campaign to excise from his own company medical record an entry that he thought could be damaging to his career. On the basis of information he volunteered while answering a computerized health-risk-appraisal questionnaire, he had been classified as a potential "problem drinker," a diagnosis he considered ridiculous since he drank relatively little but had admitted on the questionnaire that at an occasional party he might have as many as four drinks, spaced over a period of hours. When he asked Sinsky to correct the record, he was told that no one would ever know; yet he remained sufficiently uneasy that he finally wrote a formal letter of clarification to the file.

The personnel director of another division expressed similar reservations about confidentiality and described herself sitting at the computer terminal answering the same questionnaire and wondering whether the machine was recording how long she was pausing on some of the more invasive questions, while she debated how candid to be in answering them. Interviews with Sinsky himself lent credence to these managers' concerns. He had no data at all on how his programs were being used by employees or on the impact they were having and seemed incapable of developing even a simple management information system. Often he would comment plaintively that he was unappreciated by other managers, who didn't understand what an important contribution he was making to the firm. As he vented these frustrations, it seemed increasingly plausible that the pressure on him would be almost irresistible to fall back on the one source of unique power he had—information on medical fitness—and to use it in subtle but calculating ways in the hope of ingratiating himself with other managers. This is what evidently occurred, and it backfired. The word eventually spread that sensitive information was unsafe with him, and he became progressively more isolated and disgruntled.

As willing as nonmedical managers were to discuss their "paranoia" (as they often characterized it) that information about their own health would be used against them, corporate physicians (Sinsky included) denied that this was an issue. Medical directors tended to see managers as the ones responsible for pressures to breach the confidentiality of medical record. Sinsky's observations on this point were echoed by many other corporate physicians:

> I often get calls from supervisors. They're having trouble with an employee and either want to know whether I have any information that would suggest a psychiatric problem or else want me to arrange to have him evaluated psychiatrically. In the first instance I throw the question right back at them; in the second we might see the employee here in the medical department but whether or not we then have him seen by a psychiatrist is none of the supervisor's business.

In the last situation, Sinsky was doing informally what some companies handle through a formal mechanism of "fitness evaluations" to determine whether an employee's unsatisfactory performance can be ascribed to a correctable health problem. The majority of such cases involve alcohol or drug abuse. The proliferating counseling or "employee assistance programs" (EAPs) (Walsh 1982) are an extension of this thinking.

Some EAPs are housed in corporate medical departments while others reside organizationally in staff advisory, human resource, or personnel offices. Often there is competition or outright hostility between medical and employee-assistance programs that are organizationally divided, a situation Shain and his colleagues attribute in part to the different disciplines and traditions represented in the two types of program (Shain, Suurvali, and Boutilier 1986).

Close examination of the historical evolution of a particular EAP often reveals that the decision to house it elsewhere was a conscious effort to shield it from the suspicion and distrust with which employees viewed the medical department. Edward Bower, for example, had inherited a situation where the employee-counseling program was large and defiantly separate from his medical department. He called this an "artificial separation," and it bothered him:

> It was started before my time. The role model for the program is the community mental health center—it started as an organizational development kind of thing. Of course it ought to be viewed as an integral part of primary ambulatory health care. We don't have bad relations, we do interact. But when I came they were terrified that I would take them over. Of all the things I've done in my career—clinical medicine, biomedical research, teaching—administration is by far the most difficult.

A manager who had been involved remembered the separation as deliberate—and for reasons that would have to rankle a corporate medical director. "There was always a tension," the personnel vice president recalled, "as to whether and how these two functions should interrelate. But we felt the separation was important for reasons of confidentiality." For management to perceive that psychological counseling needs to be confidential to be effective and *therefore* should be independent of the medical department reflects poorly indeed on management's expectations (or experiences) concerning the medical department's handling of sensitive information.

When an EAP is separate from a corporate medical department, the question must be asked whether confidentiality has been a perceived problem. Several of the managers in Sinsky's company used the separate staff-counseling service in matters that they felt required professionalism and discretion but referred to the medical department those employees who were irritating disciplinary problems. This created a situation that could only erode the medical department's reputation over time, in a downward cycle driven by a self-fulfilling prophecy.

Where the corporate medical director was the steward for the employee fitness evaluation or wider EAP function, he would often describe the concerted effort he made to avoid having the department viewed as the employee's adversary. Dr. Isaac Kaplan, the medical director for a large public employer, described a process he had evolved over time. When a supervisor referred an employee to the medical department for an examination as part of a "performance review," the referral would be "done by memorandum" so that the employee would know, before arriving at the medical department, "exactly what is going on. It used to be done informally, and that made the physician's job much harder." The medical department would respond in writing and supply only the assessment of whether or not there was a medical explanation for the performance problem. Kaplan confirmed Sinsky's account that supervisors tend to pry: "Supervisors are always arguing that they could do a better job of managing the problem and helping the employee if we would tell them more—and they are usually sincere. But my rejoinder is that a greater good is served by preserving confidentiality, because then everyone knows the information will not be revealed. It's a classic case of competing goods."

Kaplan's classic issue of the supervisor's access to health records has long been a source of pressure on medical departments and of suspicion on the part of labor. Virtually all the medical directors in the study remembered occasions when they had had to lock the files, or confront personnel staff or line managers for "dipping into them," or change the handling or the content of the forms used in connection with the benefit program, or lecture managers on the privacy of health information.[9] Some were able in this way to solve the problem permanently, but others described a continuous process of educating supervisors and managers on the proper handling of sensitive health information. Dr. Monroe was in the former group: "When I came here and set out to hire a secretary, I noticed that the personnel files had medical information in them—that someone was on contraceptive pills or had a chronic disease. I said, 'Let's get rid of this stuff,' and no one argued with me." Dr. Lee was in the latter:

> Our records are absolutely privileged. The insurance records can come in with a diagnosis on them and, through an error, can go to a benefits person. Nothing like that can happen to the medical records. Still, there is always

---

9. In the public hearings on OSHA's proposed rule giving employees the right of access to health records, Dr. Silverstein of the United Automobile Workers cited a similar experience of a corporate physician of his acquaintance as evidence of abuses and breaches of confidentiality that "did exist" and "continue to exist, uncontrolled, in a large number of institutions" (U.S. Department of Labor 1980:35243).

someone or other in personnel who thinks he needs to know something in the medical records and challenges me on this. He'll go to one of the thirty lawyers in the legal department and the lawyer will come to me. This has happened twice in the past three years, but they keep coming back. Or an industrial relations manager who has hired poorly—a young guy who wants to be dynamic and aggressive. He wants to look at the medical records of someone with a bad productivity rate. If it doesn't come from one direction, it comes from another. The lawyer challenges me—I love arguing with him—and says, "Why can't we see the records—we all work for the same company, don't we?" And I have to convince him that it's an ethical question, not a legal one. I want to keep the rest of the medical staff from having to fight those battles. We have to maintain that line; it's a very delicate thing.

Other medical directors also talk of buffering or preserving the purity of the rest of the medical staff by themselves drawing the fire. Childress did in the case of the "unavoidable administrative functions" expected of the medical department: "I try to center those things in one person—me—so I'm the only one who's tainted, and frankly I make an effort to keep matters as quiet as possible."

In sum, the corporate medical directors as a group try, insofar as possible, to resist being drawn into the investment analyst role and, when it cannot be resisted, to structure the interaction so as to minimize the patient's perception that the medical department is an extension of the personnel office. This they do by refusing to become party to the *use* of their medical evaluations and definitions in a job action. Monroe articulated clearly the distinction corporate medical directors insistently make between their own roles and those of line managers and personnel administrators:

> I differentiate the role of the doctor and the role of the personnel officer. People always want the doctor to make administrative judgments. I've made a point of forcing the administrative people to do their own jobs. When I first came here, the personnel people would come to me and say things like, "Is this man's hand stable enough to do a welding job?" My answer would be, "I don't have any welding torches in here. I don't know whether he can do the job. Take him out and let him try." Or they would bring in a pipsqueak of a woman and want to know if she was going to be able to lift an enormous hose. Who am I to say whether or not she can lift it? It's the personnel officer's duty to take her out and try her on it. If they come in and ask me whether they should hire an epileptic, I tell them what kinds of things they can expect of someone with epilepsy and then I throw back to them the question of whether they can find a place for a person with this condition. Then I'm out of it.

Monroe added that he didn't "believe that this is idiosyncratic on my part; I believe that others in my role make that separation," and the interviews bore him out. The solution that he and others have developed to the problem of conflicts between clinical and managerial demands can be described as the punctilio of role, resting on a form of "medical Taylorism." Like the old managerial doctrine discussed in chapter 3, medical Taylorism presumes that science can provide neutral tools for resolving labor-management disputes. It thus involves what many analysts have recognized as the myth of scientific neutrality and uses that to disclaim responsibility for the uses to which scientific products are put. The implications of this are elaborated more fully in chapter 8.

Physician as Medical Comptroller Dispensing the Company's Largesse

Returning to figure 7.1, in the next set of situations the employee professes to be sick and the company disagrees. Here, the issue nearly always revolves around his entitlement to some sort of sickness benefit—absence with pay, short-term or long-term disability insurance, worker's compensation payments. The occupational physician's involvement in these conflicts is a perpetual source of tension with labor. The International Labour Organization (ILO), for example, passed a resolution on the proper conduct of an occupational health service. The resolution specified the service to be "essentially preventive," overtly excluded absence control, and argued that interest in absenteeism rates should be limited to whatever clues they could provide to the impact of hazardous conditions on the health of the workforce: "Occupational health services should not be required to verify the justification of absence on grounds of sickness. They should not be precluded from ascertaining the conditions which may have led to a worker's absence on sick leave and obtaining information about the progress of the worker's illness, so that they will be better able to evaluate their preventive progamme, discover occupational hazards, and recommend the suitable placement of workers for rehabilitation purposes" (ILO 1959).

Absence monitoring falls in a class with preplacement evaluation as an elusive activity that is condoned or reviled depending on the underlying purposes for which it is carried out. To handle this double-edged sword, many corporate medical directors resort again to the punctilio of role, adamantly separating their contribution from that of the personnel and benefits specialists whose job it is to administer the insurance programs and from line supervisors who are responsible for monitoring attendance. Dr. Lee made such a distinction:

> We are here to advise the benefits and personnel people, not to make their decisions for them. We let the benefits people orchestrate things, with the medical department giving advice *only* if requested. I do not want my physicians to play the role of policemen. They should not assume responsibilities that are not theirs, like disciplining employees. These are the skills of the labor relations, benefits administration, and personnel people. I want a lot of

proof that a person really isn't ill before being heavy-handed. I don't want to persecute an innocent person to get at a malingerer. When someone is sent to us, it is not so they will be disciplined.

Most corporate medical directors bend over backwards to be perceived on the employee's side. Yet a number—in this sample the majority—do see behind-the-scences control of absenteeism and disability benefits as part of their legitimate role, the ILO notwithstanding. They recognize that it conflicts with a patient-care mission but believe, with Dr. Poulter, that "someone has to do it, because the benefit plan is so liberal, and I believe we do it better than the personnel people would. We always monitored the sick list, but we're making it formal now. We're reorganizing to make communication with the medical department a requirement for getting benefits."

Direct reporting of absences to the medical department has been discussed in the occupational medicine literature as a way to "affect the bottom line," but the potential for conflict is normally glossed over in the published reports.[10] In private, however, corporate medical directors recognize this problem. Dr. Russell Wyman was especially open about how he handles the potential conflict between his role as physician and that of medical comptroller:

> If you give the employee the impression you don't believe he is sick, that makes you a company doctor. But there are ways to handle situations. Two weeks ago I created a miracle. One of our people who had had an operation on his knee claimed that the leg was paralyzed from the knee down. He had even seen a neurologist. It was a doctor we didn't know and we ought to have got the patient in sooner. When I was meeting with this employee I had the feeling that there was too much con mixed in with his personality.

To test his hunch, Dr. Wyman said, he "tried an experiment." He told the employee that he would send a note to his supervisor saying that he thought the disability would keep the man out of work indefinitely. When the employee asked what the consequence would be, Wyman said: "'Well, I am not ever involved in hiring and firing decisions, that is not the medical department's role, but I suspect that what will happen is that you will be fired.' That employee came back the next day with a note from his physician saying that he was ready to go back to work. So that was my miracle cure."

Behind his tongue-in-cheek reference to a miracle, Wyman was identifying what many corporate medical directors consider the high road in absenteeism control—namely, early identification of problems that they believe would otherwise tend to deteriorate. Ideologically, this position

---

10. See, e.g., Woodsides (1980), Rundle (1981), and Hartman (1982).

rests on the presumption, widespread among occupational physicians (Walters 1982), that work is therapeutic or that not working can be harmful to an employee's health. Like the military psychiatrists Daniels (1972) studied and Smith's (1986) doctors in the coal mines, they develop a therapeutic ideology that serves to rationalize their acceptance of the organization's values and economic ends. Wyman said this: "We don't accuse. We don't treat employees as though we think they are faking. Our basic goal is to rehabilitate them and get them back to work. Whether the problems are physical or psychological, we can help. If they are malingering—not common but not unheard of—there may be a psychological element to that and we may be able to help there too."

"Rehabilitation," as many company doctors tend to see it, can consist of little more than a timely and caring nudge to an indolent employee who they believe is better off on the job than "home drinking beer and watching television." Another device that enables corporate physicians to pursue the corporation's ends without seeming to run roughshod over their patients is to blame the outside physician. Ironically, in this case, their need to protect their professional integrity inside the corporation pits them against their professional peers outside. They criticize private practitioners—like the neurologist in Wyman's story—for uncritical complicity with employees who for their own good ought to be back at work. These doctors, they believe, are motivated by economic self-interest. They complain about "whim and fantasy in the community," about chiropractors indiscriminately signing disability slips to ingratiate themselves with patients, about a "quack in Queens" whose name appears with suspicion-engendering frequency on disability slips submitted by employees living in all five boroughs of New York. They criticize physicians in general for "making something major out of a back or respiratory or emotional problem that ought to be relatively minor" and highly respected but gullible practitioners who err on the side of overprotection when their patients exaggerate the strenuousness of their work. Lawrence described a process of negotiating with outside physicians who are well meaning:

> I may have to call the employee's doctor and haggle with him a little. I may have to say, "Look, this guy's job is on the line. Now we can bring him in for light duty and arrange for rest periods. We can give him whirlpool treatments and other rehabilitative care right here at work. But we're under a lot of pressure from the personnel department. Don't you think we can get him back to work in a couple weeks' time?" They generally agree when it's put to them in those terms.

Sinsky wished he could develop a system for earlier identification of employees out on disability, but he shared Lawrence's view of the importance of working closely with outside physicians and estimated that 40 to 50 percent of his time was spent on disability problems:

> It's a few people but it eats up my time. What would really help me would be to have doctors I could talk to [in the entire metropolitan area]. It's important to use outside physicians because it erects a [protective] barrier between us and the employee. If I say, "You're not sick," that's [the company] speaking, and they don't think of me as a doctor. But if a doctor out there in the community says the same thing, they'll believe him.[11]

Dr. Lloyd Opel, the corporate medical director for a large public utility, discussed an unconventional approach to the certification of disability. It seemed to serve the purpose of muting the conflict of interest between physicians inside and outside the corporation. Agreeing that employees' personal physicians tend to keep them out of work "as long as the patient desires," he described an evolution in his thinking about how to address the problem: "I used to go around to medical societies trying to impress on them the importance of getting employees back to work sooner. But one day it dawned on me that this was the wrong way to go. Now I tell them, 'We're not going to saddle you with the responsibility of getting people back to work; that's not your job.' That always brings a round of applause."

Opel did look to the personal physician for information on the employee's medical condition but said:

> *We* decide when he can come back to work. That's *our* job. We don't give a damn what his physician thinks about that. If he advised his patient to stay away from work, we tell that patient, our employee, that he should go right ahead and follow his doctor's advice, but we won't pay him for not working if we think he's capable of being on the job. His personal physician can decide whether or not he should be working, but it's our job to decide whether or not he should be paid.

Whether Opel's approach really eased relations with outside physicians was unclear, but one can imagine tensions arising in individual cases and the need for the same kind of careful "haggling" that Lawrence and others described. It was an interesting variation on the punctilio of role theme, turning it around in this instance. Here the company physician was accepting the responsibility of exercising coercive authority that the outside physicians were unwilling to shoulder.

11. Issues related to the personal physician's role in the certification of disability came to a head after Congress passed the Pregnancy Disability Act of 1978, designed to reduce discrimination against women workers. Stipulating that pregnancy and childbirth be treated like any other health problem that interferes with an individual's ability to perform his or her job, the act challenged corporations to reassess their policies covering disability (Walsh and Egdahl 1980).

As sensitive as the dealings with outside physicians must be, the corporate medical director's purview on disability certification is further complicated by the supervisor's expectations. A particular supervisor in a given instance may want the "malingering" employee back on the job or, quite often, may want him released on permanent disability to open the way for a better performer. The second case pushes the physician back into cell 3 in figure 7.1, where his role is to find more illness or "unfitness" than the patient wants to admit. But it is an ironic distortion of the real "right stuff" denial of illness, a distortion created by particular insurance-driven incentives.

Some of the senior figures in the field recount old stories that illustrate other distortions—for example, "union-busting" managers who would demand of a corporate physician that he declare a perfectly healthy union leader unfit for work. This, they claim, is a thing of the past, and none of the study subjects could recall a recent instance; "It just doesn't happen," they would say. The more usual situation creating pressure on the physician to declare a worker unfit involves a worker who has missed a lot of work, appears to have an alcohol or drug dependency, and is generally unreliable and even sometimes disruptive. Releasing him on permanent disability may cost the company money, but without coming out of the supervisor's budget it does solve his problem. Corporate medical directors try to convince managers that these are administrative issues, not medical ones. They try to portray the medical element as simply a neutral tool.

In summary, then, the investment analyst and medical comptroller's roles bring occupational medicine into a charged force field where employees, their supervisors, their personal physicians, benefits and personnel administrators, and the company as a whole all face different incentives that produce conflicting expectations of how the corporate physician can supply a medical definition fairly and in the best interests of the organization. A strategy physicians often adopt is to supply the definition but to divorce themselves from its application.

Physician as Expert Medical Witness—Letting Science Decide

In the final group of circumstances (cell 4 in figure 7.1) medical definitions are at issue in the zone of ambiguity between labor and management. There is no dispute here about the fact of illness but considerable room for maneuvering on the matter of assigning responsibility. Many corporate medical directors say they are usually able to avoid direct involvement in worker's compensation cases, leaving them to be handled by insurance carriers. A few disagree, Opel among them: "We've got to be involved. The question is which side of the fence are we on? Sometimes we testify for the company and sometimes for the employee. The issue is how objective you can be, how well you defend your position. But you've got to be willing to testify and put it up to outside review."

Bradford also believed that he had to be involved in legal proceedings to meet the company's legitimate operational needs for medical expertise. He felt the pressures increasing:

> I'm swept into this more than I used to be, for two reasons. First, the decisions awarding compensation for stress-related problems are becoming more common; second, we didn't resist worker's comp cases as much as others did in the past, but we're starting to now. And there are a lot of near-misses where we might not get called but we have to be prepared anyway. I'd say there's a potential new case every week, and one of us actually gets called to testify about once every two months.

The observation by Opel that different cases placed him on different sides of the fence was amplified by Monroe as evidence that "I call them like I see them." He spoke of a twenty-six-year-old worker who claimed that his inoperable cancer arose out of his three years with Monroe's firm, a "will-o'-the-wisp sort of thing": "His type of cancer has a long latency period and it's the wrong tumor type for any exposure he would have had here. But you can't blame him. He's going to die and he wants to cut the best deal he can for his family. My job is to put together the objective facts as carefully as I can." Another case involved a mesothelioma (a rare form of lung cancer associated with asbestos exposure) in a long-term employee. The responsibility in this case looked quite different to Monroe after he had studied the facts:

> I was the guy who elicited the nonoccupational history. When I examined this worker he told me that as a small child he had helped his father re-shingle the roof with asbestos tiles and that later, as a teenager, he had helped install a stovepipe with some asbestos casing. I reviewed the total history and, as the company doctor, I came down saying that the other exposures were inconsequential beside the exposure he received on the job. I said the cancer was courtesy of [our company]. The insurance company has been fighting the claim tooth and nail "on our behalf," but I'm out of it now. My role is to look at the information as objectively as I can and leave the rest to someone else.

Cases like these, involving a formal record and legal representation for the affected employee, are structured to provide some protection of the employee's interests. This is less true of the more opaque situations that arise earlier in the development of a potential compensation case. Here the physician may have considerable discretion in the way he influences the employee's subsequent decisions. In an analysis of the failure of worker's compensation adequately to recognize occupational disease, Barth and Hunt (1980) argue that "the role of alerting a worker to his rights is inescapably the physician's, for there is no other source that can readily link the illness to the workplace." There is, the authors argue: "an obvious problem [for company-employed physicians] in suggesting that the worker may have a compensable claim in cases that are not clear-cut. This problem may not affect the patient's likelihood of receiving medical treatment, even at no charge to himself, but it can lower the probability that a claim for compensation will follow" (Barth and Hunt 1980:266).

What Makes a "Company Doc"?

In some cases, the problem identified by Barth and Hunt may affect not only the availability of treatment but its quality and the employee's prospects for recovery. So it seems to have done in a dismal picture Dr. Cohen, the company psychiatrist, painted of the behavior of an occupational physician he termed, pejoratively, the apotheosis of a "company doc": "A woman apprentice sustained serious eye injuries in a chemical flare-up. She should have been wearing protective goggles, and the company was negligent in not seeing to it that she was." After a period in the hospital, the employee came back to work but continued to suffer some ill effects. The company physician in this instance took it upon himself to cover for the company's mistake. Instead of being a physician to this woman and helping her through a difficult time, he minimized her pain and showed no compassion. When she returned to complain of discomfort and asked for a reassignment, he told her she just wasn't readjusting well enough:

> He wasn't at all responsive. An occupational physician's job is not to minimize the fault-finding. He should hear her out and be her ally. If she wants to complain about what the company did to her he should let her vent those feelings. Instead he's a company doc and he gets less and less information and fewer and fewer people come to him and finally someone like that leaves, and who on earth will take that job next?

Cohen added, and subsequent interviews with managers in this company confirmed, that the "irony of the whole thing" was that "no one told" this company doctor to "take management's side"; in fact management would probably have told him the reverse. He was acting on behalf of "some supposed management values that weren't ever directly communicated to him," Cohen said.

Some other company doctors in the sample exhibited this tendency to exaggerate management norms, to be tougher on employees than others in management would have wanted or needed them to be. It was as if they had internalized a distorted caricature of a ruthless managerial mentality. One explanation for this can be found in Berger's observation that people in ambiguous or marginal roles tend to overrehearse and overplay their parts, in an effort to make them feel real (Berger 1963).

The picture of this "company doc" illustrates a fundamental problem for occupational medicine. A world of difference separates the "company doc" in the story and many of the corporate medical directors quoted in this chapter. But the difference is subtle, subjective, and difficult to pin down. It has to do with a whole complex of relationships, private conversations, and unwritten answers to intricate questions concerning the role the corporate physician plays in defining illness and the uses to which those definitions are put:

1. What does the physician say (or submit in writing) to supervisors and managers before and after an examination of an employee? How much variation is there in a single firm from one case to another, and from one staff physician to another, in the way this reporting is handled; and to what can the variation be ascribed?
2. What do the supervisor, the personnel officer, and the physician say (or submit in writing) to the employee or applicant before, during, and after the examination?
3. When a problem is uncovered in an examination, what explicit steps are taken to make sure the individual receives both treatment and (if applicable) just compensation, and what is done to "cushion the effect" (Taylor and Raffle 1981) on the individual?
4. When a single problem is uncovered, what mechanisms exist to link it to other evidence available elsewhere, in the firm or outside, with which it might begin to form a pattern implicating as a potential occupational stressor a substance, or a process, or a physical or social arrangement in the workplace?
5. As such patterns begin to emerge, how quickly and effectively does the company act to correct the situation and communicate the information to all parties with a need to know, which could include employees, former employees, union representatives, customers, competitors, the government, and the academic community?

Because the questions go to *uses* of information, it is often not enough to supply the definition and then look the other way, as many corporate physicians have been comfortable doing, because they say they trust their company's management to be fair. Some are tightening up on policies and procedures, in part on their own volition or that of the firm's management, in part owing to pressures from various branches of government or from employees and their representatives. This attention to policies and procedures tends to involve corporate medical directors at a higher and more strategic level of the corporate structure.

The Strategic Pole of the Management Axis

The picture just painted of the corporate medical director's operational role has, at its core, a conflict model of the labor-management relationship. Barnard's basic conception was that effective management needs to bully, cajole, or seduce labor into accepting progressively tighter constraints on freedom. Management's gain in control is labor's loss in discretion. Within that zero–sum context, some corporate medical directors negotiate their own areas of "indifference" and "nonacceptability" to govern the corporate physician's organizational role. To one degree or another they respond as best they can to the needs the organization perceives for the expertise, the imprimatur, or the professional relationships and currency unique to a physician. And when a medical definition is required to resolve a management-labor conflict in one of the areas of ambiguity, they try to supply it as objectively as they can, without becoming drawn into the dispute. To distance themselves, they espouse the specialty's credo, discussed in chapters 2 and 3. The credo holds that occupational physicians serve their organizations by giving precedence to the needs of individual employees because, as is frequently asserted, "the benefit to the company from an occupational medical program is the aggregate impact of the good that's done for its individual employees."

But some situations strain the credo. An operational manager may want the medical department not to "do good for" an individual but rather to attend to the needs of the larger organization by helping deal with an individual who is performing poorly or making demands considered unreasonable. When the credo fails, the corporate physician's second line of defense is the punctilio of role. He insists on a distinction between his function (supplying the medical definition—the supposedly neutral scientific tool) and those of personnel administrators, line supervisors, and other members of management (applying the definitional tool in a job action or in the allocation of scarce resources).

The company physician thus begins to engage in a form of passive resistance when the organization puts pressure on him to violate his credo. The physician limits his engagement with the bureaucracy so as to maintain the coherence of his professional role. If it solves the physician's problem in a temporary and tentative way, this stance leaves the organization's problem still to be addressed. It therefore creates resentment among the managers still facing the problem. So they put the physician on the defensive in the organization with a pair of debilitating stereotypes: that physicians are, first, "inept managers" and, second, "empire builders." The apparent contradiction between these two images (can inept managers build empires?) is resolved when the two criticisms are viewed as reflections on the physician's interaction style.

The corporate physician's ambivalence about the damage his organizational role can do to the patient-physician relationship he would like to create causes him to pull back from the organization's demands when they create conflicts. But this pulling back makes him seem arrogant and aloof in the eyes of his fellow managers. One plant manager reported having advised a new plant physician that she would be expected to be an actively contributing member on a management team. When she first "arrived on the scene," he said he told her this:

> If you can perform and be counted on, great. But there are four hundred other technical professionals in this organization, all with advanced degrees. They have to earn credibility and trust—it doesn't come automatically—and so, to be frank, do you. There are a lot of health-related matters where we need you involved and where your word isn't necessarily going to be law. You can't expect to influence policy if you won't participate in problem-solving at the operational level.

The physician accepted her plant manager's advice and did earn his admiration and trust. The advice, though, overlooked a crucial distinction between a plant physician and other "technical specialists" with advanced degrees. The physician differs from Ph.D. chemists and engineers, and even from corporate lawyers (whose client is the firm), in that she is or would like to think of herself as a consulting professional with a clientele. The client (or patient), more than the degree, is the source of her feeling that she ought to stand apart from the demands of the organization; the ability to enlist the trust of employees is the greater good to which Kaplan argues the manager's need to know should be subordinate.

Conflicts between the clinical and managerial roles surface most palpably at the operational end of the management axis. Company physicians there are functioning much as they do at the clinical end of the medical axis. They accept the work that comes their way and do the best they can with it on a case-by-case basis. Often they are confronted with an already charged situation—an employee whose supervisor feels he has been absent too often or too long or is performing inadequately, one who is disabled or ill and blames work exposures, others who may have been exposed to possibly harmful agents or who have to be reassigned because of an actual or potential sensitivity to a substance with which they work. In such situations it is difficult for a corporate physician, or anyone, to contribute much toward a solution that will satisfy all the principals. If, however, these problems can be anticipated through mechanisms developed in advance, then there is a greater likelihood of resolving the problems before they deteriorate. Moving away from the operational toward the strategic end of the management axis enables some corporate medical directors to become more actively involved in defining how the company will handle sensitive health issues. More important, it can give them a say in defining what functions the corporate medical department will and will not serve.

Dr. Opel stood out at the time of the study as a corporate medical director who was consciously attempting to redefine those functions for his own firm and, ultimately, for the wider profession. He presided over the corporate medical department at the New York subsidiary of a very large national firm involved predominately in a service industry. He made the case for a more strategic corporate medical department in the following terms:

> Because of the company's size, the unique New York environment, and other factors, the company's medical programs are faced with challenges and opportunities to an extent not experienced by other companies in our industry, or, indeed, by most other industries.
>
> In addition, the traditional modes of medicine generally and the country's health-care delivery systems in particular are changing rapidly and substantially. The company's involvement in the health affairs of its large population of employees and their dependents is expanding rapidly. Governmental intervention is aggressive and societal expectancy is increasingly demanding.
>
> The corporate medical director must be able to grasp the social complexities of this situation, understand the working politics of health care, stay abreast of scientific medical knowledge, properly assess the economics and realities of the company's position, and develop solutions to the problems these circumstances spawn.

To serve a 1981 population of 80,000 employees (47 percent female and averaging forty-one years of age), Dr. Opel's medical department employed 234 professional, paraprofessional, and support personnel, of whom 212 were management. Of the "paraprofessionals," 40 were nurses. The number of physicians summed to 39 full-time equivalents.

The department divided into two major functions: an operations (or service delivery) division and a research and development division. The latter comprised two physicians who, together with a doctoral-level systems director, handled systems development, planning, and implementation, using epidemiology and biostatistics. An unusual position, created in 1981, charged a "director of health resource management" with "assuring that the community health-care marketplace in which company health-care dollars are spent is managed for maximum efficiency." A nonphysician manager, he represented the company to the organized health-care community and to other corporations throughout the state interested in changing the health-care system. The rationale underlying the creation of this role was that the company's health costs, which exceeded $209 million in 1981 and continued to rise at a rate of about 15 to 20 percent a year, were a central concern of the corporate medical department. The $209 million included the costs of disability absence ($32.4 million), incidental absence ($20.9 million), health plans ($103.6 million), worker's compensation ($4.7 million), replacements for lost time ($20 million), dental plan ($18.8 million), and the costs of running the medical department ($9.1 million in 1981).

Opel differed from many other corporate medical directors in his belief that a medical department has an inescapable role to play in the management of this broadly defined assemblage of overt expenditures and covert costs ascribable to illness. He proposed to address these costs in three different ways:

1. By seeking to deal more effectively with established disease;
2. By striving both to reduce the amount of future disease and to enhance the "wellness" or coping ability of the firm's employees; and
3. By taking steps to build an integrated data system that would undergird future assessments of the efficiency and effectiveness of alternative strategies to conserve and enhance employees' health.

The first of the three objectives implied that Opel's staff physicians would find a way to oversee the personal health care of the company's employees. How to accomplish that was a problem with which Opel and his associates had been struggling for a decade and a half. As a consequence, they had gone further than most corporate physicians toward specifying and even redefining the influence occupational medicine could hope to have on the personal health-care system.

To deal more effectively with established disease, improvements in "case management" were considered essential for controlling "excess costs" associated with faulty decisions on the part of individual providers or consumers. These costs attached to unnecessary surgery, overutilization of services and procedures, and inordinate use of hospitals. But some of the increased costs of health care reflected a system-wide escalation in charges for services that, on the individual level, Opel viewed as entirely appropriate. It was to these larger structural problems that the new director of health resource management was to direct his attention, by participating actively in business coalitions, health maintenance organizations, and other community-wide efforts to rationalize the health-care system.

Individual case management was the province of a line organization, managed by a medical director for operations and providing health services to the company's employees. Those services were delivered in eight principal locations and a number of secondary facilities throughout New York state. These were expected to "deliver high-quality health services to improve employee health, resolve or minimize the adverse effects of ill health and incapacity on company operations, and support operating management in day-to-day resolution of health problems."

The commitment to tackle the broadly defined problem of health-related costs led Opel's staff to develop a concept they referred to as "health-care management," or HCM. Opel said HCM "discards a fifty-year tradition which had limited occupational medicine to concern with job-related matters and had excluded it from significant involvement in the personal health of employees." He was quick, however, to caution against overstating the differences between his approach and that of other corporate medical departments: "It's a matter of degree. Others are moving in this direction too. It's a function of pressures we're all feeling. Those pressures come out of different holes. Here they came out of the alcohol hole first. The difference is that we opened the door and let the avalanche come in." Opel adds the additional caveat that unlike firms in more hazardous industries, his firm can allocate a large proportion of its medical resources to "general health maintenance" as distinct from "environmental health concerns."

Correcting "Clinical Malfunctions"

Health-care management, as conceived, operated on three "levels." On the first, Opel's physicians sought to intervene in situations where they found "malfunctions in the present clinical system." Some involved mistakes on the part of the employee's personal physician ("improper or no diagnosis, inadequate or harmful treatment, excessive costs"). Others involved "abuse of the system" in the form of "excessive absence or employee noncompliance." Still others involved "inappropriate" or "unnecessary" costs for hospitalization, surgery, or ambulatory care. Opel cited case after case of successful interventions to redress errors of this sort. For example:

- An employee's personal physician was giving him ointments for a persistent rash on the palms of his hands until a company physician suggested that the outside practitioner order a simple blood test for syphilis. The test was positive; the disease was then treated.
- Recurrent back pain kept one employee out of work an average of two weeks a year over an eight-year period. An exercise routine the medical department prescribed, after a thorough evaluation, broke the cycle. That employee had a perfect attendance record for the subsequent four years.

- A young employee's hypertension was being treated, unaccountably, with an anti-gout drug, a situation that came to light in a company periodic health examination. The company physician arranged a consultation with a different (more competent) outside doctor, with whom the employee chose to remain as an ongoing patient. His hypertension is now under control.
- An employee scheduled for a hemorrhoidectomy checked in with the company medical department for an informal second opinion and mentioned that the surgeon's secretary had quoted a fee of $450. The company's investigations confirmed the qualifications of the surgeon and the need for the operation. "Just for good measure" and to express interest in the case, a company physician called the surgeon, discussed the patient's lack of complicating problems, and inquired what the fee would be. The answer: $250.
- The private physician of an employee with a history of heavy smoking and drinking requested that the company medical department x-ray the patient's mouth because of a lesion. The company physician suspected cancer and suggested a biopsy, to which the private physician reluctantly agreed a week later, after much prodding from the company physician. It was a carcinoma, for which the company promptly arranged treatment with a well-known specialist.
- In a return-to-work evaluation of an employee who had been hospitalized for renal stones, the company's tests suggested that the primary pathology was not the renal condition but multiple myeloma. The company physician arranged with the personal physician for a consultation with a hematologist. A bone marrow test confirmed the company physician's suspicions, and a more appropriate treatment was begun.
- Forgetting to take her lithium, a manic-depressive office worker periodically lost control, disturbed her coworkers, missed work, and was hospitalized more than once. The company medical department arranged jointly with her psychiatrist for routine company counseling and blood-lithium testing, and her "course was smoothed significantly."
- The neurosurgeon who had scheduled a disc-removal operation for an outdoor craft worker with a long history of low back pain told a company physician that he would know at what level the disc was protruding "once we get in there for a look." The company physician's preoperative examination of that patient, in the hospital, disclosed no disc protrusion at all. Advised that the insurance would not cover the procedure, the surgeon discharged the patient, who recovered and returned to work after medical treatment on an ambulatory basis.

In each of these cases, company physicians provided not therapy but "management" of situations in which established disease was being handled inefficiently or ineffectively. When they first set out to do this, Opel said, his physicians had to face the problem of how to get the authority they needed to intervene in these situations:

> We became attracted to the notion of directing more attention to the front end of the health-care system—of trying to intervene earlier. In 1968 we went to the Bronx to do primary care: not necessarily to do it ourselves but to get it done right, to manage the system. The question was, how would we do it, where would we get the forces? We couldn't get the state to set us up in business. The medical society wasn't about to give us a mandate. I woke up one morning to the realization that the key was the individual employee. If we could get him or her to give us the authority, then we could begin to manage. We could shorten hospital stays and direct people to competent doctors—anything was possible with that authorization from the employee—that would be our lever.

If employees were the lever, the fulcrum on which it rested was their confidence and trust. Use of the medical department had increased steadily over a fifteen-year span, to the point where Opel was estimating that about 60 percent of the company's employees "come through" the medical department for one reason or another during the course of a year. Some of them were being "captured" into the kind of relationship with a company physician that would provide the needed leverage should a "clinical malfunction" occur. Others were not. Opel lacked an adequate definition of the size of the population "in" his health-care management program:

> Our problem is defining what we mean by "in" HCM. We gradually develop relationships with employees. They don't come and sign up for "health-care management," we don't even use that term with them. We're trying to define the stages of progressive involvement, and eventually we'll track those in our computer system, but for now it's not quite that formalized. What typically happens is that an employee comes in and says, "Hey, doc, I hear you're interested in people, can you help me with my problem?"

From the trust standpoint, Opel viewed that employee-initiated contact as ideal; his physicians tried to create an atmosphere in which employees would feel they had direct access to the department. Whereas supervisors used to make the arrangements for employees to visit the department, whatever the circumstances, Opel and the other company physicians had begun to encourage their patients themselves to call for appointments and then to ask their supervisors for the necessary time off. But even when employees were involuntary patients, Opel and his staff physicians expressed comfort with the roles they played. His associate medical director for operations, Dr. Sarah Farmer, insisted that "issues" with employees were rare:

> We're not in the business of trying to penalize people, to make it hard for them to earn a living. We know we're making very important decisions, decisions that may influence whether a man can earn a living. They're as important in their own way as the decisions a cardiac surgeon makes. One of the interesting and rewarding things we can do is get the supervisor invested in caring about the employee's health. This is real medicine. We're making a difference. It's exciting and satisfying.

Opel differentiated "astute" from "hide-bound" occupational medicine with another anecdote illustrating his view of how health-care management could remove barriers to trust even on the part of an involuntary patient. In this hypothetical case, an employee appears at the medical department complaining of knee pain, with a "slip" from his supervisor labeling him "uncooperative."

> In the "old way" the physician says to himself that the boss wouldn't have sent this employee over if he hadn't been a problem. Although his examination of the knee is negative, he takes an x-ray and isn't surprised to find nothing abnormal. He may even arrange for the patient to come back on Friday afternoon when the orthopedic consultant will be there. The orthopod finds nothing abnormal, to no one's surprise, and the physician sends a note to the supervisor indicating that the employee can do the assigned work. He then pats himself on the back and says he's done the company a fine service. "After all," he thinks, "I was hired to make decisions and I made this decision and proved the employee was faking." The problem is that the physician has completely missed the boat.

In health-care management, as Opel conceived it, a situation like this would be handled more empathetically:

> Now imagine that the same employee walks in with the same slip from his boss, but this time there ensues a discussion in which it ultimately is determined that the employee was an only child whose family sacrificed to send him to college but he dropped out before finishing. He's now guilt-ridden and working at a more menial task than he perceives would have been his lot if he had completed his education. Moreover, because he attended college he sees himself as a "college man" and resents assignments he considers beneath his dignity. In truth he is using the knee problem as an excuse to avoid such work. The physician says, "Hey, Joe, the company's got a tuition aid program—would you like me to call the fellow who runs it and see if we can arrange to get you some help to finish college?" And he says, "Would you really do that for me, doc?" Now you've done something about the real problem. That's the art of health-care management.

A dilemma which Opel admitted was that this outcome, although palpably different for the individual and the company, often escapes notice when the medical department's contribution is being assessed. "I ask you, how do you measure what happened with Joe and get it down to the bottom line? Occasionally Joe's supervisor may come back and say, 'Doc, Joe's a new man, what on earth did you say to him?' But more often you hear nothing more and don't know until much later, if at all, whether tangible benefits resulted."

This problem reflects another constituency whose trust was essential to successful HCM—management. Opel felt he was trusted to "be careful not to throw money down ratholes." He said when it became clear that a popular fitness facility he had stated "couldn't be costed out in the black," he closed it. As another example, he trained the first nurse clinicians in industry and had established "as a constant goal" to increase the efficiency of the medical operation. His consciousness of cost-effectiveness antedated the company's reorganization, indeed permeated his thinking about how to accomplish health-care management, especially on what he termed the second HCM level, involving the attempt to reduce the amount of future disease.

Targeted Preventive Interventions

Once employees began to look to the corporate physicians for help in "getting healthy when they're not and staying healthy when they are," something called a "lifetime health strategy" was developed. It began with an initial baseline evaluation, upgraded as experience accumulated. Again, Opel warned against overemphasizing the discontinuity between this and what other corporate medical programs naturally do: "The lifetime health strategy is important conceptually, but not operationally. Essentially we do what anyone would do. We collect all the information we can, identify with the individual specific objectives for their health maintenance, and arrange future appointments for ongoing evaluation and support."

Having described this as an analogue in the medical sphere to management by objectives in the management sphere, Opel qualified that too, saying "it's really management by successive approximations." He stressed the individualization of the preventive strategies as the key not only to case-by-case success but also to macroefficiency, and again he used a specific example. Offering Pap smears annually for all 40,000 women employees would cost about a half million dollars and yield perhaps two or three cases of disability averted owing to early detection of cervical cancer. The cost per case would be $250,000. If the Pap smears were offered to only 5,000 or so high-risk women (so classified on the basis of race, heredity, sexual practices, age, and other known risk factors), then the cost of the testing program would fall to about $75,000 a year for the same yield, or $25,000 per case averted. In a further refinement, the intervention could be reserved for only those high-risk women who could also be defined as potentially high-yield candidates, because their disease would be caught at a treatable stage or for similar reasons. If there were only 1,000 such women, then the cost per successful intervention would be only $5,000, a figure that could be reduced by further refinement—for example, by varying the frequency of testing.

Opel granted that limitations in the current state of the art of preventive medicine make it virtually impossible, except in the rare case, to predict with confidence which will be the high-risk/high-yield individuals. He observed that although obesity and smoking increase the probability of specific forms of coronary heart disease and cancer, some people with these known risk factors will suffer no ill effects. Unable to predict in advance who will be the lucky ones, "we apply our preventive measures to everyone and hope that we do no appreciable harm to those who do not need it. This state of affairs might be acceptable if our interventions were salutary and attractive to the individual concerned. Unfortunately . . . most of our current energies in prevention are devoted to finding ways to get people to do things they do not want to do."

Advancing the State of the Art

For the longer term, Opel saw health-care management not only as a practical management tool but also as a possible mechanism to advance the state of the art in preventive medicine. He saw it as providing the means for collecting all available information on an individual's health and health practices over a working lifetime and integrating this into a data base that could compare individuals with statistical norms. The statistical insights would be used to modify and improve the individual's lifetime health strategy. Meanwhile, over a period of years, those experiences with individuals would be aggregated and a knowledge base built so that high-risk individuals could eventually be identified and high-yield interventions developed and applied. Then the irritating weight-watching exhortations could be reserved for only those people whose fat is portentious and who stand a reasonable chance, with some individually tailored help, of actually shedding their extra pounds.

To accomplish this longer-term goal, Opel considered it essential that corporate medical departments have integrated information systems to achieve what he called "the mass effect":

> The concept of health-care management is that the individual is the entry to the management of the group. The relationship with the individual takes cognizance of his individuality. Then you put the aggregate together and make decisions about the allocation of resources. Take the breast self-exam program. We can look over six to ten years and see how many cases we detect and make some educated projections of the program's cost effective-

ness. But you can't do that in a little demonstration project at corporate headquarters because you won't see the numbers.

Opel argued that "you get that mass effect automatically" through the kinds of multiphasic health-testing programs that were fashionable in occupational medicine until questions began to surface about their cost-effectiveness. But once the care is personalized, achieving the mass effect has to be a "conscious strategy": "No matter how well they're done, those limited demonstrations won't touch the bottom line. You've got to penetrate deeply into the employee population. That's what distinguished us from programs at some other companies where the quality is great at corporate headquarters, but there's no mass effect, and therefore little change on the bottom line."

Despite this optimism, a radical change in the competitive environment surrounding Opel's firm precipitated his early retirement and the company's partial retrenchment from his program of aggressive management of employees' health. Nevertheless, several factors are coming together in a number of other firms to underscore the logic of the more strategic approach Opel was beginning to evolve for a corporate medical department.

The strategic corporate medical director moves along both axes toward the top quadrant of the model characterizing his role. On the medical axis, he strives to accomplish the twin goals expressed by Opel. His first objective was to find a way to intervene in the medical care system so that his firm's corporate medical department could help ensure the appropriateness and quality of care its employees were receiving from outside physicians.

After more than a decade of efforts to moderate health-care costs, mostly by discouraging excessive or inappropriate use of services, corporate purchasers of health care are increasingly interested in establishing mechanisms for monitoring the quality of care. This is for two reasons. First, advocates of cost containment have made a compelling case in recent years that the provision of unneeded services has often been harmful to patients. Second, concern is building that the pendulum may swing so far that needed services will not always be available at the appropriate time. With improvements in the data analytic capabilities of the insurance carriers and other third parties administering health-care claims, and with the growing competition among organizations delivering care, profiles of provider practices are becoming increasingly commonplace. These profiles compare an individual doctor's practice style to community averages or norms: how frequently he subjects his patients to particular procedures or orders particular tests, how long he keeps patients in the hospital for particular operations, workups, or diagnoses. This kind of information converts companies from passive payers to purchasers with the ability to study and even influence patterns of community medical practice. Strategic corporate medical directors see themselves as centrally involved in this process.

One corporate medical director, employed by a computer manufacturer, has developed a formal "request for proposals" and is evaluating competitive bids in order to write a performance contract with a qualified health-services provider. The firm is beginning to approach health-care providers as potential "vendors" and their services as "products" for which it can contract, much as it does to acquire other goods and services it needs to produce its product. The contract it seeks to write will specify a comprehensive, coordinated package of health services (including inpatient, outpatient, and preventive care, counseling, and environmental health and safety services), to be administered through a single network of individual and institutional providers. A major criterion for selecting the successful bidder will be the efficiency and quality measures built into the system being proposed. Whether the complete plan can be implemented as envisaged remains to be seen. Still, it has emanated from a corporate medical director who is thinking in ways that are new to occupational medicine, ways that are essentially "strategic." This physician's orientation is anticipatory; he is seeking to integrate a group of programs that have tended, historically, to function separately, and his goal is to build a synergistic system with self-monitoring devices and feedback loops.

Other corporate medical departments are setting themselves up as "gatekeepers," authorized to assess the necessity of medical expenditures financed through the employee health benefit, and as sources of guidance to employees seeking advice on treatment alternatives. These new approaches are much more consistent with Opel's views of an expanded medical department than with old-style one-on-one occupational medicine.

Opel's second broad objective for health-care management was to encourage employees to alter their lifestyles in line with principles of preventive health maintenance. Here he was seeking to gain a "mass effect," to convert the medical department's focus of concern from an aggregation of individual patients, processed one at a time, to a large population, in which statistical probabilities would carry as much weight as would personal anecdotes. This theme, too, is building momentum in a number of firms with the advent of computerized health-risk appraisal instruments and the growing understanding, from large-scale epidemiological studies, of preventable risk factors.

On the management axis, strategic corporate physicians understand, as Opel did, that achieving long-term goals in health conservation requires winning the employee's trust. Trust has always been the ultimate challenge for the field.

8 ■ Can There Ever Be a More Strategic Role?

Throughout its modern history occupational medicine has been a profession in search of identity—a profession many of whose members practice in overwhelmingly bureaucratic settings. When social scientists write on the "bureaucratization" of professional work, they find a fundamental antipathy between professionalism and bureaucracy. Professionals treasure autonomy and self-regulation of performance. Bureaucracy regulates behavior and circumscribes autonomy. Nowhere should this discordance be more starkly evident than in the corporate physician's role, and most previous writings on the subject have sounded this as a theme.[1] Corporate physicians have been medicine's man in the middle. At this point we may ask whether there can be any way out.

Certainly this exploration has uncovered a role imbued with the logical incompatibilities and objective signs of conflict predicted by sociological theory and research—or, in C. P. Snow's more colorful metaphor, it has described a group of scientists struggling to stay afloat in deep moral waters. Snow criticized scientists for deceiving themselves into believing that they can escape moral culpability by forging technical tools—such as nuclear fusion—while abdicating any responsibility for setting limits on their use (Snow 1961:256). Starr (1982) and many other scholars[2] have unseated the popular view of medicine as a morally neutral enterprise capable of producing objective "scientific" diagnoses, divorced

---

1. For example, see Daniels (1972, 1975), Kaplan (1965), Lomas and Berman (1983), Haug (1976), Callahan and Gaylin (1978), Ben-David (1958), Nack (1979), Veatch (1977), Smith (1986), Derber (1982), Field (1953, 1957), and Walters (1982, 1984, 1985).

2. Zola (1978, 1983), Conrad and Schneider (1980), Conrad and Kern (1986), Navarro (1976), Navarro and Berman (1983), Szasz (1970), and the Ehrenreichs (1978) are among other noteworthy current writers on this theme.

from social context. "Cultural authority"—that is, influence over "definitions of reality and judgments of meaning and value"—according to Starr is often separated from the "social authority" that channels behavior and action. Modern societies make this separation as an overt device to facilitate a fair hearing of both sides when interests conflict. In this way, medicine can function unobtrusively as "a resource for social order" (Starr 1982:15) or an "institution of social control" (Zola 1978) by supplying definitions but standing apart from their application.

The moral waters rise around the corporate physician when he is cast in his social-control role, as the medical adjudicator described in chapter 7. It is there that he is called upon to supply an "expert medical opinion" to mediate between employer and employee when their interests diverge. This they do to some degree in nearly all instances involving the assignment of responsibility for the two-way interactions between work and health—both the harm arising out of work and the impact of illness on performance. Other situations introduce a higher organizational purpose that transcends individualism. These, in the corporate context, generally involve a financial imperative—conserving resources, holding down expenditures in nonproductive areas, pushing productivity, or focusing on short-term profit and loss. In addition, they may involve questions of equity, justice, and group process—whether and in what ways it is fair, wise, or expedient to arrange special dispensations for the employee with a physical (or mental) limitation. If there is an escape for occupational physicians from the conflict that has stunted the development of their roles, they will first have to recognize how paralyzing the conflict has been. Ironically, in their efforts to avoid conflict—to remain above the fray—they have constructed a wall of defenses that rests on the basic premise that the conflict can be denied or escaped without being directly confronted.

As a group, corporate physicians tend to minimize the conflict in their roles. Yet evidence is close at hand of certain recognizable devices they use in the effort to keep their heads above the waters. One is the "credo," a term applied in chapters 2 and 7 to a characteristic belief found among corporate physicians in the study. Often they insist that there is little or no conflict in *their* roles because the good they can do for the company is the aggregate good they do for individual employees. Chapter 7 analyzed potential disjunctions between individual and organizational purpose. The credo waves these away by asserting that for the physician to act in the best interest of the individual employee is by definition to serve the corporation's larger purpose. It is a form of what Derber terms "ideological desensitization," a denial of the ideological dimensions inherent in the work they do (Derber 1982).

A second device that helps to hide the conflict is referred to in chapter

2 and elsewhere as "medical Taylorism,"[3] a kind of "ideological cooptation," in Derber's lexicon, a disclaiming of responsibility for the uses to which others put one's work (Derber 1982). Based on the assertion that occupational medicine can be a neutral mediator between employer and employee, medical Taylorism seems to have surfaced contemporaneously with Frederick Winslow Taylor's "scientific management." It resembles Taylorism in its inordinate faith in objective "scientific truth" for the resolution of conflict. Like Taylorism, this medical analogue trivializes the conflict between labor and capital by asserting that truly objective science can be a neutral ground on which to resolve disputes. It requires accepting the premise that there can be a single, unanimous scientific solution, independent of social context. In return, it allows the corporate physician to fall back on the punctilio of role and define his authority as technical expertise, something he can view as qualitatively different from the fiat economic authority with which the corporation stands in relation to its employees, at least in theory or some of the time (Davis 1949).

In an extension of medical Taylorism, the profession goes on to define its problems largely in terms of credibility, competence, and other personal characteristics presumed correctable through selection or socialization techniques. The object is to recruit or train practitioners who will thereafter be "more objective," "more scientific," "more neutral," thus "more professional" as they feel their way through the bureaucratic thicket. The history of occupational medicine, as we have seen, is laced through with the familiar undertakings of an aspiring professional group (Wilensky 1964): advocacy of more and better educational programs at the graduate and postgraduate level, attempts to institute professionally controlled requirements for certification of both professional credentials and the content of programs, promulgation of a code of ethical conduct.[4]

---

3. Taylorism connotes much more than the myth of scientific neutrality. Breaking down a job into component parts—in order to control the laborer by robbing him of control over the integrated whole—is the essence of Taylorism as usually understood. The term is apposite for that connotation as well. The division of intellectual labor in corporate medicine that gives the doctor the responsibility for supplying but not applying the medical definitions divests him of control over the products of his labor. In that sense he is both Taylorizer (projecting his medical inputs as neutral when they are in fact instruments to control labor) and Taylorized (assigned a limited task that mitigates his control of his own labor).

4. Wilensky argues that the sequencing of those stages is important and that occupations that put the code of ethics first are using it as a battering ram to try to break down the walls to true professional status. It could be argued that occupational medicine is in Wilensky's terms behaving like an occupation trying unsuccessfully to achieve professional status. I make this argument elsewhere (see Walsh 1986).

Centering problems in conduct and rules, as occupational medicine traditionally has done, vitiates attention to structure and roles, for the most part ignored. This tendency, too, flows from medical Taylorism. If company physicians can maintain neutrality in management-labor conflict, as medical Taylorism holds, then it follows that there is nothing intrinsic to the structure of the company physician's role making conflict inevitable. Company doctors can identify with the moral purposes of the larger organization and serve it loyally without compromising their identity as physicians. The fiction that conflict can be avoided is thus necessary to medical Taylorism and to the company physician's self-identification as a doctor still. If it results, then, in the development of devices for masking conflict, these lead in turn to ambiguity about the essential mission of the profession. Such ambiguity can be observed in each of the major domains within which practitioners operate: on a social scale, within the profession, in relations with patients, and within the confines of the business organization.

In the broad social domain, the defensive strategies that make the mission unclear derive from the mechanism of "the doctrine of specific etiology" (Dubos 1959:117–18). This doctrine facilitated the transformation, traced in chapter 2, of an activist public health tradition that pursued its causal chains into the social and economic structures of a society to a narrow medical model that avoids confrontation with vested interests by defining illness as chiefly an individual affair (Fox 1975). The doctrine of specific etiology eclipsed the holistic Hippocratic tradition in which occupational medicine ought logically to fall, dealing as it does with a patient in the context of a complex social role—worker. This doctrine, too, is akin to medical Taylorism in its faith in "science," as in the exhortation that "the *scientific* response of the trained physician was to seek a specified medical etiology in an individual case for a specific problem." If, for example, a middle-class woman in the late nineteenth century was diagnosed with "hysteria," a "fashionable disease at the time," the "scientific" neurologist or psychiatrist would see his task as "diagnosing a medical problem with a specific etiology, a predictable course of development, and an origin in a malfunction of the uterus. The disease stemmed not from society but from an individual's sexual organs" (Bledstein 1976:109). Again, "science" narrowly construed permits comfortable pursuit of the ends of medicine, secure in the knowledge that they will not lead to a confrontation with the sometimes conflicting ends of a larger and often more powerful economic order or with those of the employing organization.

Within the professional domain, the dichotomy between "occupational" and "nonoccupational" illness serves the similarly protective function of steering occupational medicine clear of an internecine war with the outside medical profession. Chapters 2 and 3 showed this to be an engagement in which the occupational medical profession repeatedly has come out the loser. The dichotomy rests, again, on a narrow monocausal model of health and disease: occupational medicine's own doctrine of specific etiology.

While solving potential "turf" problems with the outside medical profession, the occupational versus nonoccupational dichotomy tends to isolate the discipline, to fragment the health care available to patients-as-workers, and to confound definitions of the occupational medical enterprise. In a study of worker's compensation thirty years ago, Somers and Somers noted ambiguity in the definition of occupational medicine. They accounted for it in a diplomatic footnote: "In a field developing as rapidly as occupational health, theoretical concepts inevitably lag behind practice. There is still a wide difference of opinion as to the precise definition of occupational health and the related fields" (Somers and Somers 1954:214). Three decades and numerous definitions later it seems reasonable (if perhaps undiplomatic) to ask whether the field has coalesced around a generally accepted definition of its central purpose. If not, the earlier confusion may have reflected something more fundamental than a communication lag attending the "rapid" development of a new specialty.

A current perspective on this issue was offered in an interview with Dr. Dale Ware, an internist turned occupational physician, to whom had fallen the job of organizing the continuing education offerings at the profession's annual meeting. His frustration was this:

> The problem with this specialty is that it's the world. There's no core discipline. I'm faced with the question of how to structure a learning situation and the arena is almost limitless. The result is that the pedants in occupational medicine can't cope with the broad range of problems which they ought to address. I'm no exception. I confess that when I go home and look through a professional journal it's usually the *Annals* [*of Internal Medicine*], not the *JOM* [*Journal of Occupational Medicine*].

As early as 1946, a study of physicians in industry also picked up on the problem of ambiguous boundaries. Stern perceived even then a growing emphasis on toxicology and specific external hazards. It was, he worried, tending to "sever industrial medicine from the mainstream of medicine and public health by dealing exclusively with hazards in the factory, shop, mine and mill, isolated from the worker's health in the community." He saw reducing the formal and arbitrary separation between those two worlds as the discipline's principal challenge (Stern 1946). Recent commentary on Stern's warning sees the situation deteriorating. Goldsmith and Kerr (the latter as then medical director of the

United Mine Workers of America) argued that in the intervening years "the specialization and refinement has intensified, the schism deepened, and the toll of occupational disease and disability worsened" (Goldsmith and Kerr 1982:28).

In the domain where the corporate physician comes into contact with an individual patient, the credo serves to obscure the divided loyalties that (as chapter 7 showed) are structured into the operational management sector of his role when his function for the organization is to supply medical inputs for use in nonmedical deliberations. Sometimes it is simply impossible to serve the larger organization by doing what is best for the individual employee—or what the employee believes is in his own best interest. On such occasions, corporate physicians tend to equate "absence control" with "rehabilitation." They perceive work as therapeutic for the employee out on sick leave. They tend also to emphasize that life is inherently risky and that the workplace is relatively safe. The hazards of work, they feel, are often overstated, with the result that individuals take too little responsibility for their own health. These ideological devices seem to bring into alignment the conflicting interests that might otherwise strain the corporate physician's relations with his patients.

It is in the organizational domain, finally, that medical Taylorism developed and thrives. Medical Taylorism permits the corporate physician to contribute to the organization's smooth functioning, to provide medical "interpretations" equivalent to Snow's scientific tools, and to escape responsibility for how they are used. Withholding a specific diagnostic label in order to preserve confidentiality while providing the medical interpretation on which a job action can rest begs the central issue for the employee of the use of the information in relation to his career prospects. It does serve the latent function for the corporate physician of institutionalizing one kind of organizational need for his professional expertise.

A different way to handle the insurance and absence-related medical adjudications would be to screen individual claims against statistically derived group norms. Case-by-case evaluation would then be reserved for the occasional exception and could be delegated to outside physicians, hired on a consulting basis. Some companies do structure the adjudication process this way, but in many others it remains driven by the expert medical opinion of an in-house physician. Corporate physicians often cling to the adjudication function, however problematic it may be for them, because it seems like one of the few concrete contributions they can make to the efficient operation of the corporate enterprise. Routinely being involved in medical adjudication ensures that the physician's role, however conflicted, at least remains somewhat secure.

This ambivalence about the adjudication function was clearly evident in a series of interviews with Dr. Edward Bower, as, in 1980, he was deciding to take a substantial cut in pay and resign his post as corporate medical director of a 13,000-employee manufacturing firm.[5] He had joined the nonunion company because of its reputation as a socially progressive employer and had come with "dreams" of building a popular in-house medical program. Twelve years later, disillusioned and defeated, he spoke of "agonizing reappraisals" that were haunting him: "I anticipated when I came that a large number of employees who didn't have good access to ambulatory medical care in the community, people who are using emergency rooms inappropriately, would come and use the medical department if I set it up right." When Bower's dreams failed to materialize, he struggled to comprehend why: "Somehow the medical service is inextricably linked to management. There's a general problem with institutional medicine, a perception that the people there are lower quality, and indeed it's often true. In occupational medicine we lose our credibility because we are involved in monitoring short-term disability."

He speculated about ways in which the medical department could be relieved of responsibility for monitoring disability but then caught himself—as though reliving a battle he had already lost—and said it would never happen: "Unfortunately the trend is in the other direction, toward very liberal policies and attempts to fine-tune the limitations and exclusions. A person who is out to beat the system will do so anyway. And you end up with tomatoes in your kisser either way you do it."

In fact, as others in the company understood the situation, the "trigger reason" for Bower's decision to leave was a ruling by the chief executive officer that would have had the very effect Bower claimed to want—that of insulating the medical department somewhat from the incendiary medical adjudication functions. The chief executive had ruled that an employee claiming a disability should have recourse to an outside practicing physician for a tie-breaking third opinion if Bower contradicted his own personal physician's assessment of his ability to work. This ruling had come down in the context of a grievance that had been appealed all the way to the chief executive. His reversal of Bower's judgment in that particular case, and his insistence on a tie-breaking outside medical opinion, was interpreted as a vote of no confidence in Bower, and it may have been.

More than one manager observed that Bower had "become pretty hardened," had come to feel that "everyone was ripping off the system." The notion of a "nonwork ethic" was one familiar "Bowerism"; and some senior managers spoke admiringly of his "personal belief and con-

---

5. For a case study of this incident see Walsh (1986).

viction": "He's a demanding guy. If you ask people around the company, they would say, if anything, he's on the tough side—that is, if he thinks you should be back on the job, he'll say so, and he'll say so because he believes that it's better for you to be working."

Even as they touted his tough-mindedness, however, managers were subtly conveying a concept of the medical department's mission that was fundamentally discordant with Bower's own sense of the contribution he could make. Bower was complaining of the employee's "unwillingness to assume a personal burden for health" and of management's view of the medical department as "in a class with fire extinguishers—something that ought to be seen," nothing more than "public relations," a "high-visibility benefit," "optics and hypocrisy." Meanwhile, other managers were commenting on what a "luxury" it was to have an in-house medical program, how important it was to create the impression among employees that the "company is interested in their health." They faulted Bower for a "negativeness" they sensed among employees toward the medical department because it was failing to do "enough hand-holding." While Bower was wondering whether he was "really doing anything worthwhile" and questioning the provision of in-house medical care as "just adding more intensity to an already saturated system" of overused health care, the vice president at the head of his division was expressing the view that "we want people using the corporate medical facility as much as possible." The director of the employee counseling program had this to say about "frivolous" use:

> The doctors stay in their white coats and isolate themselves in their clinics. They've been trained in a more or less self-contained system—the hospital—a self-contained society, and that's a model they have. They don't get out into the community. They worry about whether the visits are "capricious." But it may be highly functional for someone to leave the machine because the tension is building up. What's the role of the medical department? If the person can't stand to sit at the machine for another minute and so leaves it to go to the medical department for an aspirin he then throws away, is that capricious use? Maybe that's what the medical department is there for.

Clearly there was a difference of opinion; what had happened?

In the 1960s the company had recruited Bower as a well-qualified internist who would run the emerging medical program as its first full-time director. Bower thought he shared their vision when he accepted the post. But time and the experience of functioning as a medical adjudicator drove a wedge between the two conceptions—medical and managerial—of the program's basic mission. Bower came to feel embattled on all fronts. Patients, he felt, were making unreasonable demands, shirking responsibility for their own health, and showing too little respect for him. It felt to him as though they viewed him as a "vending machine," nothing more than an automated "keeper of technology" to whom they could go for a chest x-ray so they could continue smoking.

Managers gave him little credit for the success he had in streamlining the medical program by introducing nonphysician providers. And these measures had the effect of isolating him professionally as a lone physician in an ambulatory clinic processing basically healthy people. Being "an ancillary person" in management was inescapable but galling, especially when his medical advice was overruled in the name of employee relations. The medical department's authority in the organization was sharply circumscribed, bounded on one side by an active counseling program guarding its domain, on the other by a "lean" and ambitious health and safety group, equally intent on walling itself off from medical dominance. Only the clinical mission was left, and it was being subverted by the disability program. Ironically, it conferred on the physician both too much and too little power in his dealings with employees and their personal physicians. Having to "wear the black hat" seemed to distort his vision of his own role and his relations with his patients. Like the "company doc" criticized for insensitivity to the injured apprentice in chapter 7, Bower seemed somehow to have internalized exaggerated management dicta that were not really there. The internal contradictions in the corporate physician's role and a general unwillingness or inability to recognize them had created a situation where no one, least of all Bower, had a clear conception of what his mission ought to be. Lacking that, he developed a tough-guy persona that projected his increasingly cynical vision of what his management's interests really were.

Some companies are clearer than Bower's was about the mission of the medical department, but many others are not. When the conflicts in the corporate physician's role are a problem—for him or for others, in the corporation or beyond—they tend to interfere in some way with his ability to function effectively, by his own or other standards. In fact, they can be such a basic problem that they stand in the way of serious efforts to define what constitutes "effective performance" for a corporate physician. The question of effectiveness—and by whose lights—harks back to the discussion in chapter 1 where it was argued that there are potential tensions between externally derived professional norms and internally imposed organizational rules. The autonomy considered so essential an ingredient of professionalism reduces in the final instance to freedom from lay control or evaluation of the substance of job performance.[6]

---

6. Of course this is an oversimplification of an extended sociological debate that cannot be handled adequately in a footnote, although, as Perrow points out, it began in one—

The consequent barrier to evaluation creates ambiguity in the corporate physician's role. Effectiveness in an office has to relate to some conception of goals, but the goals of corporate health programs are diverse and not easily measured, the more so because few managers consider it important to try (Egdahl and Walsh 1983).

The model introduced in chapter 5 (figure 5.1) provides a way to approach the problem of how to define "effectiveness" for this multifaceted and ambigous role. Because the ambiguity arises out of conflicts within the role, the only way to begin to resolve it is to segment the role into constituent parts and look at the issue of "effectiveness" for each one separately. In each segment of the role (as role theory would predict), a different set of expectations comes from different members of the corporate physician's role set. Breaking it down in this way helps bring into focus the functions and dysfunctions in the way the role is structured. It permits the closer look discussed in chapter 1 at the various sources of social control of the physician's performance, and it points the way toward strategies for change.

The Corporate Physician's Role Revisited

The model in figure 5.1 combined a medical and a management axis to divide the corporate physician's role into four quadrants. The medical axis extended from a pole representing individually oriented clinical medicine to one representing group-focused population medicine. The poles of the management axis represented, respectively, an operational, day-to-day orientation to the company's immediate needs and a strategic, longer-term, and more anticipatory purview on potential constraints and opportunities in the future. Figure 8.1 subdivides the model further and labels the sectors. Table 8.1 summarizes salient features of the three fully developed sectors of the overall role. The fourth sector—strategy formulation—foreshadows what the future may hold.

Parsons's footnote to Weber's *Theory of Social and Economic Organizations* (see Perrow 1977:50–51). There is an inconsistency in the sociological perspectives on professional practice in bureaucracies. Theories of professionalism emphasize autonomy and freedom from role prescriptions and see this as the basic conflict with the bureaucratic emphasis on rules. (See, e.g., Freidson 1970a; Mechanic 1976, 1978; Hall 1975, 1977; Miller 1967.) Role-conflict theory, on the other hand, holds that ambiguity in a role, professional or otherwise, creates important problems of adjustment. This would seem to point in the reverse direction from that suggested by the professionalism literature. Greater specification of accountabilities and functions would emerge from role theory as a solution to the organizational professional's problems (see Kahn et al. 1964; Gross, Mason, and McEachern 1958). The scholars who specify *types* of organizational professional (in particular, see Gouldner 1957; and Larson 1977) begin to find a way out of this contradiction, which, nevertheless, persists.

184 ■ *INSIDE THE CORPORATION*

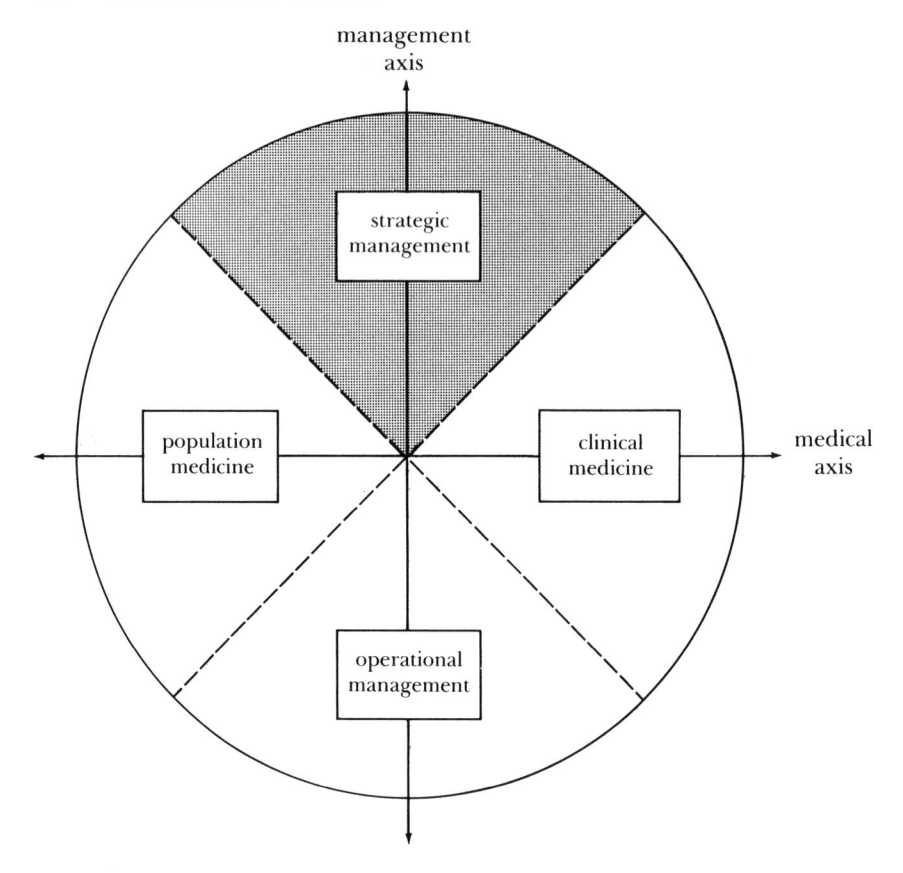

Figure 8.1.
The Corporate Physician's Role Revisited.

Medical Adjudication

The medical-adjudication function had its historical roots in the verification of eligibility for insurance (as in the early relief and benefit associations mentioned in chapter 2) and in the "doctoring for the situation" that chapter 2 showed was implied in the weighing of individual insurance claims against a common pool. Oriented primarily toward the employer's interests and needs as defined in administrative exigencies, the product of this "personnel policing" is a medical judgment for an industrial-relations application—"fitting workers to jobs" through preplacement examinations, preparing and sometimes presenting the medical evidence for worker's compensation cases, probing for a medical explanation (and solution) when a worker's performance has deterio-

Table 8.1
Salient Features of Three Major Role Sectors

	ROLE SECTOR		
	Medical adjudication	Health-care service	Environmental medicine
Historical roots	Verification of eligibility and claims processing (workers' comp. and benefit associations)	Emergency treatment in remote locations	Accident prevention and public health reforms
Functions	Medical interpretations for industrial relations applications	Early detection, health conservations, case management	Risk assessment and management; organizational intelligence
Technique/ expertise	Medical administration	Clinical medicine	Epidemiology, biostatistics, toxicology
Conflicts	Worker vs. supervisor Inside M.D. vs. outside M.D.	Organized medicine, regulators, labor, public health vs. occupational medicine	Costs vs. health mission Line vs. staff conflicts
Conflict-escaping devices	"Medical Taylorism" (science as a neutral mediator between management and labor) Work is therapeutic and abetting a malingering employee is iatrogenic behavior.	The credo: (to act in the best interest of the individual employee is by definition to serve the employer)	Life in general is hazardous and work is relatively safe. The media are alarmist in their portrayal of workplace risks.

rated, verifying the legitimacy of illness when an employee has been absent, and making arrangements for rehabilitative services, job adjustments, or other accommodations to hasten his return to work. The demands in this one sector sometimes draw the corporate physician into the circumstance described of military psychiatrists, where they are "impersonal bureaucrats, responsible *for* the welfare of patients rather than *to* the patient himself" (Daniels 1972:147).

Patients seen by a corporate physician functioning in this capacity are generally involuntary ones, and their personal physicians, as chapter 7 pointed out, are frequently regarded as a significant part of the problem. So the medical-adjudication function brings the corporate physician into a force field where the employee and his supervisor may be at odds (perhaps with personnel specialists or corporate attorneys already embroiled in the dispute) and where the outside physician may be at best oblivious to and perhaps even contemptuous of the company's perspective on his patient's condition and needs (a situation alluded to in chapter 5). How, then, in this melée, is "effective performance" to be defined? It depends on who does the defining. If, as Friere (1968) asserts, to define the world is to control it, then the cacophony of definitions can be read as a struggle for control.

The employee as an involuntary patient would surely rather avoid the encounter altogether, and his spokespersons in organized labor would (and do) insist that a corporate physician cannot perform this function at all and hope to "establish common cause with the worker" in other kinds of interactions (Samuels 1977:153). A similar position is enunciated by the International Labour Organization in a statement adopted in 1959 (ILO 1959).

For the patient's personal physician, too, the company's medical adjudications most likely represent an unwelcome intrusion. The patient's interests may be served if a corporate physician can introduce into the situation some important information about the patient's job that the personal physician would otherwise have missed. Better yet, the corporate physician may be in a position to proffer some constructive help in getting the convalescing patient's job restructured or arranging for rest breaks and medical oversight in the plant so that the job will complement the therapy. If the personal physician is mishandling the case, furthermore, the corporate physician may be able to intervene and artfully "steal" it from him, as the New York Telephone Company physicians[7] (and others in the sample) seem able to do. This kind of "medical sleuthing," it can be argued, very much serves the employee's interests if it removes him from the care of a physician who has been managing his case poorly or who perhaps has prescribed needlessly intensive treatment. It serves the company's interests as well if it hastens the employee's recov-

---

7. The New York Telephone Company innovations were principally the work of Dr. Gilbeart Collings, who retired just after AT&T went through its court-ordered divestiture. Many of his efforts at innovation slowed after he left, but his ideas remain viable, if not yet proven so. For an elaboration of them see Walsh (1983, 1984), Collings et al. (1972), Collings (1977, 1982), and Robinson and Wood (1982).

ery, thus restoring him to productive work and averting health-care expenditures financed largely through the employee health benefit plan.

Savings on health-care costs will likely win perfunctory applause from the line manager supervising the disabled employee. The supervisor's problem is to "put out the product" as efficiently and expeditiously as possible; health-care costs appear on different balance sheets and seem a very remote concern. What the supervisor wants from the company's physicians may be more complex than that they simply strive to have the injured or ill employee restored to health as soon as feasible. If the employee was injured in the line of duty, a safety-conscious firm will have strong incentives for the line manager to avoid lost-workday accidents. These "health"-motivated incentives, ironically, may create a climate in which the supervisor wants the injured worker back on the line immediately (irrespective of the possible consequences for his longer-term recovery) in order to protect the group's safety record. Responsible company physicians find themselves cast as the supervisor's adversary when this situation arises, part of the general phenomenon Dr. Monroe observed when he commented that as a company physician "you're generally in some kind of hot water or another."

If supervisors sometimes want employees back on the job sooner than may be warranted, different circumstances can as easily find them on the far side of the fence. Sometimes the supervisor's object is to enlist the physician's aid in getting rid of a troublesome employee, clearing the way for a better performer for whom allowances do not have to be made. Again, incentives create the mindset of the supervisor, for whom the substantial costs to the firm of carrying an employee on long-term disability insurance are of no immediate consequence. In theory at least, the physician can serve the corporation's financial interests by bringing these employees back to work, even if against the supervisor's wishes.[8]

These tensions reflect in part the well-documented differences between staff and line orientations (Wilensky 1967:42–48).[9] But there are staff-to-staff tensions as well. Other staff managers of concern to the corporate physician when he is functioning in this medical-adjudication domain include personnel officers and legal staff, who want the physician to provide a reasoned medical opinion and to stand behind it. Medical Taylorism helps the physician resist this pressure but creates problems

---

8. That bringing a disabled worker back on the job may not always be in the employer's economic self-interest is posited, theoretically, by Schramm in a human capital model (Schramm 1980).

9. There is an extensive literature on line and staff functions in organizations (see, e.g., Dalton 1950; Wilensky 1967:42–48) and another body of writings on the dynamics of the corporate social response process, from the initial discovery of a social issue to the institutionalization of a response (see Ackerman 1975; Bauer 1978; Stone 1975).

in his dealings with the corporate-staff peers to the extent that he sequesters himself from the "dirty work" described in chapter 1. Other managers are left with the work still to complete. They may come to view the physician who has partitioned himself off as arrogant and aloof, as not a "team player" or a competent manager. Chapter 7 speculated that the widespread impression in industry that physicians make "poor managers" has as much to do with their interaction styles—shaped at least in part by medical Taylorism—as with any particular expertise or knowledge they lack.

Health Care Service

Whether they view him as an accomplished manager or not, the corporate physician's organizational peers tend to grant his dominion over whatever medical services the company directly provides its employees. The service-delivery function tends to develop most fully in firms exhibiting one or more of the following characteristics. They may be capital-intensive (as Exxon Corporation is) or highly profitable firms trying to keep up with rapid growth (as has been the case at Digital Equipment Corporation). Like Gillette, they may have relatively few serious health hazards or large concentrations of employees in one or a few locations, or they may, as Kaiser Industries did just after World War I, operate in remote locations where medical resources are thin.

For reasons other than the remoteness of their locales, companies sponsoring the more extensive medical services may perceive the need to augment community health resources, as in the case of R. J. Reynolds when the firm moved a large food-products operation to North Carolina and created a temporary shortage of medical resources. Dr. Opel's health-care management addressed not shortage but surfeit. It was designed to shepherd the company's employees through the bewildering medical maze in metropolitan New York. Relatively extensive in-house medical services may be part of an overall corporate emphasis on its employee relations, perhaps to preserve its nonunion status or to stand out in a competitive labor market, an important motivation for firms along Boston's Route 128 and in California's Silicon Valley in the expanding electronics and computer industries. In some cases, high-quality medical services may be integral to the public image the company chooses to project as part of its overall marketing posture; the clean-living cachet of companies such as Johnson and Johnson, Kimberly-Clark, Xerox, IBM, and Campbell Soup makes sense of their visibility in the "health promotion" field. In firms that are especially stratified, such as some of the old-line banks, the medical program may parallel the executive dining room as a high-level perquisite for a select few. There was this quality to aspects of the second-opinion and confidential-advisor function that chapter 5 showed many corporate physicians serving for senior executives. In still other circumstances, an elaborated medical program may emerge, as Allied Corporation's did, out of a company response to acute external pressures following a health-related crisis. Each of these perspectives on the goals of medical services suggests a different set of criteria for assessing the effectiveness of the program and of the company's physicians in their health-care service capacity.

The influence of different perspectives is especially evident in an ongoing controversy over how the medical service can or should relate to the company's efforts to stabilize health-benefit costs. That one issue alone, and the larger question of the proper function of an in-house medical program, show the shifting nuances when the "effectiveness" of a corporate physician's performance is refracted through the divergent perspectives on his essential role.

The employee-as-patient wants the company's physicians, in their health-care service capacity, to be trustworthy, competent, accessible, empathetic, and on his side—all the qualities he wants of any physician whose services he seeks out. How many actually seek out the services of in-house medical providers is an open question. Many of the corporate physicians interviewed for the study said they do not know what proportion of the company's employees avail themselves of the services offered by the medical department (the "penetration rate"). Some go so far as to volunteer, tongue-in-cheek, that for all they know the 30,000 (or whatever number) patient encounters logged in a given year could have been three employees each visiting the medical department 10,000 times.

Most, of course, know more than that. Dr. Whitesides took pride in the fact that 97.5 percent of the 200 employees in the company's headquarters report on schedule for their voluntary periodic health examinations. He knew how this record compared with previous years and with the experience at his firm's plants and offices in other parts of the country, and he viewed the statistic as one measure of the relative performance of the medical departments under his aegis.

Some corporate medical directors in the study arrange on occasion to have questions about the performance of the medical department included in routine employee opinion surveys. Dr. Tyson had commissioned an outside market research firm to conduct a special survey, asking 15,000 of the firm's employees in two of its major locations to appraise the medical offerings there:[10] how well the location medical department handles routine illnesses and injuries or emergencies, how

---

10. The full reference for this study cannot be provided because it was shared in confidence by the medical director of the firm that commissioned it. It appears to have been competently designed and executed.

"helpful" it is, how well it does in "respecting confidential information about employees," how well it keeps them informed about the services it provides, about "programs for disease prevention," and about ways "to stay physically fit." Feeling well informed about the medical department correlated on nearly every dimension with favorable responses to it. The group that felt least well informed, interestingly, was top management: 66 percent said they were "very" or "fairly well" informed, compared to 83 percent of "general salaried workers," 76 percent of supervisors, and 68 percent of hourly workers.

On the confidentiality question—a critical one for occupational medicine—59 percent (of 807 respondents) gave a "favorable" response, 26 percent said "average," and 10 percent "unfavorable." Despite this equivocal impression about the protection of confidentiality, nearly all of the respondents used the medical department to some degree. Only 1 percent said they had not used it at all over the previous two years, 10 percent had used it once, 56 percent two to five times, 17 percent six to ten times, and 15 percent over twenty times. The bulk of these visits (49 percent) were for voluntary general physical examinations, which 90 percent of respondents rated "very" (62 percent) or "fairly" (28 percent) important to them.

The survey is worth reporting in this detail because it suggests that employees separate the physician's medical-adjudication function from his delivery of service, a separation organized labor finds problematic. The doubts expressed by nearly half of the sample about the handling of confidentiality deterred few from availing themselves of the voluntary health-examination program. The popularity of the examination program, moreover, highlights a problem created for corporate medicine by its multiplicity of goals. As noted earlier, some corporate physicians have been reassessing the medical efficiency and effectiveness of routine physical examination programs. But they know that whatever the outcome of the rational assessment, they may have difficulty convincing top management to curtail an activity that employees so value. Dr. Bower's self-diagnosed "midlife crisis" was precipitated in large measure by this overlay of an industrial relations mentality on the corporate medical role. When his considered medical advice was overruled by nonmedical logic, he came to feel used and to resent being caught up in what he termed the company's "hypocrisy," its "optics."

The popular new health programs—fitness tracks, stress-management seminars, various kinds of "employee assistance"—also become difficult for corporate physicians to resist, whatever their professional assessment of the medical case for the innovations. They look askance at the proliferating wares of the outside vendors, while feeling pressured to do "something" to stay abreast of the times.

A different sort of "outside vendor," the employee's personal physician, has a distinct perspective on the company's service-delivery function. Private practitioners' concerns, Dr. Blumgarten observed, center on "butter for their bread." With an impending doctor surplus in a constricting market for service, the available butter for physicians' bread may spread less far than it has. Competition for patients will become keener. Occupational physicians have insisted that they refer the private physician more new business than they take away. As long as the outside physician perceives this to be the case in his own practice, what he wants of the corporate physician in the service-delivery capacity is a good working relationship. Reciprocal sharing of information can make the medical systems both within the corporation and in the outside community more sensitive to the patient's health in relation to job demands and better able to intervene appropriately when the situation warrants. The claim that occupational medicine has a positive impact on the private physician's net income has rested on the premise that voluntary screening and examination programs identify previously undetected chronic disease that the company, unable or unwilling to treat on an ongoing basis, refers to community providers. Questions about the sensitivity of routine screening programs (and how much new disease they actually detect) cast doubt upon the validity of this claim. But whatever the strictly medical merits and demerits of voluntary screening programs, the belief that they generate business may serve the latent function for the corporate physician of easing relations with the outside practitioner.

Relations with other managers, staff or line, take on a different dynamic when they are "consumers" of the physician's health-care services rather than the "product" of his medical-adjudication efforts. As individuals they want of the physician what other employees-as-patients want: competence and caring. Moreover, if he cares for them well, he may develop relationships that will buoy him when the medical-adjudication waters begin to rise. If other managers in the firm respect the "professionalism" of the corporate physician, they may be more inclined to accept the argument that he should avoid the coercive use of his medical authority.

These traditional relationships become complicated, however, when health-care costs are factored in. The dominion granted the corporate physician over the medical program has rarely if ever extended to the *financing* of the employee health benefit plan. That multibillion-dollar problem (in some of the largest firms) far overshadows the three to ten-million dollars expended by the most lavish medical programs. The big-dollar item has always been the province of finance and benefits officers, who negotiate the contract with the insurance carrier or manage the company's own administrative apparatus if no carrier is involved. As the costs of the health benefit plans continue to rise, these lay managers are developing and analyzing data on the utilization of health-care services. The data pinpoint anomalies, often in the practice patterns of a few physicians whose hospitalizing, testing, and billing are excessive in comparison to community norms. How to act on that sensitive information remains a thorny question for most firms (Sapolsky et al. 1981). Because it involves professional politics, it opens an opportunity for corporate physicians to move more centrally into the management matrix. This may enhance the physician's effectiveness in the managerial domain, but not without controversy. The controversy reflects fundamental uncertainty as to whether and in what ways the corporate medical director is more physician or more manager, or a unique blend of the two.

One fresh perspective on this question came from a physician just out of training. The problem with corporate medical departments, according to Hans Emmerich, a young physician-ergonomist who had been surveying the field for a niche where he might apply his unusual combination of skills, is that they allow themselves to remain "expense propositions." He wondered:

> Why do corporate medical directors report through industrial relations departments, which are expense-generating divisions, and not through cost-saving ones? Why aren't corporate physicians responsible for quantifying the effects of their services? If corporate physicians are in part managers, then it would seem practical to expect an accountability of the managerial effectiveness of their departments, through positive return on investment, the customary yardstick for managerial decisions.

Emmerich argued, further, that corporate physicians could demonstrate a positive return on investment if they would break out of the narrow mold cast in their medical training:

> The romantic systems in medical school are the cardiovascular, respiratory, and neurological systems. The musculato-skeletal system is a backwater, relegated to nonphysician engineer types. As a consequence, human-factors issues receive much less attention than is warranted by their cost in illness, fatigue, and lost productivity. Back problems especially are much subtler than the toxicological problems that capture the limelight but affect a much smaller proportion of the workforce. If corporate physicians would attend to the cumulative pathogenic processes that purloin a worker's efficiency, health, and productivity, if they would use their medical skills to develop physical measurements to match the traditional engineering definitions of machine function and task requirements to do a job, they could convert their departments into cost-saving propositions.

Instead of pursuing these interests, Emmerich took a job as the on-camera doctor for a local television station.

A MORE STRATEGIC ROLE? ■ 193

In contrast, Dr. Julius Whitesides, corporate medical director of one of the world's largest firms, expressed reservations about efforts to quantify a corporate medical program's contribution, even though, he said, such a contribution is the program's conceptual cornerstone from a historical perspective:

> It was during the Second World War, when two or three top executives died prematurely of coronaries, that [the company] began to look on its employees as a capital asset. After that the feeling grew that we spend a fortune to maintain equipment and a health-maintenance program has the same theoretical effect. From the time that philosophy evolved, we have done much more than simply prevent harm. The reasons are not altruistic. The programs are not viewed as a fringe benefit but as a cost of doing business.

Nevertheless, he said, he had always emphatically resisted trying to justify programs in terms of what they saved:

> Our insurance carrier once came to me with some data they thought we could use as evidence that our medical programs are more effective than [some others in our industry]. We didn't even tell our management about that because we don't want them to focus on those kinds of numbers. They'll start expecting statistics like that year after year, and I don't believe they're meaningful. Management has accepted philosophically the value of preventive medicine and I don't want to muddy that with artificial data. The cost-benefit stuff is pseudo-science. It's a losing game, and I don't like to see us get maneuvered into it.

Whitesides did add that his firm, a large petroleum producer, was capital-intensive and could "afford to offer good services to all our people at a cost so modest that it doesn't make sense to waste time trying to justify the expense. Since management isn't oriented toward short-term bottom-line issues they don't ask us to be."

Dr. Lee, corporate medical director for the expanding defense contractor, depicted himself in a similarly favorable financial climate ("We're in a unique situation. We're sort of fat cats, so we can do whatever we want"). He, too, voiced distaste for measurement:

> As long as I stay a doctor, I stay respected. The minute we start asserting ourselves in management, there's a certain reservation. You're taken out of the physician's role and your image is tarnished. A lot of the physicians who go to business school lose it. In the three years I've been here, they come to me and say, "Doc, tell us what's good and we'll back you up. But let's have no paternalism. Let's not rob them of responsibility and make them so problem-oriented that they can't take care of themselves." I joke and say, "That's not the Japanese system," and we all have a laugh.

Managers in Dr. Bower's company echoed the view that physicians should go only so far in interjecting their opinions. The head of his division commented that Bower could "absorb some new responsibilities without having to give up his clinical role" but added that "we try not to tie up a lot of his time by asking him to run things." Commenting that "the status of a physician in industry is low among other managers," Bower's immediate supervisor seemed to reinforce Dr. Lee's impression that corporate doctors maintain their effectiveness by steering clear of nonmedical affairs: "Status is a problem. Ed sees it, I think, and bows out of administrative things—sometimes—but he's not always consistent. Sometimes he'll make a recommendation based on a nonmedical judgment." A comment like this is another manifestation of medical Taylorism in its support of the view that there are essential distinctions and separations to be made between medical and nonmedical input into decisions.

Some corporate physicians bridle at this distinction. Robert Ingersoll was one. An ambitious corporate medical director of a forest-products company, he wanted to try to manage "the whole ball of wax," including the employee health benefit programs. Directly responsible only for occupational health, he saw no way over the long term for companies to justify the "big salaries" they have to pay in-house physicians in order to compete with the outside opportunities available to energetic physicians. His role overlapped that of a vice president for human resources, also highly paid, and Ingersoll felt confident of his own ability to "take care of what is in my company a $50-million business." His ambition was blocked, however, and he left that company for a job with a growing consulting firm, specializing not in occupational health but in computer-intensive management of corporate health-care costs.

A late-career Bell System medical director shared Ingersoll's view that corporate physicians should be deeply involved in the management of employee health benefits: "We have a very specific and definite function in health-care policy and cost containment that nobody else has." But Dr. Arnold Bennett, who had recently joined a top firm in the information business, dissented from Ingersoll's position: "In my company there are benefits specialists who have a hell of a lot better skills than I do in managing those dollars." So did Dr. Monroe, who had held several national offices in professional organizations. He expressed scant interest in investing his energies in reducing health-care costs:

> I do not wish to participate in this economic business. My role is staff consultant, hired to deal with chemicals. To do that I must be able to present myself as a physician—to management and the bluest of the blue-collar workers. You ask why the corporate medical director is not the equivalent in a company's health affairs of a corporate counsel in legal affairs. The answer is simple. Many of these things are not medical policy. They are business policy or personnel policy. We're not talking about medical issues when we

worry about how to contain the costs of the employee benefit package. Others disagree; some are big on "management," but that's their inclination, not mine. I'm not a good manager and I really don't want to be. But I am a big shot here, the doctor that the president turns to for advice. I'm part of making the company go.

Although the benefits and medical functions in most large corporations have developed along separate tracks, new, more sophisticated thinking about how best to manage a health-care benefit—thinking that begins to recognize the inseparability of financing and service-delivery issues—raises the possibility of uniting, for the first time, the financing and service functions *inside* the corporation. As members of the medical fraternity, some corporate medical directors are now being called upon for advice on how to handle corporate relations with employees as health-care consumers and with providers of care (Belk 1983).

This is new for them and occasions some discomfort, as evidenced in the literature. One example is an article in the profession's specialty journal by a member of AOMA's ethics committee (with a coauthor). Bernard Schuman, M.D., who was then corporate medical director of the Port Authority of New York and New Jersey, sketched a new role for his colleagues in health-care cost containment and then insisted that the ethical occupational physician could and even should assert himself in his company's deliberations about how to manage health-care costs. "Participation . . . by medical department staff," he and his coauthor argued, "should insure a balanced approach and preclude cost-saving measures that promise short-term bottom-line results but that risk long-term health liabilities." Moreover, they went on to conclude that "cost containment need never constitute compromise with ethical guidelines or professional standards of occupational medicine" but "should be seen rather as a broadening of concepts and perspectives entirely consistent with the proper role of the physician in today's rapidly changing society" (Schuman and Lacis 1982:697).

Schuman's article can be viewed as a delayed reaction to a quite different position taken by another of the field's spokespersons, Dr. Irving Tabershaw. In his summary of a 1978 professional conference on the ethics of occupational medicine, Tabershaw observed that "there was a general feeling—at least . . . from the physicians—that the cost of health care to corporations was not a legitimate concern of theirs, at least not at this time" (Tabershaw 1978). The time had come, Schuman seemed to be saying, to reassess that position, however controversial the suggestion might be.

Company-sponsored alcoholism programs provide a concrete focus for thinking about complications that arise when cost containment becomes part of the medical department's overt mission. In referring to the company program an employee whose drinking is causing documented performance problems, a supervisor knows how unsatisfactory the alternatives are—either outright dismissal, possibly followed by grievances, arbitration, and temporary reinstatement, or grudgingly tolerated mercurial behavior and disruptive muddling through. Alcoholism programs have represented a rare opportunity to help the needy individual while attending to the organization's needs. Backed up as they are by the company's disciplinary apparatus, these programs operate initially in the medical-adjudication domain. But the job-performance criterion functions as a buffer separating the physician or other therapist from the tensions in that domain between supervisor and worker.

When performance is the issue, the therapist and client may together establish a treatment goal of abstinence from alcohol but that remains a treatment goal—a private matter between professional and client—and not a performance goal. The performance goal is for the supervisor and the employee to address; it and only it is considered the legitimate concern of the employer. If the employee continues drinking, damaging his liver, and using more than his share of the health care financed through the employee-benefit plan, that does not become an issue so long as he performs adequately on the job.

When the costs of the benefit plan *are* the issue, then the focus shifts to the self-destructive behavior that is unrelated to performance on the job. As detailed in chapter 7, management's zone of control penetrates deeply into what used to be the zone of ambiguity. The ability to identify "high-cost users" of health care (Zook and Moore 1980; Burton, Eggum, and Keller 1981) gives employers a scientific tool they can use to conduct witch hunts. It also raises equity questions since behavioral risk factors, like most illnesses, are concentrated in lower socioeconomic and educational strata. Moreover, if high-cost employees (for example, those who drink, smoke, or overeat) are to be a target of cost-reducing interventions, what about high-cost spouses or children? What about large families, or families that ski or engage in other high-risk sports? Where is a company to draw the lines (Walsh and Gordon 1986)? It is an intuitive and less than fully articulated sense of these troublesome distinctions that compels some corporate physicians to speak out against a role for their profession in the management of health-care costs. Nevertheless, the cost imperative does provide the kind of external mandate that Part II showed occupational medicine traditionally to need. This may seem especially compelling to a profession whose external mandate from a strong regulatory program in occupational safety and health has been stifled by a conservative retreat from regulation.

Environmental Medicine

As it was being felt in the late 1970s, the strong government mandate emphasized the environmental aspect of occupational medicine. OSHA partisans viewed medical-service delivery as certainly a distraction from the profession's true calling and possibly a deliberate smokescreen put up by irresponsible employers. A former director of NIOSH strongly expressed this opinion: "I usually feel that big corporations that get into primary care take advantage of this interest to cover up their neglect of workers and hazards in the workplace. I would love to be shown I am wrong. Should you find companies that aggressively follow up findings of occupational disease with engineering changes on the job rather than treating or blaming the victim, I'd be interested."

Without more systematic data than are available, one can only speculate on the response to this challenge. But it is reasonable to argue that some corporations develop—for whatever reason—a relatively high level of consciousness of employee health. This may conduce to greater vigilance along the entire medical axis, from the population to the clinical pole. This study at least warns against uncritically accepting the premise that health-service delivery in a firm must necessarily be traded off against environmental health protection. A priori, it need not be a zero–sum game.

In magnifying the one sector of the corporate physician's role least under his independent control, the government mandate in environmental health protection was a mixed blessing. It heightened industry's awareness of the need for health conservation but created a climate, at least in the higher-risk or more highly sensitized firms, where health was becoming too important to be left to the doctors. The nostalgia expressed by some of the veteran occupational physicians with a clinical orientation—physicians such as Whitesides and Blumgarten—reflected this change in the division of labor in the health apparatus of the large, health-hazard-conscious firms.

Meanwhile, the boundaries around this group of self-consciously hazardous firms were expanding all the time. The proliferation of chemicals in commerce and the honing of measurement techniques have been important influences. Summarizing these, a NIOSH director wrote (with a coauthor): "The chemical abstracting service has on its registry four million chemicals and makes 21,000 new entries per month. According to the Environmental Protection Agency (EPA), 45,000 to 47,000 chemicals have been produced in the last three years. It is estimated that 2,000 to 4,000 *new* chemicals are produced each year, many of which never leave the laboratory; latest EPA figures suggest that approximately 400 new chemicals will reach the market this year" (Yodaiken and Robbins 1980:468). As "occupational stress" has also become a growing concern, distinctions between occupational and nonoccupational health have tended to yield to the recognition that work and health interact in complex ways in nearly all business firms (McLean 1979; Warshaw 1979; Moss 1981).

The spread of chemicals and the lowering of thresholds of detection meant that by the early 1980s companies were admitting to themselves and their employees that their core technologies had undergone fundamental change. In one company's case, miniaturization had transformed the firm from a "box-assembly" to a chemical enterprise. Recognition of this shift came on the heels of two worrisome incidents with potentially carcinogenic substances to which customers and employees were being exposed. As a result, the company's managers began to take steps to organize a health-protection function that they hoped would reach the caliber of the longer-standing programs sponsored by leading firms in the chemical and petrochemical industries.

The waning of an accepted concept of purely "occupational disease" meant that more and more different types of companies, employing diverse technologies to produce a wide range of products, would have to pay serious attention to the environmental medicine problem. This was dramatized in a consensus document released by NIOSH in March 1982. It listed the ten "most serious occupational disease and injury categories in order of importance." The list included in nearly every case diseases of ambiguous and multiple etiology, on the job and off. Entirely too general to be localized in one or several types of production process, these broad-scale occupational health problems would seem to presage for the environmentally oriented occupational medical professional a wide and expanding mandate in large firms of nearly every industry type. Historically this is new.

The corporate physician's environmental-medicine functions have their roots in the early sanitary reforms, discussed in chapter 2, and in the "safety first" campaigns of the early 1900s. Both provide only partial sustenance to the occupational physician who fits technically but seldom ideologically into the public health discipline that mounted the sanitary reforms and ideologically but seldom technically into the engineering and industrial hygiene disciplines central to "safety first" and its subsequent campaigns. To a greater extent than the service and adjudication sectors of his role, the environmental-medicine function involves the corporate physician in an interdisciplinary collaboration which he will not necessarily dominate. The technical complexity of the task is part of the reason—the physician's output is input some other function needs, which is Drucker's criterion to distinguish a manager from a specialist

(Drucker 1973). Also, environmental interventions interfere more than medical ones do with the established routines of the organization.

In the service-delivery capacity, occupational physicians address problems in one-on-one interactions with patients. The medical-adjudication functions introduce the added complexity of supervisors and other company representatives. But still they keep the focus generally on individual employees processed one by one, even in cases where the processing includes negotiating an organizational intervention (perhaps a job adjustment or other accommodation that has to be extracted from the supervisor of a given employee-as-patient). The environmental functions, in contrast, are ineluctably organizational; they are ramified into decisions about what products the company will produce, how, when, and at what cost, and to whom, and how those products will be distributed—even, sometimes, how the consumer will use and dispose of them. The strictly medical aspect of this interdisciplinary endeavor is difficult to isolate from aspects particular to product management, industrial hygiene, engineering, industrial relations, personnel and employee education, and even marketing.

When conflicts arise over the physician's environmental-medicine role, they often reflect uncertainty about the proper mix of medical and managerial expertise necessary to accomplish tasks over which (because they relate to health) physicians often feel entitled to exercise the "professional sovereignty" that has been medicine's hallmark in noncorporate practice settings (Starr 1982). Sovereignty inside the corporation is of a different order. As one vice president noted, "The product manager around this place is a kind of king." For the corporate physician, the complexities that ensue come into sharper focus, again, when the demands on him in this environmental-medicine sector of his role are considered from different angles of vision.

The individual employee, one could posit a priori, wants full information, fair information practices, and full protection, emphasizing engineering controls that burden the boss, not him. It should be a matter of indifference to him what role the corporate physician plays in the provision of these protections, so long as they are adequately provided. They do raise equity problems that someone needs to address—many related in one way or another to the general question whether and how allowances can be made to protect certain classes of worker without discriminating unfairly against others. The types of worker possibly requiring extra protection include those with "hypersensitivities" (from exotic enzyme deficiencies to the ability to conceive a child) or chronic illnesses (like diabetes) or personal habits (like cigarette smoking) that increase their vulnerability to environmental assaults on their health.

If the corporate physician does become embroiled in balancing issues of this sort, it is as the kind of "physician for the situation" introduced in chapter 2. Like the claims-processing activities described there, these interest-balancing issues call on the balancer in "a single transaction" to represent multiple clients (the protected classes, the other employees, and the larger corporate entity). Orthodox clinicians are normally spared having to make these judgment calls because the structure of the patient-physician relationship defines their primary allegiance. Corporate physicians develop ideological devices to compensate for this diminution of structural protection. One is a logical heir of Lord Abinger's doctrine of the employee's willing "assumption of risk," discarded, as chapter 2 showed, with the advent of worker's compensation laws. Those laws recognized the inherent danger of work and sought to internalize the social costs of industrial accidents by holding employers responsible for harm befalling employees in the line of duty.

The modern-day extension of Abinger's doctrine rests on different economic thinking. It finds a willing "assumption of risk" in employees' leisuretime pursuits and from this finding infers a greater tolerance for hazards on the job than is suggested in the cry for "full" protection. Hang-gliding, stockcar racing, skiing, drinking to excess, smoking cigarettes, riding motorcycles, even driving cars or eating marbled beef or aflatoxin-contaminated peanut butter, the argument states, are demonstrably riskier than many exposures on the job. Therefore, some level of job hazard can be assumed "acceptable" to the typical employee (Smith 1976; Dinman 1980; Lowrance 1976; Hanley 1981), who if rational recognizes that the enormous economic cost of "absolute protection" could shut down his plant and put him out of work.

An alternative device is to acknowledge that employees are deeply concerned about workplace health hazards but to construe these concerns as overreactions to the "media hype" and the "regulatory excess" toward which, as chapter 6 showed, some corporate physicians express animus. Both devices require that the corporate physician see the workplace as reasonably safe, a perspective many of the corporate physicians in the sample confidently exposed.

Organized labor tends to disagree. Union spokespersons share the regulators' conviction that occupational medicine is superfluous or even malign if not wholly committed to the primacy of an urgent and largely neglected health-protection mission. In public, union spokespersons take the absolute position that introducing cost considerations or Abinger-like relativism is tantamount to "valuing a human life," an entirely unconscionable enterprise in their eyes. Physicians must always "choose life" over profit, the argument continues, but occupational physicians employed by business firms may not be permitted to do so. Medicine therefore belongs elsewhere.

The difficulty of defending a position as purely one-dimensional as this is illustrated by labor's own inconsistencies when political contradictions arise. When the Manville Corporation instituted a nonsmoking policy because of the well-documented synergy between cigarette smoking and asbestos as risk factors for debilitating lung disease, the unions publicly contested the policy and filed official grievances in three jurisdictions. Union leaders privately granted the scientific rationale for the policy. Manville had the "high ground" on the life-versus-death dimension, but the unions could not countenance what they perceived as Manville's "union-busting" tactics, having established the policy by management fiat.

Labor relations in general emerged from the study as a crucial unresolved problem for many of the corporate physicians in unionized firms, and this was evident not only in the medical-adjudication sector, where the union's role is to protect the employee's interests, but also in the environmental-medicine sector, where there ought to be a mutuality of interest in making the workplace safe (Kotin 1979). Some unions are becoming more vocal and organized on environmental health issues than has been typical in the past, and some corporate physicians see in this an opportunity to define interests in common. As in the cost-containment realm, corporate physicians can increase their leverage within the management matrix if they can carve out a role that brings them closer to the firm's "technical core" (Thompson 1967). Developing strong ties to labor—by working with union designees on collaborative scientific studies[11] or simply by opening channels of communication to discuss health-related concerns—would have this effect. Because these activities would strengthen the physician's power base, they are threatening to personnel and industrial relations specialists, who feel safest when they can maintain exclusive control over interactions with unions.

The closer the physician gets to the technical core of the firm, the more he threatens domain already claimed by someone else. An illustrative episode arose at one of the firms studied in depth. The company was in the process of redefining its occupational-medicine enterprise to meet newly perceived environmental health needs. A clinically oriented corporate medical director had retired and been replaced by Dr. Bennett, quoted in chapter 5, a physician with strong toxicological credentials. He was recruited by and reported to Samuel Perkins, a vice president for

---

11. Two well-known examples are: (1) the Tripartite Study conducted by researchers at the University of Pittsburgh with the guidance of the Steelworkers Union, the three major aluminum manufacturers, and NIOSH; and (2) the study conducted by Harvard University researchers for the Rubber Workers Union and B. F. Goodrich. Also, General Motors and the United Auto Workers Union reached an agreement on September 29, 1983, in which a GM-UAW Occupational Health Advisory Board was created.

personnel. A somewhat more senior vice president, in an engineering division, had been put in charge of a newly established unit assigned to coordinate the interactions (on staff and line levels) among all the separate functions involved in aspects of environmental health protection, including worker safety, industrial hygiene, product safety, and toxicological and epidemiological research. There was to be a "dotted line" relationship between this engineering unit and "people health and safety" under the personnel vice president and his new medical director. One of the early undertakings was to establish company-defined standards for safe exposure levels to specific toxic agents. The imbroglio surrounding the standard-setting process illustrates the tensions between medical and managerial expertise.

Perkins, the personnel vice president, wanted Bennett, his new medical director, to have the principal say in the setting of standards for employee exposure. The conflict came to a head in a semantic argument between the personnel and engineering vice presidents, the former intent on having his medical director "issue" the exposure standards, the latter insisting that the medical role should be merely to "recommend." The disagreement was appealed, level-by-level, all the way up to the chief executive officer, who passed down a ruling in the medical director's favor.

Later, Dr. Bennett said he would have resigned over an adverse ruling, but the "shoot-out," as he called it, did not stop there. He issued a standard requiring the maintenance force going out on service calls to wear protective gloves while handling a certain suspect substance contained in one of the firm's products. The marketing people became "very upset" about "what the customers would think when our service guys came in there looking like we're afraid of our own product." Several managers began to express doubts about the medical director's judgment—was he qualified to make these kinds of assessments, cutting across the entire decision matrix? Wasn't this really a question for a product manager to resolve? The industrial hygienists expressed questions about "whether medical can manage. Are they capable in the technical sense and do they have the interest? Wouldn't they rather stay with what they know—practicing medicine in industry?" Even the chief executive was sufficiently unsure of the medical director—on whom he had conferred the authority to "issue" standards—that he telephoned him to point out that $100 million was at stake. "I'm not telling you how to come down on this," the medical director recalled the CEO having said to him, "but I am asking you to listen to all the business arguments." In the end Bennett's concerns were confirmed in some additional laboratory evidence, and management fell in line behind the requirement that service engineers wear gloves.

Having won two important victories, the medical director still faced several obstacles before his authority would be securely established. He was jockeying with the engineering group for control of the toxicology labs. Also, the industrial-hygiene group was wondering if it was in their best interest to be subjected to medical authority. In most locations the industrial-hygiene and safety staffs were larger than the medical staffs, were more actively involved at the interface with line managers, who accorded them a kind of grudging respect, and sometimes were higher in the chain of command than the plant physician, who nearly always reported to the location personnel director. Bennett, as corporate medical director, had these "turf wars to fight," and even his own medical staff was "lobbing shells" at him, for having done too little with "job descriptions and performance plans." To make bad matters worse, a very senior executive took him aside one day and told him he was not "being political enough," and Bennett's marriage was showing the strain of a grueling travel schedule. Several months later, however, Bennett had begun to feel more in command and could say, optimistically, that he was "learning how to broker when I need support. You can find someone somewhere who will back you up, whether it's legal or communications or the user group." He was, in terms of the model in figure 8.1, finding ways to be more strategic.

■ *PART FOUR*
Conclusion

9 ■ Lessons

The history of occupational medicine has been anchored in the visions of a few pioneers who see challenge and fulfillment for physicians in corporate medical practice, if management can be sold on the health-conservation mission. Meanwhile, the history has been burdened by persistent clashes of this vision with the profit imperative driving the corporation. The profession's visionaries have always been attracted by the opportunity to practice true preventive medicine with a large, discrete population. And this hope has always been thwarted to some degree by bureaucratic perversities that dangle the population tantalizingly beyond reach. The corporate medical directors presiding over the strongest and best-established programs still admit that their knowledge and impact are uneven, depending as they do on the initiative of senior managers of individual locations, not to mention the ongoing cooperation of scores of supervisors. Effective corporate physicians resist deliberately choosing profit over health in a particular instance. But even they find themselves competing at a disadvantage for an adequate voice in the firm.

Simply cataloguing the medical programs that have sprung up at local management initiative in offices and plants across the country and around the world can be a major undertaking in a large, decentralized firm. Plant physicians typically report to plant managers (often through personnel officers) with a "dotted line" to the corporate medical department. Corporate medical directors in such firms have difficulty collecting program information from plant physicians (who are, at least, members of the same functional specialty). The difficulties multiply rapidly whenever anyone suggests that operational managers be asked to provide to the corporate level a standardized accounting of enough information on the work experiences and exposures of employees in the facility to support a prospectively oriented health-conservation program on a company-wide scale. The suggestion flies in the face of the emphasis current in most companies on decentralization of decisionmaking and diminution of bureaucratic controls (Peters and Waterman 1982).

In his 1977 "Ramazzini Oration," Dr. Norbert J. Roberts, then corporate medical director of Exxon Corporation, touched cautiously on this issue. He spoke of needed "changes in the organizational details of the type of decentralized management that has understandably become the norm in large organizations operating at multiple sites." Asserting that "we must now require that we receive the information that we must have to identify health effects," he granted that "any proposal that would diminish decentralization is about as popular as the plague and usually for good reasons." Nonetheless, he insisted that "this one has become a necessity and I have confidence that it will be recognized as such" (Roberts 1978b:172).

The quest for health-risk data is an extension of the longer-standing focus in occupational medicine on general, periodic health evaluations. Both involve the occupational physician in an attempt to carve out a unique and meaningful mission. In 1909, when Harry E. Mock initiated his program of physical examinations for employees of Sears, Roebuck and Company in Chicago, he was developing the technology through which company doctors could begin the transition from "finger-wrappers" to industrial physicians. Periodic physical examinations became the "core technology" (Thompson 1967) of occupational medicine and remained so for nearly a century.[1] Reiser (1978) points out, in a history of the concept of screening for disease, that the Chicago innovation was inspired by public health activists intent on stemming the spread of tuberculosis. But Mock's vision was more generic. Selleck and Whittaker (1962) reconstruct his thinking as a young physician weighing the wisdom of pursuing the "great opportunity" of a job opening at Sears. A mentor who asked what kind of opportunity he saw was told,

> Here are 15,000 people, men and women, gathered under one roof in a great industry. This is a great human laboratory. Think of the opportunity of making a complete physical examination of all these people. We have been trained to examine sick or supposedly sick people, but here I could study average normal workers and could learn what "normal" as differentiated from "sick" really is. I could catch the evidence of disease early and could warn many of these in time to prevent impending trouble.

1. The literature on issues related to screening for disease is voluminous. Among the best overviews are the Canadian Task Force on the Periodic Health Examination (1979, 1980), Collen et al. (1977), Breslow and Somers (1977), Department of Continuing Education, Harvard Medical School (1980), Sackett and Holland (1975). Nugent (1983) provides a historical account of screening in industry.

If looked upon as a vehicle to help achieve the promise Mock perceived in occupational medicine for implementing preventive medicine within a defined population, integrated data systems take on a new dimension, whatever their particular form. Not only do such systems help ensure that workers are not being harmed by exposures on the job; they also raise the possibility of bringing epidemiology into the corporate health-policy equation in two important new ways. The first harks back to Terris's thinking about epidemiologically grounded public policy in health (Terris 1980). A more critical assessment of employees' health needs, supported by progressively improved data, could stimulate a more strategic and deliberate approach to planning all the company's health interventions, not just those in the traditionally circumscribed realm of the occupational physician. Thus, data from health-risk appraisals and periodic examinations would be coordinated with passive epidemiological surveillance systems and data from insurance-claim files as a management-information system for a comprehensive program of health management, including oversight and quality assurance of care rendered by outside practitioners.

The second role for epidemiology in a strategic corporate health plan draws on Cochrane's even broader vision of epidemiology as a critital perspective (Cochrane 1971). Corporations capable of integrating the knowledge they have on the health of populations for which they are responsible would be in a position to assess more rigorously than occupational medicine has done in the past the extent to which their programs continue to commit the "sins of omission and commission" for which Cochrane takes his medical brethren to task.

The exciting opportunity that attracted Mock and others into the field depends for its realization not on niceties of technique—such as periodic evaluations or data systems—but on the possibility of truly preventing some disease. Adequate records were from the very beginning correctly perceived as crucial to the task. Also, it was perceived that these could be created only through a system of clinical encounters, building inductively to a composite picture of health patterns within the workforce. Employees had to be willing to report for examinations to make the system work, and earning employees' trust was therefore an appropriate preoccupation. That preoccupation, however, created the conflicts in the occupational physician's role, because it placed him at the mercy of competing and sometimes mutually exclusive but legitimate claims to his loyalty. The irony is that the conflicts may, in turn, have blocked other avenues to aggregate data that might have reduced the occupational physician's dependence on clinical records reflecting his own one-on-one encounters. One such avenue ran outside the corporation, the other inside. Both come to light when one considers how occupational medicine might have developed but did not.

In one plausible counterfactual scenario, occupational medicine in the United States might have grown up as a complement to an integrated and environmentally astute system of community medical practice that would have produced the clinical records with which to build a data base to track the health of a working population. That it did not speaks in large part to the way the general medical system developed in the United States, as a fragmented, specialty-dominated confederation of private practitioners, few of whom think to probe in detail the work experiences and exposures of the patients they see. It speaks also to the absence of any meaningful link between the practices of medicine inside and outside the corporation. It might have been possible to forge that link had not occupational medicine been perceived as captive of the bureaucracy and thus as a threat to professional autonomy (Starr 1982:200–06).

The other potential but unrealized source of aggregate data that occupational medicine could have used to make good its promise of preventing illness might have been insurance carriers, as fiduciary agents of the corporations. Companies with elaborate medical programs, like those in the sample for this study, paid their insurance carriers large sums of money to administer an employee health benefit program and to pay the claims, but the companies seldom if ever asked the carriers to refine that claims-paying system so that they might learn from it about the health of their employee populations. Where medicine as an institution derived much of its social and cultural power from the economic advantage it enjoyed as an intermediary between sellers and buyers of health care (Starr 1982), the corporate payers for the care kept *their* physicians outside the financial loop. The structure and financing of the benefit package were negotiated with the insurance carriers by specialists in finance and personnel, advised by officers in industrial relations. Medical guidance was seldom if ever sought. The benefit package was clearly defined as a device to help employees purchase health care on their own, entirely distinct from the company's in-house medical apparatus. It was therefore not set up in such a way that medical questions could fruitfully be asked of it.

Redefining Occupational Medicine

If these conditions are now changing—if Starr is right that "a corporate ethos in medical care" is going to alter the structure of the medical-care system, and if the new corporate consciousness of health-care costs is going to drive the insurers to produce new aggregate data (Walsh

1980)—then the conditions may be right for strategic corporate physicians to redefine occupational medicine.

Functioning at the operational pole of the management axis, corporate medical directors are responding to exigencies and needs defined by the organization. These are summarized in table 9.1. Moving toward the strategic pole, they become increasingly successful at manipulating the organization's perception of how it can use their medical expertise. In this respect, they become strategic not only about the place of a medical function within a corporate enterprise but also about the role they themselves can properly and comfortably play as professionals in bureaucratic organizations. They rechannel expectations and reinvent rules of role. It can therefore be argued that the movement along the management axis from the operational to the strategic pole gives occupational physicians a way to shake the pack of problems that has dogged their heels.[2]

At the heart of many of these problems is the reality that operational managers have to concern themselves with short-term profit and loss while health is necessarily a longer-term issue. A longer-term corporate-wide purview on health is essential to the mission of a corporate medical program with a truly preventive outlook. A longer view is the ultimate conflict-resolving device for occupational medicine, capable of producing a more satisfactory and more lasting solution than rationalizations such as the credo and medical Taylorism. Herein resides the corporate physician's real hope of making the credo more than a slogan for masking the subordination of individual needs to larger organizational purposes. The longer-term purview reads the credo the other way around; it seeks to redefine and reshape the organization's larger purpose so that it *will* be consistent with individual needs. This interpretation of the credo implies that the object of the environmental health task (of which medicine is one of several elements) is to understand as fully as possible the interactions between individual and organizational needs. In turn, this requires collecting all possible inputs bearing on associations between work and health and converting them to "organizational intelligence," Wilensky's term for policy-relevant "information—questions, insights, hypotheses, evidence" (Wilensky 1967). The intelligence must then be interpreted and disseminated—to employees and their repre-

---

2. For essays by practitioners and others cognizant of challenges faced by the profession, see, e.g., Belk (1983), Block (1977), Bundy (1976), Carrick (1975), Collings (1982), Coye (1979), Dunning (1961), "Ethics in Occupational Medicine" (1980), Herbert (1975), Hollinshead (1981), Jend (1973), Johnstone (1961), Karrh (1979, 1983), Keene (1974), Kehoe (1959b), Kerr (1973), Kotin (1980, 1982), Kotin and Gaul (1980), Legge (1938), Magnuson (1976, 1978), Samuels (1979, 1983), Shepard (1960), Tabershaw (1975, 1976, 1977), and Warshaw (1966, 1971, 1976, 1978).

Table 9.1
Summary of Criteria for Effective Performance of a Corporate Physician Functioning in Various Role Sectors

Expectations	ROLE SECTOR		
	Medical adjudication	Health-care service	Environmental medicine
Employee-as-patient	Be fair and objective and on the employee's side.	Be trustworthy and discreet, medically competent, accessible, and empathetic.	Anticipate and remove hazards without diminishing employee's job status or prospects.
Organized labor	Do not perform this function for the company and expect to make common cause with the workers in other situations.	Leave medicine in the community where it belongs.	Provide access to records. Engage in no "union-busting" (via fiat or unilateral decisions).
Patient's personal physician	Do not interfere or second-guess; personal M.D. has patient's interests at heart.	Leave butter for our bread. Share relevant information. Restructure jobs when necessary.	Inform private physicians about patient's work exposures.
Line manager	Help move problem employees out of my domain; reduce absenteeism, increase productivity.	Be competent and caring.	Spend as little money as possible and don't interfere with production.
Staff manager	Make medical judgment and stand behind it. Expect no special exemptions from the dirty work.	Concentrate on running the medical service and don't build empires.	Be a team player on an interdisciplinary health and safety staff.

sentatives (including personal physicians and organized labor), managers, suppliers, customers, government regulatory agents, and academic researchers—so that they can act upon it. This means tapping into the most effective and appropriate "action channels" (Allison 1971) throughout the firm and to and from relevant parts of the external environment. It also means that the problems created by the decentralization of authority in the firm must somehow be resolved.

Evidence suggesting that intelligence and its conveyance are crucial to the corporate medical task is available in the post hoc observations by managers knowledgeable about what happened in companies that mishandled environmental health problems, as Allied did kepone, Manville did asbestos, and B. F. Goodrich did vinyl chloride. Good organizational intelligence alerts wellmeaning managers to the consequences of alternative courses of action (Wilensky 1967:xi). "Mending the information net," in Stone's terminology, is a necessary if not always sufficient step toward promoting corporate social responsibility (Stone 1975). The organizational structures that limit the passage of health-pertinent intelligence are created, not given. People make them; people can improve them.

One proposal to try to improve the flow of information relevant to workers' health would be to relocate the occupational physician so that he is accountable equally to management and labor. Many labor leaders believe this kind of restructuring of accountability is the only practical way to "liberate the occupational health professional" (Mazzocchi 1981). Another possibility would bring the government into the equation in an arrangement modeled after that of the air traffic controllers. They, like corporate physicians, perform jobs where lives are at stake.

Several European governments—for example, those of Italy, France, Belgium, and Germany—employ physicians to conduct inspections of worksites and examinations of employees and mandate employer-financed occupational health services in sizable plants (Ashford 1976: 501–10; Altenstetter 1981). A 1978 law in Ontario requires employers to establish joint health and safety committees, to inform workers about possible hazards, and to conduct medical monitoring of employees exposed to designated substances. Other Canadian provinces are also experimenting with laws designed to move occupational-medical programs onto neutral ground, away from direct management control (Walters 1985).

Although highly unlikely in the United States, given the political and economic climate of the 1980s, arrangements such as these would presumably go far toward reducing the conflicts that this study has found are sapping the corporate physician's role. That presumption is lent support by the finding here that some company-paid physicians are taking steps to build their own new structures, through new "health information nets" and through a reconceptualization of the physician's accountabilities inside the firm and outside. In terms of the model, they are moving corporate medical programs up into the strategic sector. No single corporate physician has yet woven all the pieces together, but the efforts of a dozen or so leaders in the field are giving shape to a protean and potentially more strategic role.

Cementing Relations with the Employee-as-Patient

To become a more strategic medical director, the corporate physician needs to find a way to produce "organizational intelligence" that can support corporate health policies directed at restraining problem-causing activities and promoting problem-solving ones. It will then be important to persuade employees throughout the firm to cooperate voluntarily with location medical programs. This will be the action channel through which baseline data can be collected for assessing the health effects of work. Dr. Whitesides's 97.5-percent participation rate becomes an important target. This will also be an important channel for communicating reciprocally with employees about their perceived health problems and needs, options available to them for health-care services, and actions they and the firm can take to protect and promote health.

With this as a goal, the traditional medical-adjudication functions emerge as counterproductive: they alienate employees and their personal physicians. Three general strategies are discernible among the corporate physicians who have perceived this problem and taken steps to surmount it. The first involves deliberately sloughing off the medical-adjudication activities, contracting some out to insurance carriers or to outside medical consultants who have impeccable credentials ("carriage trade" was one corporate physician's term for the consulting physicians he used to resolve disputes) and who are kept at arm's length. A sharp demarcation is also drawn between the medical function and adjudication responsibilities properly belonging to supervisors and personnel officers. Whereas medical Taylorism supplies medical tools to be used in the administrative decisions and then looks the other way, this approach challenges the appropriateness of using internally generated medical tools at all. Dr. Monroe, as we saw, insisted that he was in no position to assess whether a "pipsqueak of a woman" was strong enough to lift "an enormous hose" and told the personnel manager to "take her out and let her try."

When adjudication functions cannot be sloughed off, a second line of defense, available in firms that have a critical mass of physicians, is to localize the contentious work in an individual physician whom the majority of employees are least likely to see clinically. Childress, the university medical director quoted in chapter 6, made sure that he and only he ruled on controversial cases so that his clinical staff would not become tainted in the eyes of potential patients. This also helped him ensure that the difficult judgments were handled with the utmost discretion.

A third strategy recognizes, as does the second, that some medical-adjudication functions may be unavoidable. Instead of enveloping them in mystery, however, the third approach takes explicit steps to build in formal protections. Procedures are clearly specified, in writing, in advance. Negative impacts on employees are cushioned to the extent possible. For example, those who are moved off a job for a health reason are guaranteed "rate retention," a roughly equivalent job at an equivalent rate of pay, seniority, and benefits.[3] Or written fair-information policies are promulgated throughout the firm so that employees sent to the medical department know what to expect and have true access to their records and a good understanding of the extent of and limits on the confidentiality the medical department can meaningfully ensure. The supervisors who send them also appreciate that theirs is the responsibility for monitoring job performance. Beyond this, some firms in the sample had or were contemplating the organization of joint labor-management committees to set ground rules and anticipate potential new problems in the medical-adjudication realm. In effect, these strategies address C. P. Snow's concerns about scientific responsibility. The strategic corporate physician consents to provide the medical tools that management needs but also plays an active role in specifying boundary conditions for their use.

Building Bridges to Labor

Relations with labor, unionized or not, are crucial to the physician who would play this strategic role. Several examples now exist of joint or tripartite studies where labor and management, and sometimes also the government, set research priorities or identify a particularly pressing research question in occupational health, arrange to support a piece of high-quality research, and constitute an expert panel capable of interpreting the research findings, when available, and charged with hammering out in advance an acceptable protocol, timetable, and procedure for communicating the results to relevant parties. Coye (1982:443–49) has proposed an extension of this approach, involving formal peer review of industry-sponsored occupational health research, using an administrative mechanism modeled after the Institutional Review Boards established to protect human subjects in studies funded by the National Institutes of Health. Coye elaborates "operational guidelines" for occupational health research that would adequately protect and respect workers, emphasizing anticipatory arrangements. The approach,

---

3. OSHA's lead standard included, as an innovative element, a "medical removal protection" clause requiring employers to move workers with elevated blood-lead levels to alternative jobs without prejudice to their pay, seniority rights, and benefits (see Yodaiken and Robbins 1980:467).

she feels, "would be an opportunity for academically based groups to be more involved and learn more about the practical problems of field trials and, in many cases, it would offer industry groups an opportunity to initiate their projects with less chance of future charges of bias based simply on criticism of their industry funding" (Coye 1982:447). Basic to any such approach is the idea that, instead of "letting science decide" in the patronizing and unilateral fashion implied in old-style medical Taylorism, mechanisms can be established that recognize the rarity of an ultimate scientific "truth" and provide an open forum for "letting science debate." Full and timely disclosure would be accorded the workers with legitimate interests in the outcome. Their intelligence and good sense would not be underestimated.

Forging Alliances with Outside Medicine

The outside physician, as Ramazzini knew, is also crucial to a serious effort at occupational health conservation. The more strategically oriented corporate physicians see as a major target of opportunity the need to engage with employees' outside physicians in a constructive and prospective policy of managing disability cases early in the illness career. There is a widespread intuitive impression among corporate physicians that an employee's disability career progresses through distinct stages, becoming increasingly intractable as time wears on.[4] The outside physician is seen as a facilitator of this destructive process; he is, in the eyes of corporate physicians, creating iatrogenic illness. Assuming that the problem involves competent and well-intentioned private physicians responding to their patients' presumed wishes, the corporate physician can perhaps improve the situation by demonstrating to the outside medical community the company's willingness to be flexible about job requirements to hasten the employee's recovery. Strategically minded corporate physicians make an effort to be part of the local medical community so that lines of communication will be open. They "run the poison control center for the boys" or sit on the hospital's quality assurance committee, help the Red Cross struggle with policy for AIDS, or even moonlight in the emergency room.

Like the disability management problem, which has been on the corporate physician's agenda for years, the more recent issue of how to manage overall community health-care costs calls for cooperative relations which strategic corporate physicians are working to develop with outside medical providers. Several companies are developing statistical

---

4. Although not to my knowledge recognized as such, this intuitive understanding of the dynamics of disability resembles Lemert's theories of primary and secondary deviance (see Lemert 1951).

profiles of the practice patterns of physicians in areas where they have large concentrations of employees. Some are exploring the possibility of using this information to identify or organize groups of more parsimonious, "preferred" providers from whom employees would be encouraged (through minor reductions in their out-of-pocket expenses) to purchase health care financed through the employee benefit plan. For the most part stimulated by the benefits and financial specialists in large firms, this thinking is being shaped also by some of the more strategically oriented corporate physicians, who see in it an opportunity to strengthen the links between the health systems inside and outside the firm.

Carving Out a Management Niche

Dr. Bennett was learning first-hand a lesson that was taught in the abstract by a management team from Exxon USA in a seminar for corporate physicians.[5] Asked what they can do when they "run out of organizational power," participants were led to the response that this is the time to "borrow some power from someone who has more than enough." Bennett was being coached by his boss, Perkins, and others (including the senior manager whose advice it was that he "be more political"). They believed he would succeed once he learned his way around the organization. Other physicians in the sample had mentors too. When one was being groomed for a vice presidency of health and safety, his predecessor died suddenly. Top management reshuffled itself to create a new reporting relationship where the partially groomed new vice president would be taken in hand by "a corporate geography mentor" of suitably high rank to have a vice-presidential-level physician reporting to him.

With or without the help of mentors, strategic corporate physicians learn organizational survival techniques—how to "build a business case for the relevance of their programs" and excite top management about some of the innovative things they want to accomplish, how to forge coalitions and alliances inside and outside the firm from which they can "borrow power" when theirs seems insufficient, how to provide enough structure and leadership for the medical programs under their direction or dissuade their own people from "lobbing shells" at them, and where to run for cover when shells start detonating. They learn, in sum, to recognize the separate sectors of their roles, to respect the competing ex-

5. Entitled "Impacting an Organization's Management," the course was offered as a "postgraduate seminar" at the Joint Conference on Occupational Health in Nashville, Tenn., on October 13, 1981, and again at the American Occupational Health Conference in Toronto on April 17, 1982. Course director was Frances X. Mahoney, Exxon USA, P.O.Box 2180, Houston, Tex. 77001.

pectations that they inevitably face, and even to harness the energy behind these expectations to help them accomplish professional ends in an overwhelmingly bureaucratic milieu.

Instead of limiting their involvement with the bureaucracy in the vain hope of avoiding the conflicts its economic ends insinuate into their roles, they engage wholeheartedly with it. Using the means it makes available, they build the coalitions and the "business cases" with which to challenge purely economic ends with more humanistic ones. But they succeed at this only in corporations that choose, for a variety of reasons, to permit them to do so.

In such organizations, strategic corporate physicians can function (together with other members of the health team) as internal auditors,[6] making sure the company is doing all it can to avoid the kind of social backlash Drucker says inevitably attends an unmanaged impact (Drucker 1973). Internal auditors are given license to probe and prod at will. (A lighthearted reminder of this appeared in a small sign on the wall of the auditor's office visited in the course of the study. It said, "In God we trust. . . . Everyone else we audit.") However unpleasant the news that internal auditors uncover in this way, managers prefer to hear it from them, with recovery time still remaining, than from an outside auditor who arrives after the action window has passed (Ackerman 1975). But the license given the internal auditor—whether financial or medical—depends on the credibility of the outside auditor as a legitimate threat.

The history of occupational medicine, as portrayed in part II, has brought progress for the profession only when the external environment has impinged on the corporation, when the external health auditor, in whatever guise, is being announced at the plant gate. The gradual progress in the field reflects the gradual increase in society's demand that employers assume responsibility for the health effects of work. Companies have remained free, however, to define their physicians' roles pretty much as they wish. How those roles will evolve in future will depend on a few major contingencies.

If toxic wastes and other environmental health issues rise to crisis proportions, then it is conceivable that corporate physicians, at least in firms dealing with chemicals, will be driven more and more into the environmental health sector of their overall role. Some of the younger corporate medical directors interviewed for the study see environmental health and toxicology as their discipline's frontier. They are most likely to be proven right if, as seems plausible, environmental health issues in general develop an increasingly strong political constituency. Such a sce-

---

6. I am indebted for this metaphor to Richard H. Egdahl, M.D., Ph.D.

nario seems probable if there continue to be galvanizing incidents like the 1985 Bhopal disaster in India and the 1986 Chernobyl nuclear accident in the USSR. In some companies, on the other hand, and perhaps for the field as a whole, a strong environmental health movement could entirely engulf the world of occupational medicine. If environmental health pressures build from the outside, new opportunities will emerge for occupational physicians, but they will arrive with an urgency that will demand rapid adaptation. If company physicians fail to rise to the challenges—fail to become more strategic as envisaged here—strong pressures (if they develop) will create new organizational forms that will close down their options and paint them even farther into a corner.

If, after the Reagan administration, occupational health is restored to the national agenda and OSHA is revitalized, strategic corporate physicians who can be effective internal auditors may yet have their day. But as long as the social and political environment remains quiescent, occupational medicine with an environmental focus is likely to stagnate and even to slip back to the status quo ante-OSHA. An alternative form of pressure, however, when regulation fails, is litigation in the courts, through such personal-injury and product-liability suits as were brought against the Manville Corporation or even through criminal sanctions. In 1984, for the first time in legal history, three officers of a corporation located outside Chicago were indicted for murder in connection with the death of a worker. The president, a plant manager, and a foreman of the now-defunct company were each convicted and sentenced to twenty-five years in jail. What this says is that a pro-business ideology at the federal government level offers no guarantee of immunity at least in extreme cases of malfeasance. How far the precedent could spread remains to be seen.

Irrespective of what government does, the Japanese influence on labor relations, the expanding service economy, and the so-called wellness revolution could result in an increasingly strong emphasis in American industry on "human resources," the quality of working life, and the pursuit of health. Such an emphasis seems particularly plausible if a convincing case is built that company sponsorship of health-enhancement programs is cost-effective. Some suggestive evidence to this effect has been developed by Johnson and Johnson,[7] which now intends to market to other companies the "Live for Life" program developed initially for its own employees. Economists express skepticism that prevention actually pays (Russell 1986), but if the encouraging results reported by a few innovating companies can be replicated, worksite health promotion

7. See Wilbur (1983), Settergren et al. (1983), Wilbur and Garner (1984), and Blair et al. (1986).

could become more than the fad it seems to be now. Should this occur, corporate physicians could find themselves functioning chiefly in the health-service delivery sector of their roles, redefined and expanded. The sector would become increasingly strategic, combining a clinical with a population orientation and defining the health service broadly to anticipate and treat all sorts of occupational stresses.

Impetus for a growing health-service role within the corporation could come as well from the general ferment in medicine. Basic changes now taking place in the medical profession may well favor the corporate practitioner. Gone is the self-sufficient solo practitioner against whose idealized image the company doctor stood in stark, invidious contrast. Rare is the practicing physician who can claim to have pure relations with his patients, uncomplicated by third-party intrusions and other conflicts of interest. Beyond the outside influences of insurance carriers and the government and the bureaucratic demands of hospitals and other institutional care settings are the basic contradictions within medicine itself, where halfway technologies (Thomas 1977) in an era of chronic degenerative diseases have written for medicine a crowded agenda of painful choices concerning when and how to begin and end life, regulate behavior, and ration scarce resources. Seen in this light, the ethical conflicts that have plagued occupational medicine lose some of their glare. The prospect of an overabundance of physicians in the years just ahead makes it all the more conceivable that physicians in training may look more favorably than they have in the past on one of the few specialties believed genuinely in need of new recruits.[8]

Even the medical-adjudication sector, as reactive as it traditionally has been, could become the springboard for a more strategically oriented role for corporate medicine, given changes now taking place in the financing and delivery of medical care. The cost-containment imperative has driven care out of inpatient hospitals while restructuring the delivery of medicine more and more into systems of "managed care." The presumption has been that major efficiencies in medical practice patterns can be achieved without serious harm to patients. Having themselves played a central and conscious role in creating the incentives to drive these changes, large employers may become concerned about their impact on the quality of care. Pressure may build for the creation of mechanisms to monitor for insufficient and inadequate care. Among the kinds of tracers and mechanisms that might be developed to assure quality, some could be established within corporate medical departments to

---

8. Statistics on medical manpower are available from the American Medical Association in Chicago. Projections of future supply were made by NIOSH (1978) and GEMENAC (1980).

monitor post-hospital convalescence as well as overall trends in morbidity and mortality among employees and their dependents. Whether corporate physicians will perceive and rise to this challenge is another question without an answer at this time.

Issues for the Future

An exploration ranging as widely as this study inevitably raises more questions than it answers. Much remains to be done in refining and testing the model developed here and using it to map the existing universe of occupational medical programs and practitioners, industry by industry and firm by firm. Doing so would bring an order to that universe heretofore conspicuously lacking.

Another line of research that follows naturally from this exploration would be to gauge in more structured studies the variety of expectations—the conflicting definitions summarized in table 9.1—for corporate occupational medicine. What do employees and their physicians really want from a company's health program, and how can they be brought into more fruitful interactions with it? What do other managers—line and staff—understand as the medical director's essential contribution? A hypothesis worth testing is whether a good "fit" between the corporate medical director's sense of his mission and the views of other relevant actors in the company correlates with other possible indicators of effectiveness such as levels of use, influence, satisfaction, and trust.

In addition, the numerous operational issues touched on in this study provide fertile ground for future investigation and practical experimentation. Among many such issues, the following stand out as particularly worthy of sustained attention.

1. Medical adjudication
   - Can in-house occupational physicians be more actively and aggressively involved in trying to improve outside practitioners' handling of chronic disease and disability? This could have important implications for health-care and disability costs, inside corporations and more generally. Where are the most promising new models for early intervention, rehabilitation, and case management, how effective and efficient are they, for what conditions, and under what circumstances are they replicable?
   - What are the essential "fair information practices" in occupational medicine, where are they most difficult to enforce, and what can be done to upgrade performance on this divisive issue? How successful in this regard are the various joint labor-management structures

being developed, and what general lessons do they suggest about how to define and pursue areas of mutual interest in occupational health protection? Is OSHA's "hazard communication" rule going to have an effect?

2. Health-care service
   - Is the delivery of health care a diversion from the more important health-protection task facing occupational medicine as hazards proliferate? Or does some amount of in-house primary care create a "health consciousness" that spills over into health conservation, broadly defined? Systematic comparisons (international, inter- and intra-industry, inter- and intra-firm) would begin to resolve this question.
3. Environmental health
   - What are the barriers to the creation of integrated data systems, and how can they be overcome? Is legislation needed to create positive incentives or at least mitigate negative ones? Could the creation of such systems be mandated? As an adjunct or alternative to corporate-sponsored systems, can a useful national occupational-health registry be developed?
4. Strategy formulation
   - Is there a new breed of occupational physician? Should there be? This last is the question that flows most directly from the current research.

A New Breed of Corporate Physician?

Whether or not there is developing (or indeed can develop) a new breed of occupational physician, and with what essential characteristics, is an empirical question of some moment for the profession and those who would play a part in charting its future course. Medical school curricula, corporate recruiting and training techniques, professional education and support programs, and government standards for medical monitoring of the workplace all rest on untested premises about the actual and potential motives behind occupational medical careers.

The available information on career patterns and choices is sketchy, anecdotal, and dated. One of the very few empirical studies to have pursued the specific point found among members of the British Society of Occupational Medicine that "less than a quarter (24 percent) of the full-time doctors [N = 390] stated that occupational medicine had been a first choice of career" (Sawtell and Cooper 1975:40). Earlier studies of the choice of public health careers (Back et al. 1958; Coker et al. 1966; Cahalan, Collette, and Hilmar 1957) were informative but probably do not apply in the radically different professional environment of the 1980s. Nor do they specifically describe an occupational medical career.

Interviews with the physicians in the present study tended to support the general impression that the specialty is for the most part entered mid-career, often more by accident than by design. One of the most eminent (Julius Whitesides) described himself as having been "seduced" into the field by an incumbent medical director with a forceful personality. Convinced that the opening would offer "the opportunity to practice an idyllic form of medicine" (in a well-endowed in-house medical program at the corporate headquarters of a highly profitable, capital-intensive firm), he entered occupational medicine directly out of his postgraduate training and stayed his whole career.

This direct path has been traveled infrequently. More common is the pattern several physicians described. They started working for a corporation on a part-time basis, often to supplement income during the lean early years of practice, and gradually slipped into full-time roles. Typically, they continued in the companies where their part-time involvement had enabled them to feel out the management and develop a modus operandi.

Finances were often a background consideration, and sometimes a triggering one. In the interchange quoted earlier between Harry Mock and an older mentor, Mock (who became a pioneer in the field) freely admitted at the outset to a mixture of motives: an idealistic vision of the opportunities in occupational medicine and a pragmatic need for money so that he could get married. Similarly, the vice president for health and safety who was assigned a "corporate geography mentor" when his predecessor suddenly died had previously been well established in academic occupational medicine. But he "looked at the demographics" and "got fed up with earning a salary that meant I was subsidizing the college educations of everyone else's kids while wondering if I was going to be able to scrape together the tuition for my own."

Many apparently shed the physician's natural antipathy toward institutional medicine during a period of military service, where they also became comfortable with the intrusion of organizational purpose into a clinical relationship. Some were escaping from traps—an assistant professorship that was beginning to look as though it would not eventuate in tenure; a house officership that failed to materialize because of trouble with the Selective Service Board; a wife who was having miscarriages and wanted her husband home more often than his private practice permitted; several group practices so successful that the hours and workload became "overwhelming," and another that foundered because some of the senior members were not bringing in their share of income; a private pediatric practice that was too "painful"; and other such personal reasons.

In these situations, the corporate post was often viewed as a temporary, temporizing move, a way to earn a steady income while reassessing and redirecting a "real" medical career. Perhaps corporate practice often does serve such a function; physicians who cycled through a corporation and returned to private practice would not be part of the sample of a study designed as this one has been. But a striking pattern among those who were in the sample was the regularity with which they mentioned having initially reacted negatively to the prospect of practicing in a business firm or having set out with the intention of leaving at the first opportunity. Dr. Ware, the corporate medical director at one *Fortune* top-ten company, offers a case in point: "The plant needed another full-time doctor and I needed to make a break. So I said I would stay for six months while I made arrangements with some colleagues to buy a building and start up a group practice. One thing led to another—maybe I'm just a procrastinator—but here I still am some twenty years later."

Procrastination is seldom the full explanation—for that physician or for others. The literature in occupational medicine often recognizes and decries this career pattern of inadvertence. The field, its representatives caution, ought not to be viewed as "a refuge"; corporate posts are not "sinecures" (Warshaw 1977). Even among the physicians in this sample who entered the field inadvertently or half-heartedly there appears to have occured at some later point a more complicated decision process than simply to coast in an undemanding or lucrative job—the sinecure notion. Many developed a sense of excitement, of challenge, in response to the opportunity to enhance the health of large numbers of people. The extrinsic rewards of the job (salary, benefits, security, and comfort) may have been the initial attraction, but the intrinsic rewards (the challenge itself) were often cited as a sustaining motivation. This, of course, may be a rationalization, especially if, as seems possible, external mobility becomes constricted once a physician enters the full-time employ of a business firm. Often it was couched in a slightly apologetic tone: "It may be pie in the sky," they would say, "but . . .", or "Then there's the odd duck like me" who thinks he can make a difference.

A few—not more than five physicians in this sample of thirty-seven—seemed to give the challenge precedence over all other considerations. They either avoided clinical roles after their training or quickly became restive in them. They felt they could "do more" with their "talents and training" than process "doorknob turners" one by one. One left a thriving family practice in search of a "broader experience" in life so that he would not become a "boring old doctor" twenty years hence. The career of Alvin Schoenleber at Standard Oil of New Jersey (Schoenleber 1950) was the early prototype for this "new breed" of occupational physician as corporate gamesman (Maccoby 1976).

If medical schools are to improve their education for occupational medicine[9] and if companies are to enhance their recruiting of new talent, then a better understanding is needed of the decisive stages in successful occupational medical careers. How, when, and why do incumbents enter the field? What are their expectations? How are these frustrated and satisfied? Are the answers to these questions fundamentally different for occupational physicians than for other groups of physicians? Are there within-group differences among occupational physicians, and how do these correlate with corporate settings and contingencies? Do different expectations and career patterns produce noticeably different conceptions of the essential mission of occupational medicine, the license and mandate entailed, the extent of occupational health hazards, and the nature of justice in the workplace when competing interests collide? How clearly is it possible to describe "effective performance" in the field?

These questions require fuller answers before it will be possible to predict with confidence whether there is in fact a significant trend toward an expanded role for corporate physicians. If there is such a trend, this study has suggested the direction it should take—movement along the medical axis from a clinical to a population orientation and along the management axis from an operational to a longer-term outlook. The result of the trend, if there is one, should be the emergence of a new breed of occupational physicians who can perform effectively and with enthusiasm as scientifically and organizationally astute strategic corporate managers, with an eye on a population and a commitment to confronting and managing long-term health risks whatever their genesis.

Lessons for the Practice of Medicine

Whatever the future may hold for occupational medicine, there are generic lessons to be extracted from the past. The "coming of the corporation" (Starr 1982) into the health-care system has fueled such concern about external pressures on modern medical practice that the experiences of company physicians—the pressures they have felt, the tradeoffs they have faced, and the lines they have endeavored to draw—are becoming increasingly pertinent for physicians everywhere.

At the heart of these experiences are inescapable tensions between individual and organizational purpose, summarized most succinctly as a balancing of the physical and emotional health of the employee with the economic viability of the firm. As these interests converge and diverge,

---

9. For writings on deficiencies in educational and training programs in occupational medicine, see Gima (1982), Kammer (1953), Kehoe (1959a), Levy (1981), Mazzocchi (1977), and Suskind (1978).

medical information and expertise can be a passive accomplice or a decisive weight in tipping the balance of power.

For the practice of medicine in what has come to be accepted as "an era of limited resources," the individual patient's needs stand juxtaposed to the demands of a particular organization and a larger social reality. As hospitals, HMOs, and newer health-care enterprises develop corporate missions and mystiques, imperatives other than "health" intrude on the patient-physician interaction. Physicians in these settings can try to wall themselves off and just be good doctors. But the experience of occupational medicine suggests that this stance is hard to sustain in a structure that divides the physician's loyalty.

Alternatively, physicians can take a cue from the more strategic of the corporate physicians, build a political base, and learn to make "business cases" for tempering short-term economic ends with longer-term, more humanistic ones. In the larger medical context, such cases will rest (as they do in corporate occupational medicine) on approaching the long-term risks to health that will attend shorter-term cutting of corners in the name of efficiency. Succeeding at this requires playing as effective members on a management team, ceding the unchallenged status as "captain" (Fuchs 1974) of a smaller medical team where everyone defers to them but they lack influence in the larger organization. As they succeed, they can begin to refine the rules of the game, in particular to ensure that policies on how medical information will be handled are as clear and fair as possible, so that affected individuals are fully informed participants in discussions and decisions concerning what is best for them. This means pushing the following kinds of issues as high as possible on the organization's agenda:

1. What organizational and economic leverage against the uncooperative patient (or the "high-cost user of health care") do physicians have in these more complex relationships with their patients? The fact that an industrial medical service has the economic authority of the employer as an implicit prod to foster compliance is revealed in the case of alcoholism and drug dependency when the "leverage of the job" becomes an explicit therapeutic device known as "constructive confrontation" (Walsh 1982). Whether or not they are recognized, organizations house other sources of equally strong coercive power; these diminish in importance as the authority of the organization wanes.
2. Where there is such power, physicians need to recognize it and to ensure that adequate protections are in place. This means defining fair information practices and communicating them effectively. One lesson from occupational medicine is that there should never be occasion to discuss an employee's medical suitability for a position or be-

nefit he or she wants without that individual's knowledge and prior consent.
3. As the organization's control becomes increasingly strong, an effort needs to be made to examine and sort out competing claims on limited resources in the context of different notions of justice—of who is bearing risks and reaping rewards. It is here that occupational medicine is a microcosm for trends in medical practice. Company physicians have struggled in settings where resources available to conserve health have been sharply constrained. They have weighed tradeoffs on chemical toxins, when the probabilities were unknown and the cost of another increment in knowledge lay beyond the reach of their budgets. They have faced the reality of having to stop short of absolute safety and accept a level of risk. They have served as medical adjudicators, balancing individual and organizational claims. And what this experience shows is how difficult it is to escape the gray zones of moral ambiguity when medicine is practiced in a closed financial system.

Some company physicians have handled these pressures poorly, accepting a degree of callousness and myopia as an inevitable consequence of the profit imperative or allowing themselves to be coopted by the blandishments of corporate life. But others have raised the level of debate in the corporation and fought successfully for greater attention to the longer-term health consequences of business decisions. Because this typically occurs only when outside pressures on the company are making it possible for in-house physicians to function like internal auditors—when the outside auditor is a legitimate threat—another lesson of occupational medicine is that simply elevating the physician's status within the organization may not be sufficient to preserve what is best at the core of his role. His voice inside the organization may have to be amplified by externally generated demands, such as those from organized labor, government regulatory agencies, public-interest groups, and the press. As medical practice is absorbed more and more by large bureaucracies, public-interest efforts on behalf of health-care consumers will assume increased importance.

If what we are now seeing for modern medical practice is a passing of the age of innocence into a long period of constraints and choices, then physicians are losing the protection they derived from insisting on a decision rule driven by single-minded devotion to each individual patient. This will occasion a growing need for the kinds of doctor-managers into which some occupational physicians have begun to evolve: conscious of moral dilemmas, politically skilled and astute, sensitive to conflicting demands on their loyalty, accepting of limitations on both resources and knowledge but committed to future progress, meanwhile doing their best to apply their expertise in search of defensible but imperfect solutions to complex problems.

Constantly importuned to enlarge their mandates and broaden their notions of health to include threats such as tobacco and alcohol advertising, seat-belt use, poverty and malnutrition, even nuclear war, physicians may seem unlikely nominees for "the management teams" of organizations in which they work. Perhaps they should stick to what they do best—just as some have argued that the business of business is to turn a profit, resisting the diversion of other social demands. Indeed, the case is sometimes made for medicine that "in the long run the social obligation of the physician is to ignore society" (Halberstam 1974). Drucker (1973) enlarged the discussion of corporate social responsibility by pointing out how failing to manage impacts on society can cost companies a social backlash that erodes or even forecloses future profits. The omen from occupational medicine, finally, is how self-defeating it will be, as physicians are absorbed by complex bureaucracies, for them to overlook issues of structure, mission, policy, politics, roles, and role conflicts. These issues will ordain the way physicians can practice. To ignore them will be to jeopardize much of the trust that has long been the foundation of effective medical practice.

Appendix 1 ■ Company Physicians and Others Quoted in Chapters 4 through 9

SYDNEY ALLEN, M.D. [pseud.] As the staff member representing occupational medicine at a national professional society, he worried that cost pressures would further erode his specialty's potential influence in corporations. He had been a corporate medical director in stints at two large firms.

ARNOLD BENNETT, M.D. [pseud.] The newly appointed chief medical officer in a top information firm, he was concerned about the oversight of fifty full-time physicians in the company's growing medical department. Also, he described a series of "shoot-outs" he was having with management.

MANFRED BLUMGARTEN, M.D. [pseud.] He was corporate medical director, with almost thirty years' experience at an international chemical firm employing 125,000 people in 60 countries and 320 operating companies, based in Europe. As the titular head of a medical staff of 173 physicians world-wide, he worried about the encroachment of ever more stringent regulations and described efforts to "keep the black spots off [his] white coat."

EDWARD BOWER, M.D. [pseud.] Having just resigned his post at a 13,000-employee company in New England after twelve years as corporate medical director there, he was retreating to a job at a midwestern university at a substantial cut in pay and gave vent to considerable frustration over what he termed the "hypocrisy" of management at his former company, where his "dreams" of expanding the medical service had been dashed.

RALPH BRADFORD, M.D. [pseud.] The medical director for a company based in New England with 35,000 employees, he described things he did to align himself with the employees in disciplinary actions and also told of inviting medical students in to expose them to occupational practice, but he spoke of it in a way that made it sound routine and uninspiring.

JAMES CHILDRESS, M.D. [pseud.] After ten years as medical director of a large and active university health service, he worried a lot about how to create a climate of trust. In this he saw close parallels between university-based occupational medicine and industrial practice, in which he had previously engaged part-time.

GERALD COHEN, M.D. [pseud.] A part-time staff psychiatrist with a midwestern firm in the metals business, he told an anecdote to characterize how a physician deteriorates into a "company doc" in the pejorative sense and discussed his own work interviewing employees being assigned to international posts.

HANS EMMERICH, M.D. [pseud.] Just out of training as a physician and Ph.D. ergonomist, he was consulting to several firms and trying to find a niche for his unusual blend of skills. In the end, he took a job as an on-camera doctor for a television station.

SARAH FARMER, M.D. [pseud.] Associate medical director in a large New York firm with a group-practice-style in-house service, she took palpable pleasure in the personal relationships she sustained with patients and former patients. For the first seven and a half years of her involvement with the firm, she had worked as an OB-GYN consultant a half day a week and remarked on "how different" occupational medicine is from the dominant stereotypes other physicians carry.

TREVOR GOTTLIEB, M.D. [pseud.] Vice president and corporate medical director of a large company struggling with very serious health hazards, he had previously been a government scientist and, in his new corporate role, was outspoken in his criticism of government regulators and the press.

ROBERT INGERSOLL, M.D., J.D. [pseud.] As corporate medical director of a forest products company in the West, he wanted responsibility for the "whole ball of wax"—not just employee health services, but benefits and human resources too. When that did not materialize, he left and took a job on the East Coast as a principal in a small entrepreneurial firm specializing in health-care cost management.

ISAAC KAPLAN, M.D. [pseud.] The medical director for a large public firm, he had been a member of the committee that drafted the American Occupational Medical Association's Code of Ethical Conduct. He argued that a "greater good" is served by scrupulously preserving the confidentiality of employee medical records, so that programs can be effective.

ARTHUR LAWRENCE, M.D. [pseud.] An internist with experience in both a university-based group practice and another industrial firm, he was hired to replace Dr. Bower, who, he believed, had "painted himself into a corner," where he was experiencing an intolerable loss of clinical acuity.

FRANK LEE, M.D. [pseud.] Corporate medical director for a 40,000-employee defense contractor and computer parts manufacturer, he had left his private practice three years before for the corporate job and described his new role with zest, tempered with a touch of regret at having been shut out of "the cloakroom" of private medical practice.

THOMAS MAXWELL, M.D. [pseud.] The senior corporate physician with a healthcare products firm strongly emphasizing employee wellness, his background was in toxicology, the area, in his view, "where the action is for occupational medicine."

JACK MCCARTHY, M.D. [pseud.] Corporate medical officer for one of the ten largest chemical manufacturers, he argued that building epidemiological data bases was in industry's long-term interest, although an explosion of occupational disease was in his view unlikely to occur.

MARY MCDONALD, M.D. [pseud.] A young physician-epidemiologist on the part-time payroll of one of the large international unions, she took a stand on worker privacy distinctly at odds with corporate physicians' views. The physician's imperative, she believed, was to protect the worker's secrets from his employer.

HAROLD MONROE, M.D. [pseud.] At a 10,000-employee chemical firm, he was a corporate medical director who clearly saw his role as dedicated to employee health protection. He also served as an officer in several national professional organizations and called himself an "odd duck" because he followed a "formal pathway" to occupational medicine, with a master's and doctorate in public health and then a residency in an occupational medical unit in a corporation.

STANLEY MORRISON, M.D. [pseud.] Former vice president and corporate medical director at a large metals manufacturer with mines all over the world, after his death his philosophy was still evident in the comments of several physicians still at his firm, including Drs. William Neeley, Gerald Cohen, and Bernard Tyson.

WILLIAM NEELEY, M.D. [pseud.] A plant physician in Tennessee, he started with the company at ten hours a week while he maintained his private practice. During the next two years he gradually expanded his time with the company to eight hours a day, five days a week, still conducting his private practice, but only at night. After ten years he closed his private practice; he had grown weary of billing and of demanding patients.

LLOYD OPEL, M.D. [pseud.] This corporate medical director of a large public utility was especially conscious of relations with outside physicians. He saw no way for a company physician to avoid involvement in disability management and argued for an aggressive approach that essentially took the private practitioner "off the hook."

SAMUEL PERKINS [pseud.] The personnel vice president to whom Arnold Bennett reported, he was "coaching" him on how to survive in the corporate thicket. Also he was especially conscious of mounting concerns among employees about the hazards to which they were being exposed on the job.

JUSTIN POULTER, M.D. [pseud.] The only full-time physician employed by a public utility of about 4,000 employees, he had tried unsuccessfully to find a way to secure formal training in public health, while continuing on the job.

NORMAN SCHULTZ, M.D. [pseud.] A vice president and corporate medical director for a large consumer-products firm headquartered in the Midwest, he spoke of the need upper-level managers have for access to occasional professional counsel from an organizational peer who can exercise the utmost circumspection.

CHARLES SINSKY, M.D. [pseud.] For eighteen years the vice president and corporate medical director at a large New York bank, he voiced concerns about the quality of care the bank's employees were receiving from their outside physicians and wanted to define an activist role second-guessing those treatment decisions. His influence was sharply limited, though, and other managers criticized his indiscretion.

MICHAEL SWIFT [pseud.] The nonphysician director of health and safety for a large chemical manufacturing firm, he felt the need for expanded and integrated data systems and advances in epidemiological capabilities.

FRED TYLER, M.D. [pseud.] Elevated to corporate medical director after fourteen years in the field as a division medical director, he was reflecting on the adjustment that the change in status entailed.

BERNARD TYSON, M.D. [pseud.] In his view there is a real conflict, often denied by his colleagues, between winning the trust of employees, as their advocates, and the respect of managers, as effective members of the management team. He saw the two issues as intertwined because advocating for employees often involves calling for expensive changes that it takes effective management to shepherd through successfully.

DALE WARE, M.D. [pseud.] An internist only recently attracted to occupational medicine, he remarked on how ambiguous the boundaries were around his new specialty and described the somewhat inadvertent process through which he had entered the occupational medical field.

JULIUS WHITESIDES, M.D. [pseud.] At one of the world's largest firms, a petrochemical producer with 100,000 employees worldwide and 400 full-time health professionals, about 40 at headquarters, he was corporate medical director for over a decade. Nearing retirement, he was mindful of massive changes in expectations for occupational medicine in his thirty years of practice, but also of his specialty's failure to overcome its problems of trust.

RUSSELL WYMAN, M.D. [pseud.] This medical director for a firm with 35,000 employees insisted that he was "not a company doctor" because a company doctor is "four-square against the employee," and then he described how he effected a "miracle cure" by indirectly threatening the job of an employee who had "too much con in his personality."

Appendix 2 ■ Profile of Interviews

Table A.1
Overview of the Data Base

	Subjects	Interviews
Exploratory interviews		
Occupational physicians	25	41
Managers of physicians	3	3
Other health managers	4	4
Labor	4	4
Academics, government, other informants	8	9
Total	44	61
Structured case studies: five firms, 3–5 days/firm		
Occupational physicians	12	30
Personnel/industrial relations/directors	6	11
Operations managers, engineers	3	3
Industrial hygiene, safety, nursing staff	7	10
Employee benefits staff	4	6
Counseling, EEO directors	4	4
Biostatisticians, epidemiologists	2	2
Total	38	66
Grand Total	82	127
Other observations/ interactions[a]		
Occupational physicians (in addition to the 37 accounted for above)	18	
Total occupational physicians	55	

Note: Interviews were conducted between February 1978 and October 1982.

a. Significant interactions at professional meetings and conferences, as well as round-table discussions convened expressly for purposes of the study.

Table A.2
The Sample of Corporations (N = 29)

Rankings (1982 sales, *Fortune* 500 listing)	
Top 10 industrial	3
Top 10 financial	4
10–50	2
51–100	5
101–200	6
201–250	2
Unranked	7
Total	29
Industry types	
Chemical	2
Banking	2
Electronics, appliances	2
Glass, concrete, abrasives	1
Insurance	2
Measuring, scientific, photographic equipment	1
Metals manufacturing	1
Metal products	1
Office equipment	3
Paper, fiber, wood products	2
Petroleum refining	1
Pharmaceuticals	3
Public agency	1
Rubber, plastic products	1
Textiles, vinyl flooring	1
University	1
Utilities	4
Total	29
Employment size	
Range	3,800–404,000
Mean	72,591
Unionized	
Yes	17
Mostly not	12
Headquarters location (U.S. census regions)	
Northeast	24
New York/New Jersey/Connecticut	13
Massachusetts	9
South	1
North central	2
West	2

Table A.2 (*continued*)

Geographic configuration		
Concentrated		10
Moderately dispersed		10
Dispersed		9
Physician-employee ratio		
mean (N = 25)	1:15,870	
low	1:63,000	
high	1:205	
(Full-time physicians, domestic operations: total employees, worldwide)		

Table A.3
The Intensive Case Studies

	Fortune rank (1981 sales)	Industry type (SIC)	Markets	Employment size (approx.)	Union	Geographical[a]	Hazards[b]	Corporate structure type[c]	Principal role sector[d]
Firm A	150–200	Metal products	Consumer	30,000	No	International, mostly concentrated units	Negligible	Type II	Health-care Service
Firm B	250–300	Measuring, scientific and photographic equipment	Consumer and industrial	17,000	No	Mostly concentrated in five major locations	Moderate but dynamic (chemicals in batch processing)	Type II	Medical Adjudication
Firm C	Unranked	Utility	Consumer and industrial	50,000	Yes	Dispersed over a limited region (northeastern U.S.)	Moderate and stable (physical and chemical)	Type II	Medical Adjudication
Firm D	Top 10	Office equipment	Business, consumer and industrial	200,000	No	International, highly decentralized and dispersed with some large manufacturing units	Moderate and dynamic (chemicals in fast-moving technology)	Type I	Environmental medicine/strategy formulation

Table A.3 (*continued*)
The Intensive Case Studies

	Fortune rank (1981 sales)	Industry type (SIC)	Markets	Employment size (approx.)	Union	Geographical[a]	Hazards[b]	Corporate structure type[c]	Principal role sector[d]
Firm E	50–100	Metals	Industrial	45,000	Yes	International, moderately dispersed; mostly large units	Extensive but stable (physical and chemical)	Type I	Environmental medicine/strategy formulation

a. All are headquartered in the northeastern United States.
b. The classification of hazards as negligible, moderate, or extensive combines impressionistic evidence about two dimensions of occupational health hazards: how many different hazardous substances are involved in production and what proportion of the workforce works with those substances? The dynamic/stable dimension reflects the firm's pace of technological development and whether the hazards it confronts are mostly well-known to the company (and to the field) or are new and fast-breaking.
c. Typology is developed in chapter 4, figure 4.2.
d. Role sectors are developed in chapter 5. See figure 5.1.

■ References

Abrams, William. 1976. "Industry Beckons MDs." *New York Times* (28 November): 1.
Ackerman, Robert W. 1975. *The Social Challenge to Business.* Cambridge: Harvard University Press.
Agran, Larry. 1977. *The Cancer Connection.* New York: St. Martin's Press.
Alderman, Michael H., and Ellie E. Schoenbaum. 1975. "Detection and Treatment of Hypertension at the Work Site." *New England Journal of Medicine* 293: 65–68.
Allison, Graham. 1971. *Essence of Decision.* Boston: Little Brown.
Altenstetter, Christa, ed. 1981. *Innovation in Health Policy and Service Delivery: A Cross-National Perspective. Research on Service Delivery,* vol. 3. Cambridge, Mass.: Oelgeschlager, Gunn & Hain.
Altman, Lawrence K. 1979. "The Doctor's World." *New York Times* (29 May). C1.
American Occupational Medical Association. 1976. "Code of Ethical Conduct for Physicians Providing Occupational Medical Services." Chicago: The Association.
———. 1979. "Scope of Occupational Health Programs and Occupational Medical Practice." Chicago: The Association.
———. 1981. "Careers in Occupational Medicine." Chicago: The Association.
Ames, Bruce N. 1979. "Identifying Environmental Chemicals Causing Mutations and Cancer." *Science* 204:592.
Arnstein, Robert L. 1986. "Divided Loyalties in Adolescent Psychiatry: Late Adolescence." *Social Science and Medicine* 23: 797–802.
"An Asbestos Bankruptcy." 1982. *Newsweek* (6 Sept.):54–57.
Ashford, Nicholas A. 1976. *Crisis in the Workplace.* Cambridge: MIT Press.
Auerbach, Joseph. 1984. "Can Inside Counsel Wear Two Hats?" *Harvard Business Review* (September/October): 80–86.
Back, Kurt W., Robert E. Coker, Jr., Thomas G. Donnelly, and Bernard S. Phillips. 1958. "Public Health as a Career of Medicine: Secondary Choice within a Profession." *American Sociological Review* 23:533–41.
Bailyn, Lotte, and Edgar H. Schein. 1980. *Living with Technology: Issues at Mid-Career.* Cambridge: MIT Press.

REFERENCES

Barber, Bernard. 1967. *Drugs and Society.* New York: Russell Sage Foundation.

Barnard, Chester I. 1968. *The Functions of the Executive*, 30th anniversary ed. Cambridge: Harvard University Press.

Barth, Peter S., and H. Allen Hunt. 1980. *Workers' Compensation and Work-Related Diseases.* Cambridge: MIT Press.

Bauer, Raymond A. 1978. "The Corporate Response Process." *Research in Corporate Social Performance and Policy* 1:99–122.

Bayer, Ronald. 1982. "Reproductive Hazards in the Workplace: Bearing the Burden of Fetal Risk." *Milbank Memorial Fund Quarterly/Health and Society* 60:633–56.

Becker, Howard S., Blanche Greer, Everett C. Hughes, and Anselm L. Strauss. 1961. *Boys in White: Student Culture in Medical School.* Chicago: University of Chicago Press.

Belair, Robert R. 1981. "Employee Health Record Privacy and the Occupational Physician." *Occupational Health Law. See* LaDou 1981.

Belk, H. Dean. 1983. "Results of AOMA Member Survey on Medical Care Cost Containment." *Journal of Occupational Medicine* 25:233–37.

Bell, Daniel. 1973. *The Coming of Post-Industrial Society.* New York: Basic Books.

Ben-David, Joseph. 1958. "The Professional Role of the Physician in Bureaucratic Medicine: A Study in Role Conflict." *Human Relations* 2:901–11.

Berger, Peter. 1963. *Invitation to Sociology: A Humanistic Perspective.* Garden City, N.Y.: Doubleday (Anchor).

Berman, Daniel M. 1977. "Why Work Kills: A Brief History of Occupational Safety and Health in the United States." *International Journal of Health Services* 7: 63–87.

———. 1978. *Death on the Job.* New York: Monthly Review Press.

Bingham, Eula. 1982. "Introduction," in *Occupational Safety and Health. See* Goldsmith and Kerr 1982.

Blair, S., P. Piserchia, C. Wilbur, and J. Crowder. 1986. "A Public Health Intervention Model for Work-Site Health Promotion." *Journal of the American Medical Association* 255: 921–26.

Bledstein, Burton. 1976. *The Culture of Professionalism.* New York: W. W. Norton.

Block, Duane L. 1977. "The Quest for Competence." *Journal of Occupational Medicine* 19:315–18.

Bloom, Samuel W., and Robert N. Wilson. 1979. "Patient-Practitioner Relationships." In *Handbook of Medical Sociology. See* Freeman, Levine, and Reeder 1979.

"Blue Book of Industry." 1938. *Industrial Medicine* 7: 141.

Blum, John. 1983. "Potential Liability in Corporate Medical Programs." In *Corporate Medical Departments. See* Egdahl and Walsh 1983.

Boden, Leslie I. 1982. "Presumptive Standards: Can They Improve Occupational Disease Compensation?" In *Legal and Ethical Dilemmas in Occupational Health. See* Lee and Rom 1982.

Bond, M. B., J. E. Buchwalter, and D. K. Perkin. 1968. "An Occupational Health Program." *Archives of Environmental Health* 17:1–8.

Bosk, Charles L. 1979. *Forgive and Remember: Managing Medical Failure.* Chicago: University of Chicago Press.

Brandes, Stuart. 1976. *American Welfare Capitalism*. Chicago: University of Chicago Press.

Braverman, Harry. 1974. *Labor and Monopoly Capital*. New York: Monthly Review Press.

Breslow, Lester, and Anne R. Somers. 1977. "The Lifetime Health Monitoring Program: A Practical Approach to Preventive Medicine." *New England Journal of Medicine* 296:601–08.

British Medical Association. 1980. "The Occupational Physician." London: The Association.

Brodeur, Paul. 1974. *Expendable Americans*. New York: Viking Press.

———. 1977. *The Zapping of America: Microwaves, Their Deadly Risk, and the Cover-up*. New York: W. W. Norton.

———. 1985. *Outrageous Misconduct: The Asbestos Industry on Trial*. New York: Pantheon.

Brown, E. Richard. 1979. *Rockefeller Medicine Men*. Berkeley: University of California Press.

Bucher, Rue. 1962. "Pathology: A Study of Social Movements within a Profession." *Social Problems* 10:40–51.

Bucher, Rue, and Strauss Anselm. 1961. "Professions in Process." *American Journal of Sociology* 66: 325–34.

Bundy, Merle. 1976. "How Do We Assure That the Worker's Health is the Occupational Physician's Primary Concern?" *Journal of Occupational Medicine* 18:671–73.

Bunker, John D., Benjamin A. Barnes, and Frederick Mosteller, eds. 1977. *Costs, Risks and Benefits of Surgery*. New York: Oxford University Press.

Burchard, Waldo W. 1954. "Role Conflicts of Military Chaplains." *American Sociological Review* 19: 528–35.

Burton, Wayne N., Paul R. Eggum, and Phillip J. Keller. 1981. "'High Cost' Employees in an Occupational Alcoholism Program." *Journal of Occupational Medicine* 23:259–62.

Cahalan, Don, Patricia Collette, and Norman A. Hilmar. 1957. "Career Interests and Expectations of U.S. Medical Students." *Journal of Medical Education* 32:557–63.

Callahan, Daniel, and Willard Gaylin. 1978. "The Psychiatrist as Double Agent." *Hastings Center Report* 4:12–14.

Canadian Task Force on the Periodic Health Examination. 1979. "The Periodic Health Examination." *Canadian Medical Association Journal* 121:1193–1254.

———. 1980. *Periodic Health Examination Monograph*. Hull, Quebec: Canadian Government Publishing Centre.

"Can You Pass the Job Test?" 1986. *Newsweek* (5 May):46–53.

Carrick, David. 1975. "The Company Doctor." *Journal of Occupational Medicine* 17:652–53.

Chandler, Alfred D., Jr. 1962. *Strategy and Structure: Chapters in the History of the Industrial Enterprise*. Cambridge: MIT Press.

———. 1977. *The Visible Hand: The Managerial Revolution in American Business*. Cambridge: Harvard University Press.

Cochrane, A. L. 1971. *Effectiveness and Efficiency.* London: Nuffield Provincial Hospitals Trust.

Coker, Robert E., Jr., Kurt W. Back, Thomas G. Donnelly, Norman Miller, and Bernard S. Phillips. 1966. "Medical Careers in Public Health." *Milbank Memorial Fund Quarterly/Health and Society* 44: part I, entire issue.

Collen, Morris F., Sidney R. Garfield, Robert H. Richart, James H. Duncan, and Robert Feldman. 1977. "Cost Analyses of Alternative Health Examination Modes." *Archives of Internal Medicine* 137:73–79

Collings, Gilbeart H., Jr. 1977. "Health—A Corporate Dilemma; Health Care Management—A Corporate Solution." In *Background Papers on Industry's Changing Role in Health Care Delivery. See* Egdahl 1977.

———. 1982. "Managing the Health of the Employee." *Journal of Occupational Medicine* 24:15–17.

Collings, Gilbeart H., Jr., and Loring W. Wood. 1972. "Health Care Delivery in Industrial Medical Departments." Unpublished paper presented at the 19th annual meeting of the American College of Preventive Medicine, 13 November, in Atlantic City, N.J.

Committee on Public Information in the Prevention of Occupational Cancer, National Academy of Sciences. 1977. "Public Information in the Prevention of Occupational Cancer: Proceedings of a Symposium," December 1976. Springfield, Va.: National Technical Information Service.

Commoner, Barry. 1977. "The Promise and Perils of Petrochemicals." *New York Times Magazine* (25 September): 38–73.

Conrad, Peter, and Rochelle Kern. 1986. *The Sociology of Health and Illness: Critical Perspectives.* New York: St. Martin's Press.

Conrad, Peter, and Joseph W. Schneider. 1980. *Deviance and Medicalization: From Badness to Sickness.* St. Louis: C. V. Mosby.

Coser, Lewis A. 1971. *Masters of Sociological Thought.* New York: Harcourt Brace Jovanovich.

Coye, Molly Joel. 1979. "Crisis: Control in the Workplace—A Review of Three Major Works in Occupational Health." *International Journal of Health Services* 9: 169–83.

———. 1982. "Ethical Issues of Occupational Medicine Research." In *Legal and Ethical Issues in Occupational Health. See* Lee and Rom 1982.

Coye, Molly Joel, Mark Douglas Smith, and Anthony Mazzocchi. 1984. "Occupational Health and Safety: Two Steps Forward, One Step Back." In *Reforming Medicine,* ed. Victor W. Sidel and Ruth Sidel. New York: Pantheon Books.

Dalton, Melville. 1950. "Conflict between Staff and Line Managerial Officers." *American Sociological Review* 15:342–51.

Daniels, Arlene Kaplan. 1969. "The Captive Professional: Bureaucratic Limitations on the Practice of Military Psychiatry." *Journal of Health and Social Behavior* 10:255–65.

———. 1972. "Military Psychiatry: The Emergence of a Subspecialty." In *Medical Men and Their Work. See* Freidson and Lorber 1972.

———. 1975. "Advisory and Coercive Functions in Psychiatry." *Sociology of Work and Occupations* 2: 55–78.

Davidson, Ray. 1970. *Peril on the Job*. Washington: Public Affairs Press.
Davies, Celia. 1983. "Professionals in Bureaucracies: The Conflict Thesis Revisited." In *The Sociology of the Professions*. *See* Dingwall and Lewis 1983.
Davis, Kingsley. 1949. *Human Society*. New York: Macmillan.
Davis, M. F., K. Rosenberg, D. C. Iverson, T. M. Vernon, and J. Bauer. 1983. "Worksite Health Promotion in Colorado." *Public Health Reports* 4:45–55.
Davis, Michael M. 1932. "Transactions of College of Physicians of Philadelphia." 4th series, 1934, 2:65. Quoted in *Occupational Health in America*. *See* Selleck and Whittaker 1962.
Department of Continuing Education, Harvard Medical School. 1980. "Periodic Health Exams in Perspective." *Harvard Medical School Letter* 5:1–4.
Derber, Charles. 1982. *Professionals as Workers: Mental Labor in Advanced Capitalism*. Boston: G.K. Hall.
Dingwall, Robert, and Philip Lewis, eds. 1983. *The Sociology of the Professions*. New York: St. Martin's.
Dinman, Bertram D. 1980. "Occupational Health and the Reality of Risk—An Eternal Dilemma of Tragic Choices." *Journal of Occupational Medicine* 22:153–57.
"The Doctors Doctors Go To." 1981. *Boston Magazine* 73:126.
Doll, Richard. 1981. "Relevance of Epidemiology to Policies for the Prevention of Cancer." *Journal of Occupational Medicine* 23:601–08.
Donnelly, Patrick G. 1982. "The Origins of the Occupational Safety and Health Act of 1970." *Social Problems* 30: 13–25.
Drucker, Peter F. 1973. *Management: Tasks, Responsibilities, Practices*. New York: Harper and Row.
Dubos, René. 1959. *Mirage of Health*. New York: Harper and Row.
Dunning, P. M. 1961. "Occupational Health: An Executive Philosophy." *Archives of Environmental Health* 3: 111–13.
Eastman, Crystal. 1910. *Work-Accidents and the Law*. New York: Charities Publication Committee, Russell Sage Foundation.
Egdahl, R. H. 1977. *Background Papers on Industry's Changing Role in Health Care Delivery*. New York: Springer-Verlag.
Egdahl, R. H., and D. C. Walsh, eds. 1977. *Payer, Provider, Consumer: Industry Confronts Health Care Costs*. New York: Springer-Verlag.
———. 1978. *Health Services and Health Hazards: The Employee's Need to Know*. New York: Springer-Verlag.
———. 1983. *Corporate Medical Departments: A Changing Agenda?* Cambridge: Ballinger.
Ehrenreich, Barbara, and John Ehrenreich. 1978. "Medicine and Social Control." In *The Cultural Crisis of Modern Medicine*, ed. J. Ehrenreich. New York: Monthly Review Press.
Epstein, Samuel S. 1978. *The Politics of Cancer*. San Francisco: Sierra Club Books.
Equal Employment Opportunity Commission, Civil Service Commission, Department of Labor, and Department of Justice. 1978. "Adoption by Four Agencies of Uniform Guidelines on Employee Selection Procedures." *Federal Register* 43:38290–315.

"Ethics in Occupational Medicine." 1980. *The Lancet* (19 July): 134.
Etzioni, Amitai. 1964. *Modern Organizations*. Foundations for Modern Sociology Series. Englewood Cliffs, N.J.: Prentice-Hall.
Felton, Jean S. 1976. "200 Years of Occupational Medicine in the U.S." *Journal of Occupational Medicine* 18:809–17.
Ferguson, Allen R., and E. Phillip LaVeen, eds. 1981. *The Benefits of Health and Safety Regulation*. Boston: Ballinger.
Field, Mark G. 1953. "Structured Strain in the Role of the Soviet Physician." *American Journal of Sociology* 58: 493–502.
———. 1957. *Doctor and Patient in Soviet Russia*. Cambridge: Harvard University Press.
Fielding, Jonathan E. 1982a. "Effectiveness of Employee Health Improvement Programs." *Journal of Occupational Medicine* 24:907–16.
———. 1982b. "Appraising the Health of Health Risk Appraisal." *American Journal of Public Health* 72:337–40.
———. 1984. "Health Promotion and Disease Prevention at the Worksite." *Annual Review of Public Health* 5:237–66.
Fielding, J. E., and L. Breslow. 1983. "Health Promotion Programs Sponsored by California Employers." *American Journal of Public Health* 73:538–41.
Fishbein, Gershon W. 1982. "Don't Economize on Health and Safety, Cowan Tells Industry—But, But." *Occupational Health and Safety Letter* 12:1.
Follman, Joseph F., Jr. 1978. *The Economics of Industrial Health: History, Theory, and Practice*. New York: AMACOM (A Division of American Management Associations).
Foulkes, Fred K. 1973. "*Learning to Live with OSHA*." Harvard Business Review (November/December): 57–66.
———. 1980. *Personnel Policies in Large Nonunion Companies*. Englewood Cliffs, N.J.: Prentice-Hall.
Fox, Daniel M. 1975. "Social Policy and City Politics: Tuberculosis Reporting in New York, 1889–1900." *Bulletin of the History of Medicine* 49:169–95.
Fox, Renée C. 1961. "Physicians on the Drug Industry Side of the Prescription Blank: Their Dual Commitment to Medical Science and Business." *Journal of Health and Human Behavior* 2: 3–16.
Freedman, Audrey. 1981. *Industry Response to Health Risk*. New York: The Conference Board.
———. 1983. "Dilemmas in the Company Response to Health Risk." In *Corporate Medical Departments*. See Egdahl and Walsh 1983.
Freeman, Howard E., Sol Levine, and Leo G. Reeder, eds. 1979. *Handbook of Medical Sociology*. Englewood Cliffs, N.J.: Prentice-Hall.
Freidson, Eliot. 1970a. *Profession of Medicine*. New York: Dodd, Mead.
———. 1970b. *Professional Dominance: The Social Structure of Medical Care*. New York: Aldine.
———. 1984. "The Changing Nature of Professional Control." *Annual Review of Sociology* 10:1–20.
———. 1986. *Professional Powers*. Chicago: University of Chicago Press.
Freidson, Eliot, and Judith Lorber, eds. 1972. *Medical Men and Their Work*. Chicago: Aldine.

Friedland, John. 1978. "The Challenge of Informing Workers of Job-Related Health Hazards." In *Health Services and Health Hazards. See* Egdahl and Walsh 1978.
Friere, Paulo. 1968. *Pedagogy of the Oppressed.* Trans. by Myra Bergman Ramos. New York: Seaburg Press.
Fuchs, Victor R. 1974. *Who Shall Live?* New York: Basic Books.
Galbraith, John Kenneth. 1967. *The New Industrial State.* Boston: Houghton Mifflin.
Gellman, Robert M. 1986. "Divided Loyalties: A Physician's Responsibilities in an Information Age." *Social Science and Medicine* 23:817–26.
GEMENAC (Report of the Graduate Medical Education National Advisory Committee to the Secretary, Department of Health and Human Services II). 1980. Washington, D.C.:GPO.
Gima, Alfred S. 1982. "Orienting Medical Students in Occupational Medicine." *Journal of Occupational Medicine* 24:44–46.
Ginzberg, Eli. 1977. *The Limits of Health Reform.* New York: Basic Books.
Glasser, Melvin A. 1976. "Workers' Health." *American Journal of Public Health* 66:529–31.
Goffman, Erving. 1952. "On Cooling the Mark Out: Some Aspects of Adaptation to Failure." *Psychiatry* 15: 451–63.
Goldman, Peter. 1983. "The American Dream," *Newsweek* (special anniversary issue) 101:passim.
Goldner, Fred H., and R. R. Ritti, 1967. "Professionalization as Career Immobility." *American Journal of Sociology*: 489–502.
Goldsmith, Frank, and Loren Kerr. 1982. *Occupational Safety and Health. The Prevention and Control of Work-Related Hazards.* New York: Human Sciences Press.
Goldstein, Bernard, Lawrence G. Northwood, and Rhoda L. Goldstein. 1960. "Medicine in Industry: Problems of Administrators and Practitioners." *Journal of Health and Human Behavior* 1: 259–68.
Goldstein, Rhoda L., and Bernard Goldstein. 1967. *Doctors and Nurses in Industry: Social Aspects of In-Plant Medical Programs.* New Brunswick, N.J.: Institute of Management and Labor Relations.
Gompers, Samuel. 1910. "The Price We Pay." *American Federationist* 17.
Gorlin, Harriet. 1981. "Personnel Practices III: Employee Services, Work Rules." Bulletin 95. New York: The Conference Board.
Gouldner, Alvin W. 1957. "Cosmopolitans and Locals: Toward an Analysis of Latent Social Roles—I." *Administrative Science Quarterly* 2: 281–306.
———. 1978. "The New Class Project." *Theory and Society* 6:2.
Green, Robert W., ed. 1959. *Protestantism and Capitalism: The Weber Thesis and Its Critics.* Boston: D. C. Heath.
Greer, William E. R., W. Kantowitz, and P. S. White. 1977. "Comprehensive Care through Physicians Serving in Both Corporate and Private Practice." In *Background Papers on Industry's Changing Role in Health Care Delivery. See* Egdahl 1977.
Gross, Neal, Ward S. Mason, and Alexander W. McEachern. 1958. *Explorations in Role Analysis: Studies of the School Superintendency Role.* New York: John Wiley & Sons.

REFERENCES

Gruenberg, Barry. 1980. "The Happy Worker: An Analysis of Educational and Occupational Differences in Determinants of Job Satisfaction." *American Journal of Sociology* 86:247–71.

Gurin, Joel. 1981. "Alien Chemicals, Fragile Earth." *Think* (July/August): 36–46.

Halberstam, Michael J. 1974. "Professionalism and Health Care." In *Ethics of Health Care*, ed. L. R. Tancredi. Washington: National Academy of Sciences.

Hales, Dianne. 1979. "Doctors in Hard Hats." *American Medical News* (23 November): 8–9.

Hall, Richard H. 1975. *Occupations and the Social Structure*. Englewood Cliffs, N.J.: Prentice-Hall.

———. 1977. *Organizations: Structure and Process*. Englewood Cliffs, N.J.: Prentice-Hall.

Hamilton, Alice. 1943. *Exploring the Dangerous Trades*. Boston: Little, Brown.

Hanley, John W. 1981. "Monsanto's Early Warning System." *Harvard Business Review* (November/December): 107–22.

Hardin, Garrett. 1968. "The Tragedy of the Commons." *Science* 162:1243–48.

Hardy, Harriet L. 1983. *Challenging Man-Made Disease*. New York: Praeger.

Hartman, Brady. 1982. "Control of Disability and Sick Leave—Cost Container?" *San Diego Physician* (October): 35.

Haug, Marie R. 1976. "The Erosion of Professional Authority: A Cross-Cultural Inquiry in the Case of the Physician." *Milbank Memorial Fund Quarterly/Health and Society* 54: 83–106.

Hazard, Geoffrey C., Jr. 1978. *Ethics in the Practice of Law*. New Haven: Yale University Press.

Hazlett, T. Lyle, and William H. Hummel. 1957. *Industrial Medicine in Western Pennsylvania*. Pittsburgh: University of Pittsburgh Press.

Herbert, Henry. 1975. "The Pros and Cons of Relicensure and Recertification." *Journal of Occupational Medicine* 17:771–74.

Herzlinger, Regina E., and David Calkins. 1986. "How Companies Tackle Health Care Costs: Part III." *Harvard Business Review* (January/February): 70–80.

Hewitt Associates. 1984. *Company Practices in Health Care Cost Management*. Lincolnshire, Ill.: Hewitt Associates.

Hirschman, Albert O. 1970. *Exit, Voice, and Loyalty: Responses to Decline in Firms, Organizations, and States*. Cambridge: Harvard University Press.

Hobsbawm, E. J. 1962. *The Age of Revolution, 1789–1848*. New York: Mentor.

Hogan, Joyce C., and Edward J. Bernacki. 1981. "Developing Job-Related Preplacement Medical Examinations." *Journal of Occupational Medicine* 23: 469–76.

Hollinshead, Ariel C. 1981. "Occupational Safety and Health: The Years Ahead." *American Journal of Industrial Medicine* 2:273–91.

Howe, Edmund G. 1986. "Ethical Issues Regarding Mixed Agency of Military Physicians." *Social Science and Medicine* 23: 803–16.

Howe, Henry F. 1964. "Is Management Support of Occupational Medicine Diminishing?" *Journal of Occupational Medicine* 6:5–8.

Hughes, Everett C. 1958. *Men and Their Work*. Glencoe, Ill.: Free Press.

———. 1962. "Good People and Dirty Work." *Social Problems* 10: 3–11.

———. 1965. "Professions." In *The Professions in America*, ed. K. S. Lynn. Boston: Houghton Mifflin.

Illich, Ivan. 1975. *Medical Nemesis: The Expropriation of Health*. London: Calder & Boyers.

———. 1977. *Disabling Professions*. London: Marion Boyers.

ILO (International Labour Organization). 1959. "Recommendation Concerning Occupational Health Services in Places of Employment." New York: United Nations.

Jend, William. 1973. "Where do We Want to be in Occupational Medicine?" *Journal of Occupational Medicine* 15:577–79.

Johnstone, Rutherford. 1961. "Occupational Medicine—The Captive Specialty." *Journal of Occupational Medicine* 3: 283–86.

Johnstone, Rutherford T., and Seward E. Miller. 1960. *Occupational Diseases and Industrial Medicine*. Philadelphia and London: W. B. Saunders.

Jones, W. H. S., trans. 1948. *Hippocrates*, 1. London: Wm. Heinemann.

Kahn, Robert L., Donald W. Wolfe, Robert P. Quinn, and J. Diedrick Snoek. 1964. *Organizational Stress: Studies in Role Conflict and Ambiguity*. New York: John Wiley and Sons.

Kammer, A. G. 1953. "Graduate Training in Occupational Medicine." *Industrial Medicine and Surgery* 22: 149–52.

Kanter, Rosabeth Moss. 1977. *Men and Women of the Corporation*. New York: Basic Books.

Kaplan, Norman. 1965. "Professional Scientists in Industry: An Essay Review." *Social Problems*: 13:88–97.

Karrh, Bruce W. 1978. "Workplace Health Hazards: The Responsibilities to Assess, to Report, to Control." In *Health Services and Health Hazards*. See Egdahl and Walsh 1978.

———. 1979. "The Confidentiality of Occupational Medical Data." *Journal of Occupational Medicine* 21:157–60.

———. 1983. "The Critical Balance: The Influence of Government Regulation, Past and Present." *Journal of Occupational Medicine* 25:21–25.

Keene, Clifford. 1974. "The Credibility of Occupational Medicine." *Journal of Occupational Medicine* 16:309–12.

Kehoe, Robert. 1959a. "Backgrounds and Policies Involved in Certification." *Journal of Occupational Medicine* 5: 262–68.

———. 1959b. "Occupational Medicine—Whither and How." *Journal of Occupational Medicine* 1: 1–6.

Kelman, Steven. 1981. *Regulating America, Regulating Sweden: A Comparative Study of Occupational Safety and Health Policy*. Cambridge: MIT Press.

Kerr, Loren E. 1973. "Occupational Health—A Discipline in Search of a Mission." *American Journal of Public Health* 63:381–85.

———. 1977. "Impact of National Health Insurance on Occupational Safety and Health Services for Small Businesses." *See* NIOSH 1977a.

Kiefhaber, Anne K., and Willis B. Goldbeck. 1984. "Worksite Wellness." In *Health Care Cost Management: Private Sector Initiatives*, ed. P. D. Fox, W. B. Goldbeck, and J. J. Spies. Ann Arbor, Mich.: Health Administration Press.

Knowles, John H., ed. 1977. "Doing Better and Feeling Worse: Health in the United States." *Daedalus* 106.

Kornhauser, William. 1963. *Scientists in Industry*. Berkeley: University of California Press.

Kotin, Paul. 1979. "Standards in the Workplace: Crisis, Crusade, or Crucible?" *Journal of Occupational Medicine* 21:557–61.

———. 1980. "Smoking in the Workplace: A Hazard Ignored." *American Journal of Public Health* 70:575–76.

———. 1982. "Carcinogenesis: Problems and Paradoxes." *Journal of Occupational Medicine* 24:290–94.

Kotin, Paul, and Lois Anne Gaul. 1980. "Occupational Ill-Health—A Review of the Symptoms and Signs—A Critique." *Journal of Occupational Medicine* 22:471–74.

Krizay, John, and Andrew Wilson. 1974. *The Patient as Consumer*. Lexington, Mass.: Lexington Books.

Kusnetz, Stanley, and Marilyn K. Hutchinson. 1979. *A Guide to the Work-Relatedness of Disease*. Washington, D.C.: U.S. Departments of Health, Education and Welfare, National Institute of Occupational Safety and Health (DHEW [NIOSH] pub. no. 79-116).

LaDou, Joseph, ed. 1981. *Occupational Health Law: A Guide for Industry*. New York: Marcel Dekker.

Lalonde, Marc. 1974. *A New Perspective on the Health of Canadians—A Working Document*. Ottawa, Ontario, Canada: Ministry of National Health and Welfare.

Larson, Magali Sarfatti. 1977. *The Rise of Professionalism: A Sociological Analysis*. Berkeley: University of California Press.

Lasch, Christopher. 1978. *Haven in a Heartless World*. New York: Basic Books.

Law, Sylvia A. 1976. *Blue Cross: What Went Wrong?* New Haven: Yale University Press.

Lee, Jeffrey S., and William N. Rom, eds. 1982. *Legal and Ethical Dilemmas in Occupational Health*. Ann Arbor, Mich.: Ann Arbor Science Publishers.

Legge, Robert T. 1938. "Industrial Medicine of Tomorrow." *Journal of the American Medical Association* 3:291–93.

———. 1952. "Progress of American Industrial Medicine in the First Half of the Twentieth Century." *American Journal of Public Health* 40:909.

Lemert, Edwin M. 1951. *Social Pathology*. New York: McGraw-Hill.

Lerner, Sidney. 1981. "Editorial Response" to "Developing Job-Related Preplacement Medical Examinations," by J. C. Hogan and E. J. Bernecki. *Journal of Occupational Medicine* 23:475–76.

Levy, Barry S. 1981. "Medical Schools' 'Lame' Approach to Work-Related Medicine." *Occupational Health and Safety* 50: 6–9.

Levy, Barry S., and David H. Wegman, eds. 1983. *Occupational Health: Recognizing and Preventing Work-Related Disease*. Boston: Little, Brown.

Lilienfeld, Abraham M., and David E. Lilienfeld. 1980. *Foundations of Epidemiology*. New York: Oxford University Press.

Lomas, Harvey D., and Jonathan D. Berman. 1983. "Diagnosing for Administrative Purposes: Some Ethical Problems." *Social Science and Medicine* 17:241–44.

Lowrance, William W. 1976. *Of Acceptable Risk: Science and the Determination of Safety*. Los Altos: William Kaufman.
Lusterman, Seymour. 1974. *Industry Roles in Health Care*. New York: The Conference Board.
Maccoby, Michael. 1976. *The Gamesman: The New Corporate Leaders*. New York: Simon & Schuster.
MacLaury, Judson. 1981. "The Job Safety Law of 1970. Its Passage Was Perilous." *Monthly Labor Review* 104:18–21.
Magnuson, Harold. 1976. "An Open Letter to Professor Dr. Bernardino Ramazzini." *Journal of Occupational Medicine* 18:221–23.
———. 1978. "Ten Years' Progress—Real or Imagined." *Journal of Occupational Medicine* 20:247–50.
Mancuso, Thomas. 1976. *Help for the Working Wounded*. Washington, D.C.: International Association of Machinists.
Marcson, Simon. 1960. *The Scientists in American Industry: Some Organizational Determinants in Manpower Utilization*. New York: Harper & Brothers.
Mayo, Elton. 1945. *The Social Problems of an Industrial Civilization*. Cambridge: Harvard University Press.
Mazzocchi, Anthony. 1981. "Confidentiality and Access to Public Records." Unpublished paper presented at Joint Conference on Occupational Health, 13–16 October, in Nashville, Tenn. Mimeographed.
Mazzocchi, Susan. 1977. "Training Occupational Physicians: Suppose They Gave a Profession and No One Came?" *Health/PAC Bulletin* 75: 7.
McCahan, Jermyn F. 1983. "Physicians' Frustrations with Management." In Egdahl, R. H., and D. C. Walsh, eds., *Corporate Medical Department*. See Egdahl and Walsh 1983.
McDonagh, Thomas. 1982. "The Physician as Manager." *Journal of Occupational Medicine* 24:99.
McGuire, E. Patrick. 1979. *The Product-Safety Function: Organization and Operations*. New York: The Conference Board.
McKeown, Thomas. 1976. *The Role of Medicine: Dream, Mirage, or Nemesis?* Oxford: Nuffield Provincial Hospitals Trust.
McKiever, Margaret, ed. 1965. *Trends in Employee Health Services*. Washington, D.C.: U.S. Public Health Service, Division of Occupational Health (pub. no. 1330).
McKinlay, John. 1982. "Toward the Proletarianization of Physicians." In *Professionals as Workers*. See Derber 1982.
McLean, Alan A. 1979. *Work Stress*. Reading, Mass.: Addison-Wesley.
Mechanic, David. 1976. *The Growth of Bureaucratic Medicine*. New York: Wiley-Interscience.
———. 1978. *Medical Sociology*. New York: Free Press.
———. 1979. "Physicians." In *Handbook of Medical Sociology*. See Freeman, Levine, and Reeder 1979.
Mendeloff, John. 1980. *Regulating Safety: An Economic and Political Analysis of Occupational Safety and Health Policy*. Cambridge: MIT Press.
Merton, Robert K. 1968. *Social Theory and Social Structure*. New York: Free Press.

Merton, Robert K., George Reader, and Patricia L. Kendall, eds. 1957. *The Student-Physician.* Cambridge: Harvard University Press.

Miller, George A. 1967. "Professionals in Bureaucracy: Alienation among Industrial Scientists and Engineers." *American Sociological Review* 32:755–58.

Miller, S. M. 1963. *Max Weber: Selections from His Work.* New York: Thomas Y. Crowell.

Mintz, Benjamin W. 1984. *OSHA: History, Law, and Policy.* Washington, D.C.: Bureau of National Affairs.

Mitchell, James W., ed. 1982. "Occupational Medicine Forum." *Journal of Occupational Medicine* 24: 265–67.

Monson, Richard R., and Elizabeth Delzell. 1981. "An Estimate of the Percentage of Occupational Cancer Among a Group of Rubber Workers." In *Quantification of Occupational Cancer. See* Peto and Schneiderman 1981.

Morton, William E. 1977. "The Responsibility to Report Occupational Health Risks." *Journal of Occupational Medicine* 19:258–60.

Moss, Leonard. 1981. *Management Stress.* Reading, Mass.: Addison-Wesley.

Mulryan, Lawrence E., Kevin J. McCarthy, and Joseph LaDou. 1981. "Cumulative Injury and Occupational Stress." In *Occupational Health Law. See* LaDou 1981.

Munts, Raymond. 1967. *Bargaining for Health.* Madison: University of Wisconsin Press.

Murray, Thomas H. 1986. "Divided Loyalties Dilemmas for Physicians: Social Context and Moral Problems." In *Social Science and Medicine* 23: 827–32.

Nack, William. 1979. "Playing Hurt: The Doctors' Dilemma." *Sports Illustrated* 50: 99–103.

Nader, Ralph. 1973. Introduction to *Bitter Wages. See* Page and O'Brien 1973.

Naschold, Frieder. 1981. "Two Roads toward Innovation in Occupational Safety and Health in Western Countries." In *Innovation in Health Policy and Service Delivery. See* Altenstetter 1981.

National Research Council. 1983. *Video Displays, Work, and Vision: Panel on Impact of Video Viewing on Vision of Workers.* Washington, D.C.: National Academy Press.

Navarro, Vicente. 1976. *Medicine under Capitalism.* New York: Prodist.

Navarro, Vicente, and Daniel M. Berman, eds. 1983. *Health and Work under Capitalism.* Farmingdale, N.Y.: Baywood Publishing.

Nelson, David, and Stuart Campbell. 1972. "Taylorism versus Welfare Work in American Industry: H. L. Gant and the Bancrofts." *Business History Review* 46:1–16.

Nelkin, Dorothy, and Michael S. Brown. 1984. *Workers at Risk: Voices from the Workplace.* Chicago: University of Chicago Press.

Nichols, Albert L., and Richard J. Zeckhauser. 1977. "Government Comes to the Workplace: An Assessment of OSHA." *The Public Interest* 49:39–69.

NIOSH (National Institute for Occupational Safety and Health). 1977a. *Proceedings of Clinic-Based Occupational Safety and Health Programs for Small Businesses.* Washington, D.C.: U.S. General Printing Office.

―――. 1977b. *The Right to Know: Practical Problems and Policy Issues Arising from*

Exposures to Hazardous Chemical and Physical Agents in the Workplace. Washington, D.C.: U.S. Department of Health, Education, and Welfare.

———. 1978. "A Nationwide Survey of the Occupational Safety and Health Work Force." Washington, D.C.: U.S. GPO. (DHEW [NIOSH] pub. no. 78–164.)

Northrup, Herbert R., Richard L. Rowan, and Charles R. Perry. 1978. *The Impact of OSHA.* Labor Relations and Public Policy Series, no. 17. Philadelphia: University of Pennsylvania, The Wharton School Industrial Research Unit.

Nugent, Angela. 1983. "Fit for Work: The Introduction of Physical Examinations in Industry." *Bulletin of the History of Medicine* 57:578–95.

O'Donnell, Michael P., and Thomas H. Ainsworth, eds. 1984. *Health Promotion in the Workplace.* New York: John Wiley & Sons.

Office of Technology Assessment. 1985. *Preventing Illness and Injury in the Workplace.* Washington, D.C.: U.S. GPO (Office of Technology Assessment pub. no. OTA-H-256).

Page, Joseph A., and Mary-Win O'Brien. 1973. *Bitter Wages.* New York: Grossman.

Parkinson, Rebecca S., et al., eds. 1982. *Managing Health Promotion in the Workplace.* Palo Alto: Mayfield.

Parsons, Talcott. 1951. *The Social System.* New York: Free Press.

Pederson, David H., W. M. Karl Seiber, and David S. Sundin. 1986. "Health Care Trends in United States Industry." Third U.S.-Finnish Joint Science Symposium, 21–24 October, Frankfort, Kentucky.

Perrow, Charles. 1977. *Complex Organizations: A Critical Essay.* Glenview, Ill.: Scott, Foresman.

Peters, T. J., and R. H. Waterman, Jr. 1982. *In Search of Excellence.* New York: Harper & Row.

Peto, Richard, and M. Schneiderman. 1981. *Quantification of Occupational Cancer.* New York: Cold Spring Harbor Laboratory.

Posner, Richard A. 1972. "A Theory of Negligence." *Journal of Legal Studies* 1:29–96.

Pott, Percivall. 1775. *The Chirurgical Works of Percivall Pott.* 5 vols. London: Lowndes.

Powles, John. 1974. "On the Limitations of Modern Medicine." In *The Challenges of Community Medicine*, ed. R. L. Kane. New York: Springer-Verlag.

Prescott, Eleanor. 1977. "The Hazards of Caring for the Company." *Medical Dimensions* 6:23–27.

Privacy Protection Study Commission. 1977. *Personal Privacy in an Information Society.* Washington, D.C.: U.S. GPO (stock no. 052-003-00395-30).

Ramazzini, Bernardino. 1713. *De Morbis Artificum Diatriba.* Trans. Wilmer Grave, 1940. Chicago: University of Chicago Press.

Randall, Willard S., and Stephen D. Solomon. 1977. *Building 6: The Tragedy at Bridesburg.* Boston: Little, Brown.

Reiser, Stanley Joel. 1978. "The Emergence of the Concept of Screening for Disease." *Milbank Memorial Fund Quarterly/Health and Society* 56:403–26.

Rich, Spencer. 1986. "Imagine a Doctor Having to Take a Salary Cut to Get a Job." *Washington Post National Weekly Edition*, 19.

Richter, Elihu D. 1981. "The Worker's Right to Know: Obstacles, Ambiguities, and Loopholes." *Journal of Health Policy, Politics, and Law* 6:339–46.
Ritardi, Albert F. 1983. "Problems and Satisfactions in Managing Physicians." In *Corporate Medical Departments*. See Egdahl and Walsh 1983.
Ritzer, George. 1975. "Professionalization, Bureaucratization, and Rationalization: The Views of Max Weber." *Social Forces* 53:627–34.
Robens, Lord. 1972. *Safety and Health at Work: Report of the Committee 1970–1972*. Presented to Parliament by the Secretary of State for Employment. London: Her Majesty's Stationery Office.
Roberts, Norbert J. 1974. "Medicine at Work." *The Lamp* 56:20–25. New York: Exxon Corporation.
———, ed. 1978a. "Conference on Ethical Issues in Occupational Medicine." *Bulletin of the New York Academy of Medicine* 54.
———. 1978b. "Some Current Challenges in Occupational Medicine." *Journal of Occupational Medicine* 20:169–72.
Robinson, Harry, and Loring W. Wood. 1982. "The New York Telephone Company Medical Information System." *Journal of Occupational Medicine* 24:840–43.
Roemer, Milton I. 1981. *Ambulatory Health Services in America*. Rockville, Md.: Aspen Systems.
Rom, William N., ed. 1983. *Environmental and Occupational Medicine*. Boston: Little, Brown.
Rosen, George. 1958. *A History of Public Health*. New York: MD Publications.
———. 1979. "The Evolution of Social Medicine." In *Handbook of Medical Sociology*. See Freeman, Levine, and Reeder 1979.
Rothstein, Mark A. 1984. *Medical Screening of Workers*. Washington, D.C.: Bureau of National Affairs.
Royal College of Physicians. 1980. "Guidance on Ethics for Occupational Medicine." London: Faculty of Occupational Medicine.
Rundle, Rhonda. 1981. "GM Enlists Physicians to Battle Claims Abuse." *Business Insurance* 15: 3.
Russell, Louise. 1986. *Is Prevention Better than Cure?* Washington, D.C.: Brookings Institute.
Ruttenberg, Ruth, and Randall Hudgins. 1981. *Occupational Safety and Health in the Chemical Industry*. New York: Council on Economic Priorities.
Ryan, William. 1972. *Blaming the Victim*. New York: Random House.
Sackett, David L., and Walter W. Holland. 1975. "Controversy in the Detection of Disease." *The Lancet* (23 August): 357–59.
Sahin, Kenan E., and Amy K. Taylor. 1979. "Employee Acquisition of Health Care Facilities: A Possible Outcome of Escalating Premiums?" *Sloan Management Review* 20: 61–75.
Samuels, Sheldon W. 1977. "The Problems of Industry-Sponsored Health Plans." In *Background Papers on Industry's Changing Role in Health Care Delivery*. See Egdahl 1977.
———. 1979. "The Fallacies of Risk-Benefit Analysis." *Annals of the New York Academy of Sciences* 329:267–73.
———. 1983. "Ethics and Ethical Codes in Occupational Medicine." In *Environmental and Occupational Medicine*. See Rom 1983.

Samways, Margaret C. 1982. "Informing Those with a Need to Know." *Journal of Occupational Medicine* 24:387–92.

Sapolsky, Harvey M., Drew Altman, Richard Greene, and Judith D. Moore. 1981. "Corporate Attitudes toward Health Care Costs." *Milbank Memorial Fund Quarterly/Health and Society* 59:561–86.

Sawtell, Ivor J., and Jane Cooper. 1975. "Medical Officers in Industry." *Journal of the Society of Occupational Medicine* 25:38–49.

Schilling, R. S. F., ed. 1981. *Occupational Health Practice*, 2nd ed. London: Butterworths.

Schoenleber, Alvin Willis. 1950. *Doctors in Oil*. New York: Standard Oil Company.

Schramm, Carl J. 1980. "Evaluating Industrial Alcoholism Programs: A Human Capital Approach." *Journal of Studies on Alcoholism* 41:702–13.

Schuman, Bernard J., and Anu Triefeldt Lacis. 1982. "The Role of the Occupational Medical Department in Health Care Cost Containment." *Journal of Occupational Medicine* 24:696–97.

Scott, W. R. 1966. "Professionals in Bureaucracies—Areas of Conflict." In *Professionalization*, ed. Howard Vollmer and Donald Mills. Englewood Cliffs, N.J.: Prentice-Hall: 265–91

Selby, Clarence D. 1919. "Studies of the Medical and Surgical Care of Industrial Workers." Washington, D.C.: United States Public Health Service Bulletin no. 99.

Selleck, Henry B., and Alfred H. Whittaker. 1962. *Occupational Health in America*. Detroit: Wayne State University Press.

Settergren, Susan K., Curtis S. Wilbur, Tyler D. Hartwell, and John H. Rassweiler. 1983. "Comparison of Respondents and Nonrespondents to a Worksite Health Screen." *Journal of Occupational Medicine* 25: 475–79.

Shain, M., H. Suurvali, and M. Boutilier. 1986. *Healthier Workers: Health Promotion and Employee Assistance Programs*. Lexington, Mass.: D. C. Heath.

Shepard, William. 1960. "The Practice of Industrial Medicine—What It Takes." *Journal of Occupational Medicine* 29: 255–59.

———. 1961. *The Physician in Industry*. New York: McGraw-Hill.

Shevitz, Jeffrey M. 1979. *The Weaponsmakers: Personal and Professional Crisis during the Vietnam War*. Cambridge: Schenkman.

Sicherman, Barbara. 1984. *Alice Hamilton: A Life in Letters*. Cambridge: Harvard University Press.

Sigerist, Henry E. 1960. "The Place of the Physician in Modern Society." In *Henry E. Sigerist on the History of Medicine*, ed. M. I. Roemer. New York: MD Publications.

Sloan, Alfred P., Jr. 1963. *My Years with General Motors*. Garden City, N.Y.: Doubleday Anchor.

Smith, Barbara Ellen. 1986. "Black Lung: The Social Production of Disease." In *The Sociology of Health and Illness*. See Conrad and Kern 1986.

Smith, Robert Stewart. 1976. *The Occupational Safety and Health Act: Goals and Achievements*. Washington, D.C.: American Enterprise Institute.

Snow, C. P. 1961. "The Moral Un-Neutrality of Science." *Science* 133:255–62.

Somers, Anne R., ed. 1971. *The Kaiser-Permanente Medical Care Program: A Symposium*. New York: Commonwealth Fund.

Somers, Herman M., and Anne R. Somers. 1954. *Workmen's Compensation: Prevention, Insurance, and Rehabilitation of Occupational Disability*. New York: John Wiley and Sons.

———. 1967. *Doctors, Patients, and Health Insurance*. Washington, D.C.: Brookings Institution.

Spangler, Eve. 1986. *Lawyers for Hire*. New Haven: Yale University Press.

Spender, Dale. 1980. *Man Made Language*. London: Routledge & Kegan Paul.

Stallones, Reuel A. 1980. "To Advance Epidemiology." *Annual Review of Public Health* 1:69–83.

Starr, Paul. 1982. *The Social Transformation of American Medicine*. New York: Basic Books.

Stearns, Norman B., and Edward B. Roberts. 1982. "Why Do Occupational Physicians Need to Be Better Managers?" *Journal of Occupational Medicine* 24:219–24.

Stellman, Jeanne. 1977. *Woman's Work, Women's Health*. New York: Pantheon.

Stellman, Jeanne M., and Susan M. Daum. 1973. *Work Is Dangerous to Your Health*. New York: Pantheon.

Stern, Bernhard J. 1946. *Medicine in Industry*. New York: Commonwealth Fund.

Stevens, Rosemary. 1971. *American Medicine and the Public Interest*. New Haven: Yale University Press.

Stillman, Nina. 1980. "A Legal Perspective on Pregnancy Leave and Benefits." In *Women, Work and Health*. *See* Walsh and Egdahl 1980.

Stone, Christopher D. 1975. *Where the Law Ends: The Social Control of Corporate Behavior*. New York: Harper and Row.

———. 1977. "A Slap on the Wrist for the Kepone Mob." *Business and Society Review* 22: 4–11.

Stone, Deborah. 1979a. "Diagnosis and the Dole: The Function of Illness in American Distributional Politics." *Journal of Health Politics, Policy, and Law* 4:507–21.

———. 1979b. "Physicians as Gatekeepers: Illness Certifications as a Rationing Device." *Public Policy* 27:227–54.

Strumpf, George B. 1981. "Historical Evolution and the Political Process." In *Group and IPA HMOs*, ed. D. L. Mackie and D. K. Decker. Rockville, Md.: Aspen Systems.

Suskind, Raymond R. 1978. "Occupational Health Education: Transition and Challenge." *Journal of Occupational Medicine* 20:173–78.

Syme, S. Leonard, and Lisa F. Berkman. 1986. "Social Class, Susceptibility, and Sickness." In *The Sociology of Health and Illness*. *See* Conrad and Kern 1986.

Szasz, Thomas S. 1970. *Ideology and Insanity*. New York: Doubleday.

Tabershaw, Irving R. 1975. "Whose 'Agent' Is the Occupational Physician? An Evaluation and a Suggested Solution." *Archives of Environmental Health* 30:412–16.

———. 1976. "How Is the Acceptability of Risks to the Health of the Worker to Be Determined?" *Journal of Occupational Medicine* 18:674–76.

———. 1977. "The Health of the Enterprise." *Journal of Occupational Medicine* 19:523–26.

———. 1978. "Summary." In "Conference on Ethical Issues in Occupational Medicine." *See* Roberts 1978a.

Taylor, Frederick W. 1911. *Principles of Scientific Management.* New York: Harper and Row.
Taylor, P. J., and P. A. B. Raffle. 1981. "Preliminary Periodic and Other Routine Medical Examinations." In *Occupational Health Practice.* See Schilling 1981.
Tepper, Lloyd B. 1980. "The Right to Know; The Duty to Inform." *Journal of Occupational Medicine* 22:433–37.
Terris, Milton. 1980. "Epidemiology as a Guide to Health Policy." *Annual Review of Public Health* 1:323–45.
Thomas, Lewis. 1977. "On the Science and Technology of Medicine." *Daedalus* 106: 35–36.
Thompson, James. 1967. *Organizations in Action.* New York: McGraw-Hill.
Toulmin, Stephen. 1986. "Divided Loyalties and Ambiguous Relationships." *Social Science and Medicine* 23: 783–88.
Tourier, Robert E. 1979. "Alcoholics Anonymous as Treatment and as Ideology." *Journal of Studies of Alcohol* 40: 230–39.
Trasko, Victoria M. 1964. "Socioeconomic Aspects of the Pneumoconioses." *Archives of Environmental Health* 9: 521–28.
Tudor, Bynum E. 1977. "A New Corporate Prepaid Health Plan." In *Background Paper on Industry's Changing Role in Health Care Delivery.* See Egdahl 1977.
Twaddle, Andrew. 1974. "The Concept of Health Status." *Social Science and Medicine* 8:29–38.
U.S. Department of Commerce, Bureau of the Census. 1981. *Statistical Abstract of the United States.* 102nd ed. Washington, D.C.: U.S. GPO.
U.S. Department of Health, Education, and Welfare, Public Health Service. 1976. *Forward Plan for Health, 1978–1982.* Washington, D.C.: U.S. GPO (pub. no. 017-000-00172-8).
———. Office of the Assistant Secretary for Health. 1978. *Disease Prevention and Health Promotion—Report of a Departmental Task Force.* Washington, D.C.: U.S. GPO (DHEW [PHS] pub. no. 79-55071B).
U.S. Department of Labor. 1974. "Employment of the Handicapped, Affirmative Action Obligations of Contractors and Subcontractors." *Federal Register* 39:20566–71.
———. Occupational Safety and Health Administration. 1980. "Access to Employee Exposure and Medical Records: Final Rules and Proposed Rulemaking." *Federal Register* (May 23):35212–303.
U.S. House of Representatives, Committee on Science and Technology. 1982. "Hearings before the Subcommittee on Investigations and Oversight: Genetic Screening and the Handling of High-Risk Groups in the Workplace." October 14–15, 1981. Washington, D.C.: U.S. GPO (pub. no. 53).
Veatch, Robert M. 1977. *Case Studies in Medical Ethics.* Cambridge: Harvard University Press.
Waldron, H. A. 1978. *The Medical Role in Environmental Health.* London. Nuffield Provincial Hospitals Trust.
Wallick, Franklin. 1972. *The American Worker: An Endangered Species.* New York: Ballantine.
Walsh, Diana C. 1980. "The Health Insurance Industry: Structural and Strategic Issues in an Uncertain Environment." *Health Care Management Review* 5: 71–85.

———. 1982. "Employee Assistance Programs." *Milbank Memorial Fund Quarterly/Health and Society* 60: 492–517.

———. 1983. "Medicine as Management: The Corporate Medical Director's Complex and Changing Role." Ph.D. dissertation, Boston University. Ann Arbor, Mich.: University Microfilms.

———. 1984. "Is There a Doctor In-House?" *Harvard Business Review* 62: 84–94.

———. 1985a. "Employee Assistance Programs and Untested Assumptions." *Corporate Commentary* 1: 1–10.

———. 1985b. "Medicine and Management at the Ardsley Company." Dover, Mass.: Lord Publishing.

———. 1986. "Divided Loyalties in Medicine: The Case of Corporate Medical Practice." *Social Science and Medicine* 23:789–96.

Walsh, Diana C., and Nancy P. Gordon. 1986. "Legal Approaches to Smoking Deterrence." *Annual Review of Public Health* 7: 127–49.

Walsh, Diana C., and Richard H. Egdahl. 1977. *Payer, Provider, Consumer: Industry Confronts Health Care Costs.* New York: Springer-Verlag.

———, eds. 1980. *Women, Work, and Health: Challenges to Corporate Policy.* New York: Springer-Verlag.

Walsh, Diana C., and Eileen J. Tell. 1984. "In-House Corporate Medical Programs." In *Health Care Cost Management: A Changing Agenda?*, ed. P. D. Fox, W. B. Goldbeck, and J. J. Spies. Cambridge: Ballinger Publishing.

Walters, Vivienne. 1982. "Company Doctors? Perceptions of and Responses to Conflicting Pressures from Labor and Management." *Social Problems* 30: 1–12.

———. 1984. "Company Doctors: Standards of Care and Legitimacy: A Case Study from Canada." *Social Science and Medicine* 19: 811–21.

———. 1985. "The Politics of Occupational Health and Safety: Interviews with Workers' Health and Safety Representatives and Company Doctors." *Canadian Review of Sociology and Anthropology* 22:57–79.

Ware, Beverly. 1979. "Ford Motor Company's Health Education Program." Unpublished paper presented at Washington Business Group on Health Seminar on Health Promotion, 20 June, in Detroit. Mimeographed.

Warshaw, Leon J. 1966. "Patterns and Perspectives." *Journal of Occupational Medicine* 8:353–57.

———. 1971. "Industry's Role in the Delivery of Health Care." *Journal of Occupational Medicine* 13:418–21.

———. 1976. "Confidentiality versus the Need to Know." *Journal of Occupational Medicine* 18:534–36.

———. 1977. "Opportunities for Physician Employment in Industry." *Journal of American Medical Women's Association* 32:351–60.

———. 1978. "Employee Health Services for Women Workers." *Preventive Medicine* 7:385–93.

———. 1979. "Managing Stress." Reading, Mass.: Addison-Wesley.

Washington Business Group on Health. 1978. "A Survey of Industry-Sponsored Health Promotion, Prevention, and Education Programs." Washington, D.C.: unpublished.

Weber, Max. 1930. *The Protestant Ethic and the Spirit of Capitalism*, trans. Talcott Parsons. New York: Charles Scribner's Sons.

---. 1947. *The Theory of Social and Economic Organization*, trans. Talcott Parsons. New York: Free Press.
Westin, Alan F. 1976. *Computers, Health Records, and Citizens' Rights*. Washington, D.C.: U.S. GPO (stock no. 003-003-0168-1).
Westin, Alan F., and Stephen Salisbury. 1980. *Individual Rights in the Corporation*. New York: Pantheon.
Wikler, Daniel I. 1978. "Persuasion and Coercion for Health." *Milbank Memorial Fund Quarterly/Health and Society* 56:303–38.
Wilbur, Curtis S. 1983. "The Johnson & Johnson Program." *Preventive Medicine* 12: 672–81.
Wilbur, Curtis S., and David Garner. 1984. "Marketing Health to Employees: The Johnson & Johnson Live for Life Program." In *Marketing Health Behavior*, ed. Lee W. Frederiksen, Laura J. Solomon, and Kathleen A. Brehony. Plenum Publishing.
Wilensky, Harold L. 1964. "The Professionalization of Everyone?" *American Journal of Sociology* 70: 137–58.
---. 1967. *Organizational Intelligence*. New York: Basic Books.
Wolf, Stewart, John G. Bruhn, and Helen Goodell. 1978. *Occupational Health as Human Ecology*. Springfield, Ill.: Charles C. Thomas.
Wolfe, Tom. 1979. *The Right Stuff*. New York: Farrar, Straus, Giroux.
Wolinsky, Frederic D. 1980. *The Sociology of Health*. Boston: Little, Brown.
Woods, David. 1978. "The Occupational Health Physician's Occupation." *Canadian Medical Association Journal* 118:73–75.
Woodsides, Kenneth D. 1980. "Yes, Management, Your Medical Department Can Affect the 'Bottom Line.'" *Journal of Occupational Medicine* 22:232–34.
Yale Law Journal. 1981. "Occupational Health Risks and the Worker's Right to Know." *Yale Law Journal* 90: 1792–1810.
Yodaiken, Ralph E., and Anthony W. Robbins. 1980. "Occupational Ill-Health—A Review of the Signs and Symptoms." *Journal of Occupational Medicine* 22:465–74.
Zenz, Carl, ed. 1975. *Occupational Medicine: Principles and Practical Applications*. Chicago: Yearbook Medical Publishers.
---. 1980. *Developments in Occupational Medicine*. Chicago: Yearbook Medical Publishers.
Zola, Irving Kenneth. 1978. "Medicine as an Institution of Social Control." In *The Cultural Crisis of Modern Medicine*, ed. J. Ehrenreich. New York: Monthly Review Press.
---. 1983. *Socio-Medical Inquiries*. Philadelphia: Temple University Press.
Zook, Christopher, and Francis Moore. 1980. "High-Cost Users of Medical Care." *New England Journal of Medicine* 302: 996–1002.

■ Index

AAIP&S. *See* American Association of Industrial Physicians and Surgeons
AAOM. *See* American Academy of Occupational Medicine
Abinger, Lord, 36, 200
Absenteeism: non-work-related illnesses and, 55–56; monitoring of, 154–58, 179–81. *See also* Medical adjudication; Private physicians, disability certification and
Accident prevention, 36–41
Accountability: social-control role and, 14; institutional programs and, 88; information flow and, 213. *See also* Authority; Cost-effectiveness
Accountability, corporate. *See* Corporate accountability
Administrative functions. *See* Corporate health programs, organizational function of; Managerial role
Aircraft industry, 23
Airs, Waters, and Places (Hippocrates), 29
Alarmism, 121–22, 124–25. *See also* Hazards
ALCOA, 23, 79
Alcohol abuse: fitness evaluations and, 150–51; disability certification and, 158. *See also* Employee assistance programs
Allied Corporation, 72, 189, 213
Allied-Signal, 22
AMA. *See* American Medical Association
American Academy of Occupational Medicine (AAOM), 59
American Association of Industrial Physicians and Surgeons (AAIP&S), 57–58; founding of, 42–43; growth of, 49–50, 57–59; specialty-board problem and, 53. *See also* American Occupational Medical Association
American College of Preventive Medicine, 65
American Cyanamid, 22
American Medical Association (AMA): occupational medicine specialists in, 6, 65, 68; development of industrial medicine and, 51–55; national health insurance and, 52; occupational vs. nonoccupational illness and, 95
American Occupational Medical Association (AOMA): membership of, 58, 65, 67–68, 70; standardization and, 71–72; titles and, 84; code of ethics, 136–39, 147, 176
American Public Health Association, 65
Amoco, 22
AOMA. *See* American Occupational Medical Association
ARCO, 22
Asbestos: hazard control and, 129; synergistic effects and, 142, 201; compensation claims and, 159, 213
Assumption of risk doctrine, 36, 200
AT&T, 22
Authority: hierarchy of, 79–82; sources of, 84–89, 168, 191, 201–03; charismatic, 86
Automation, 76
Automobile industry, 23
Autonomy: theories of, 16–17; professionalism and, 18–19, 182
Aviation medicine, 8

259

Bacon, Francis, 31
Baltimore and Ohio Railroad, 33
Barnard, C., 139, 140, 162
Barth, P. S., 159–60
Becker, H. S., 17
Ben-David, J., 9
Benefit associations, 37, 39
Benefit plans, 95, 132, 217. *See also* Corporate health programs; Health-care costs; Insurance benefits
Benefits staff, 77–78, 194–95
Benzene standard, 123, 124
Berger, P., 160–61
Bethlehem Steel, 23
Biological monitoring, 75
Boeing, 22
Bosk, C. L., 17–18, 19–20
Brandeis, Louis D., 38, 47
British Society of Occupational Medicine, 222
Brodeur, P., 125
Brokering function, 97–98
Bulletin 99 (Selby), 45–46, 57, 145
Burchard, W., 9–10
Bureaucracy: medical practice and, 7–10; professionalism and, 10–12, 174; Weberian analysis of, 85–89
Bureau of Labor Standards, 56

Campbell Soup, 188
Capital-intensive firms, health-care services in, 188, 193
Carcinogens. *See* Hazards
Career advancement: physicians and, 79–82; health information and, 139, 149–50
Caterpillar Tractor, 22
Chandler, A. D., 47, 48, 51
Chemical industry, 23, 96, 123; potential hazards and, 120–23, 127
Chemicals. *See under* Hazards
Chevron, 22
Chrysler, 22
Citibank, 84
Clinical role, 73–75, 93–116; historical precedents, 29–30, 31, 33–35, 55; health-care services and, 95–99, 193–94; direct patient care and, 100–01, 102–08; clinical stimulation and, 104–08; policymaking and, 107–08; clinicians vs. scientists and, 114–16; population-based medicine and, 119–20, 134–35
Clinical skills: maintenance of, 104, 105–07; importance of, 114–15
Clinical staff: routine examinations and, 106; morale of, 106–07; administrative functions and, 153; adjudication function and, 214
Coal Mine Safety and Health Act, 60
Cochrane, A. L., 117
Code of ethics, 49, 137–39, 147
Collective bargaining. *See* Organized labor
Communications industry, 23
Community health: working conditions and, 32; cooperative interactions and, 216–17
Company doctor role, 71, 160–61. *See also* Management thinking
Company doctor system, 33–41
Compensation claims: industrial medicine and, 37–40; physician's role and, 140–41, 158–60; unclear cases and, 141–42, 159–60
Computers. *See* Integrated data systems; Visual display terminals
Concepts, idiographic vs. nomothetic, 85
Conference Board, 64–65, 68–69
Confidentiality: epidemiological data and, 138–39; employees' concerns about, 138–39, 147, 151–52, 179, 190, 215; managers' concerns about, 149–50; counseling programs and, 151–52
Conflicts of interest: professional role and, 8–10, 11; *Bulletin 99* and, 46–47; part-time physicians and, 111–12, 113
Conoco, 23
Consulting function, 19, 109–11
Contract practice, 29, 38, 52, 54
Control, concept of, 17–20
Cooptation thesis. *See* Management thinking
Corporate accountability, 21–22, 28, 36, 140–42. *See also* Compensation claims; Hazards; Worker's compensation laws
Corporate health programs: elements of, 66; functions of, 71–78; discretionary services, 72; classification of, 73; clinical function of, 73–75, 93–116; environmental medicine in, 75–77, 185, 197–203; data interpretation on, 76–77; organizational function of, 77–78; struc-

tures of, 78–83; institutional vs. idiosyncratic, 86–89; role sector model of, 93–94, 183, 184–96, 212; medical adjudication in, 184–88; health-care services in, 185, 188–96
Corporations, large: preeminent employers of physicians among, 22–23; health-risk data in, 207–08. *See also specific corporations*
Cost-effectiveness: physician's role and, 71, 191–96; potential hazards and, 120–23; health-care management and, 170, 172, 189, 194–95
Counseling programs. *See* Employee assistance programs
Counseling role, 109–10, 188–89
Coye, M. J., 215–16
Credo: labor-management conflict and, 162–63; role conflict and, 175, 179; longer-term purview and, 211
Criminal sanctions, 219

Data systems. *See* Integrated data systems
Davis, K., 12
Defense industry, 193
Demographic information, on corporate physicians, 63–71
Derber, C., 9, 16–17, 175, 176
Digital Equipment Corporation, 188
Dinman, B. D., 120
Disability certification, 77, 155, 156–58
Disciplinary role, 13–14. *See also* Absenteeism
Disease prevention, aggregate data and, 209–10
Doctor for the situation, 38–40, 47, 200
Doctor-managers, practice of medicine and, 225–28
Doctor-patient relationship: legal status of, 12n; utilitarian calculus and, 15–16; management-labor conflict and, 162–63, 178–79; organizational demands and, 226
Doctrine of specific etiology, 30, 31, 118–19, 177
Dow Chemical, 22
Drucker, P. F., 142, 198–99, 218
Drug abuse: physicians' disciplinary role and, 13–14; fitness evaluations and, 150–51; disability certification and, 158. *See also* Employee assistance programs

Dubos, R., 30, 31
E. I. Dupont, 22
Dust diseases, 49, 50

EAPs. *See* Employee assistance programs
Eastman, C., 35
Eastman Kodak, 22
EEOC. *See* Equal Employment Opportunity Commission
Effectiveness. *See* Performance criteria
Ehrenreich, B., 141
Ehrenreich, J., 141
Electronics industry, 23
Emergency care, 74
Employee: as capital asset, 33, 49, 95; relations with, 84–85, 214–15; hazard concerns of, 121–22, 126–27; as involuntary patient, 168–70, 186; expectations of, 199, 212
Employee assistance programs (EAPs), 151, 195–96
Employee benefit packages, *See* Benefit plans; Health-care costs
Employee-initiated contacts, 168–70
Employee opinion surveys, 189–90
Employer-employee relations, employed physicians and, 4
Engineers, industrial safety and, 37
England, occupational medicine in, 97, 115
Environmental health movement, 219
Environmentalists, hazards and, 125
Environmental medicine: clinical role and, 101, 102–03, 199; epidemiological data and, 117–20, 171–73; wellness programs and, 132–33; as role sector, 185, 197–203; conflicts in, 199–203; organizational intelligence in, 211–14; performance criteria for, 212; future issues in, 218–19, 222
Environmental Protection Agency (EPA), 197–98
Environmental risk: assessment of, 119–20. *See also* Hazards; Integrated data systems
EPA. *See* Environmental Protection Agency
Epidemiology, 31, 70, 209; health policy and, 117–19
Equal Employment Opportunity Commission (EEOC), 149
Ergonomics, 76, 192

INDEX

Ethical issues: nonoccupational health care and, 52; in managerial role, 136–39. *See also* Code of ethics; Conflicts of interest
Europe: concerns about hazards in, 121–23; government intervention in, 213
Expatriate employee, 108–09
Expectations, corporate physician and, 199, 212, 221
Exposures, monitoring of, 75, 128, 131–32
Exposure standards, 49, 123, 124, 127, 202, 215*n*
External control, 19–20
Exxon Corporation, 98, 188
Exxon USA, 22, 217

Factory laws, 35–36
Federal Aviation Administration (FAA), 148
Federal Department of Transportation (DOT), 148
Financial institutions, 82–83
Fitness evaluations, 150–51
FMC Corp., 23
Ford Motor Co., 22
Foreign medical resources, 108–09
Framingham heart study, 119
Freedman, A., 128
Freidson, E., 18–20, 141

Gamesmanship, 108
Gatekeeping examinations. *See* Preplacement physical examinations
Gates Rubber Company, 98, 100
Gauley Bridge disaster, 50
Geier, Otto, 47
GEMENAC report, 64*n*
General Electric Co., 22, 84
General Foods, 84
General Mills, 84
General Motors Co., 22, 48
General practice, industrial medicine and, 55
Gentillini, J. -L., 134
Germ theory of disease, 30, 31
Gettlefinger, Pete, 15
Gillette, 98, 100
Goffman, E., 15
Goldsmith, F., 178–79
Gompers, S., 35

B.F. Goodrich, 213
Gorlin, H., 69
Gouldner, A. W., 88
Government intervention, 35–36; workers' health and, 32, 33, 56; in Europe, 213; information flow and, 213–14. *See also* Regulation
Great Depression, history of field and, 29, 50
Gross, N., 83, 121
Group practice programs, 103–04

Hamilton, A., 7*n*, 34–35, 54; working conditions and, 36, 43–44; hazards and, 49, 118
Handicapped workers, 146–47
Hardy, Harriet, 7*n*
Hazard-abatement procedures, 76
Hazards: chemical, 43–44, 121–22, 123–24, 128, 130, 198; invisible, 49–50, 60, 75–76, 128; corporate health programs and, 75–76, 202; potential, 120–23, 197–98; employee concerns about, 121–22, 126–27, 200; alarmism and, 121–22, 124–25; regulation and, 123–26, 127, 129; customer concerns about, 126–27, 202; data systems and, 128–32
Hazlett, T. L., 37
HCM. *See* Health-care management
Health and safety programs, 71 73
Health-care costs: health-care services and, 99, 165–70, 187, 195–96; worksite "wellness" movement and, 132–33; statistical approach and, 164–65, 166–67, 172–73, 191–92; provider practices and, 172–73
Health-care management (HCM), 166–73
Health-care providers, corporate relations with, 172–73, 195–96
Health-care services: pros and cons of, 95–99; cost-effectiveness and, 96–97, 98; realities of, 99–108; as role sector, 185, 188–96; financing of, 191–96; performance criteria for, 212; human resources emphasis and, 219–20; future issues in, 222. *See also* Health-care management
Health education programs, 75, 76–77
Health information nets, 213

Health insurance, 59, 95
Health maintenance organizations (HMOs), 8, 226
Health professionals, company medical departments and, 77–78
Health-promotion programs. *See* Worksite wellness programs
High-cost employees, 196
Hippocrates, 29–30, 31
HMOs. *See* Health maintenance organizations
Hospitals, 7–8, 226
Hughes, E., 10, 13, 88
Human capital argument, 33, 49
Human resources: investment analyst role and, 142–46; as future emphasis, 219–20
Hummel, W. H., 37, 39
Hunt, H. A., 159–60

IBM Corp., 22, 76–77, 79, 188
Ideal types, medical departments and, 85–89
Ideological desensitization, 175
Illinois Bell, 23
Illness: occupational vs. nonoccupational, 59, 95, 102–03, 177–78, 198; social factors in, 118–19; responsibility for, 140–42. *See also* Occupational disease
ILO. *See* International Labour Organization
Immigration, health examinations and, 143
Industrial accidents. *See* Industrial safety; Safety department; Worker's compensation laws
Industrial hygiene, 56, 82, 203
Industrial Medical Association. *See* American Occupational Medical Association (AOMA)
Industrial revolution, public health and, 27, 31–32
Industrial safety, 27, 28, 29, 35–41, 82, 141–42
Industrial safety movement, 37
Industrial scientists, 11
Industry, early use of physicians in, 33–41
Industry Response to Health Risk (Freedman), 128
Information, individual, uses of, 138–39, 161, 179

Information systems. *See* Integrated data systems
Insurance. *See* Third-party payment
Insurance benefits, physician's role and, 38–40, 140, 141, 154–58
Insurance companies, medical director's role in, 82–83
Insurance underwriting: health examinations and, 143–44; health-risk data and, 209, 210
Integrated data systems, 76, 128–129; health-care management and, 171–73; data gathering and, 207–10; epidemiology and, 209
Interdisciplinary collaboration, 198–99
Internal auditor role, 218, 219
Internal control, 17–18, 19
International Labour Organization (ILO), 154, 186
Involuntary visits, strategic handling of, 168–70
ITT, 23

Jet-set medicine, 108–09
Job fitness: medical examinations and, 45–46; physician's role and, 140, 141, 142–45, 150–51, 196. *See also* Preplacement physical examinations
Job security, health information and, 139–42
Job stress. *See* occupational stress
Johnson and Johnson, 72, 76–77, 79, 188

Kaiser Industries, 98, 100, 188
Kanter, R. M., 51
Kaplan, N., 10
Kendall, P. L., 17
Kepone, 72, 213
Kerr, L., 84, 178–79
Kimberly-Clark, 76–77, 84, 188

Labor. *See* Organized labor
Labor-management relationships. *See* Management-labor relationships
Larson, M. S., 11
Lawyers, corporate, 11
Lead poisoning, 49
Lead standard, 123, 127, 215*n*
Legge, Robert, 52
Legitimacy, authority and, 86

Life-style: health-risk appraisal and, 119–20; "wellness" programs and, 132–33; health maintenance and, 173
"Lifetime health strategy," 170–71
Line managers, relations with, 187, 191, 212
Litigation: knowledge about hazards and, 129–30; environmental focus and, 219. *See also* Medical adjudication
Longer-term perspective, 211–13, 226–27
Lowman, John B., 39–40
Lung disease, 50
Lusterman, S., 68–69

McEachern, A. W., 83
Machinery industry, 23
McKeown, T., 31, 117
Malingering, handling of, 155–58
Managed care systems, 220–21
Management, professionalization of, 47–49, 51
Management-labor relationships: physician's role in, 61, 139–42; zones in, 139–40; conflict in, 139–45, 162–66, 177
Management thinking: regulation and, 123–26; population-based medicine and, 135; therapeutic ideology and, 156; internalization of, 160–61, 182
Managerial role, 77–78, 93, 136–73; ethical dilemmas in, 136–39; management-labor conflict and, 139–42; job fitness and, 142–45, 146–47; employee trust and, 145–54; sickness benefits and, 154–58; compensation cases and, 158–60; "company doc" perspective and, 160–61; strategic approach to, 162–73, 217–21; health-care management and, 166–73; longer-term issues and, 211–13, 226–27
Managers vs. corporate medical directors, 51, 163
Manpower conservation, 42, 43, 55
Manville Corporation, 72, 201, 213, 219; nonsmoking policy of, 201
Marketing posture, health-care services and, 188
Marx, Karl, 3
Mason, W. S., 83
Mass effect, 171–72, 173
Medical adjudication: statistical norms and, 179; role conflict and, 179–82; as role segment, 184–88, 190, 220–21; performance criteria for, 212; private physicians and, 214; employee relations and, 214–15; future issues in, 221–22
Medical police, 32
Medical practice: employer-employee relations and, 4; structures of, 6–10
Medical profession: trends in, and corporate practice, 220; lessons for, 225–27
Medical records: right of access to, 14n, 147, 149, 152n, 215; maintenance of, 74. *See also* Confidentiality; Integrated data systems; Trust issue
Medical school curricula, 5, 52, 176, 222, 225
Medical Taylorism: scientific objectivity and, 49; role conflict and, 153–54, 176–79, 194; staff-to-staff tensions and, 185, 187–88
Medicine, technical advances in, 44–45
Mental health, 55
Merton, R. K., 17, 83
Metals industry, 23
Metropolitan Life, 22
Military medicine, 8, 42n
Military psychiatry, 9, 185–86
Mining industry, 33
Mitchell, J. W., 146n
Mobil Oil, 22
Mock, H. E., 39, 51, 208, 209, 223
Monsanto, 23
De Morbius Artificum Diatriba (Ramazzini), 30
Mountain Bell, 23

National health insurance, 52
National Institute for Occupational Safety and Health (NIOSH), 65, 197, 198
National Labor Relations Board, 72–73
National Occupational Exposure Survey, 65
National Occupational Hazards Survey, 65
New Deal, 29
News media, hazards and, 121–22, 125–26
New York Telephone, 23, 98–99, 186
NIOSH. *See* National Institute for Occupational Safety and Health
Nonoccupational health factors: corporate health programs and, 52, 74; productivity and, 55–56; hazards and, 200
Nurse practitioners, 106, 107

Objectivity, role conflict and, 174–83
Occupational disease: worker's compensation laws and, 49–50; awareness of problem, 60; management response to, 125; broad-scale interpretation of, 198. *See also* Illness, occupational vs. nonoccupational
Occupational medicine, field of: number of practitioners in, 5–6, 63, 65–68; women in, 7*n*; evolution of, 27–89; motives for, 34–35; professional recognition and, 51–55; nonoccupational illness and, 55–60; approaches in, 70; standardization and, 71–72; as career choice, 104, 222–25; definition of, 178, 210–21
Occupational Safety and Health Act (OSHA): history of field and, 29, 60–62; regulatory excess and, 123–24, 127; screening and, 145, 148*n*; environmental emphasis and, 197
Occupational stress: corporate health programs and, 75–76, 198; as hazard, 75–76, 128, 198; integrated data systems and, 128; compensation claims and, 141
Oil, Chemical, and Atomic Workers Union, 72, 127
Oil industry, 23
Operational role, *See* Managerial role
Organizational survival techniques, 217–18
Organized labor: welfare capitalism and, 34; between the wars, 47–49; discretionary health services and, 72–73; cooptation and, 84–85; health and safety issues and, 125, 127, 200–01; medical-adjudication and, 186; relations with, 201, 215–16; expectations of, 212; accountability to, 213
Organized medicine: alliances with, 51–55. *See also* American Medical Association; Private physicians
OSHA. *See* Occupational Safety and Health Act
Outcome assessment, 69–70

Paraprofessionals, 164
Parsons, T., 14, 18
Part-time physicians: clinical skills and, 102; conflicts of interest and, 111–12, 113

Passive epidemiological surveillance, 128–31, 209
Patient-physician relationship. *See* Doctor-patient relationship
Peer review, research and, 215–16
Penetration rate, 189
Pennsylvania Railroad, 33
PepsiCo, 72, 76–77
Percival, Thomas, 32
Performance criteria, 69–70; clinical visits as, 103, 189–90; roles and, 182–83, 189; by role sector, 212
Perkins, Frances, 56
Petrochemical industry, 23
Pharmaceutical firms, medical director's role in, 83
Physical examinations. *See* Job fitness; Preplacement physical examinations; Screening examinations
Physician for the situation, 38–40, 47, 200
Physician's assistants, 106, 107
Policymaking: company medical departments and, 77–78; clinical role and, 107–08; strategic approach and, 164
Political environment, trends in field and, 219
Population, as patient, 117–35
Pott, P., 31
Powles, J., 15–16
"Preferred providers," 217
Pregnancy Disability Act of *1978*, 157*n*
Preplacement physical examinations, 142–46; trust issue and, 146–54
Preventive medicine: evolution of, 37, 40; industrial medicine as branch of, 54; as business cost, 95, 193; epidemiology and, 117–20; individual vs. population focus of, 120; vs. curative medicine, 133–35; population-based, 133–35; health-care management and, 170–71. *See also* Environmental medicine; Health-care services
Primary-care services. *See* Corporate health programs; Health-care services
Private physicians: relations with, 52, 56, 74, 214, 216–17; oversight responsibility and, 110–11, 166–70; disability certification and, 156–58, 185, 186, 214, 216–17; expectations of, 191, 212; strategic approach and, 216–17
Proctor & Gamble, 23

Product lines, discretionary health services and, 72
Product safety, 76, 126–27. *See also* Safety department
Professional certification, 53–54
Professionalism: bureaucracies and, 10–12, 88–89, 174; autonomy and, 18–19, 174, 182
Professional organizations, 64, 67. *See also specific organizations*
Public health approach, 54–55, 70, 75–77. *See also* Environmental medicine
Public health movement, 29–33, 198
Public Health Service, 56–57

Radium poisoning, 49
Raffle, P. A. B., 146n
Railway surgery, 36
Ramazzini, B., 30, 49, 63, 216
Rate retention, 215
Reader, G., 17
Recruiting, 104–05, 222, 225
Regulation: occupational medicine and, 61; screening examinations and, 72; as excessive, 123–26, 129, 200; safety department and, 127; environmental focus and, 197, 218–19, *See also* Occupational Safety and Health Act
Rehabilitation, 156. *See also* Employee assistance programs
Rehabilitation Act, 147, 149
Reiser, S. J., 208
Reporting relationships, 79, 84–85; data gathering and, 207–08; strategic approach and, 217
Research and development staff, 77–78
R. J. Reynolds, 98, 188
Reynolds Metals, 23
Ritzer, G., 10
Roberts, N., 84; "Ramazzini Oration" of, 208
Rohm & Haas, 23
Role conflict: adjudication function and, 41, 179–82; clinical vs. managerial, 63–64, 162–64; recognition of, 175–76
Roles: structurally defined, 79–83; sector model and, 93–94, 183, 184–96, 212; typology of, 140–42
Role set, 83
Role theory, 83–89, 183
Rules of role, 86
Ryan, W., 141

Safe exposure limits. *See* Exposure standards
Safety department, 127, 203
"Safety first" campaigns, 37, 40, 198
Salaried practice. *See* Medical practice, structure of
Sanitation reform, 31, 33, 198
Schoenleber, Alvin, 34–35, 54, 224
Schuman, B., 195
Scientific management, 48–49, 176
Screening examinations: history of field and, 37, 39–40, 41, 45–46, 51, 208; health certification and, 37–40; corporate policies and, 72, 74, 148; preventive medicine and, 132, 134, 145; employees' view of, 146–54, 190. *See also* Preplacement physical examinations
Sears, Roebuck and Company, 39, 51, 208
Second opinion function. *See* Counseling role
Selby, C. D., 45–46, 145
Selleck, H. B., 45, 208
Service industries, 164–66
Shell Oil, 23
Silicosis, 50
Snow, C. P., 174–75, 215
Social control: physicians as agents of, 12-16, 175; of medical work, 16–24
Socialization, social control and, 17–18
Social Security Act, 56
Somers, A. R., 35, 178
Somers, H. M., 35, 178
Specialty board designation, 53–54
Sports medicine, 8
Staff managers, relations with, 187–88, 191, 212
Stallones, R. A., 118
Standard Oil Company of New Jersey, 34–35, 224
Starr, P., 36, 44, 174–75
State intervention. *See* Government intervention; Regulation
Statistical approach, 117–19
Stern, B. J., 178
Stone, C. D., 213
Strategic approach: motivations for, 172–73; redefinition of field and, 210–21; employee relations and, 214–15; implementation of, 214–21; relations with labor and, 215–16; future issues in, 222–25

Surgery vs. medicine, 44
Szasz, T. S., 141

Tabershaw, I., 195
Taylor, Frederick Winslow, 48, 176
Taylor, P. J., 146*n*
Taylorism, 48, 176*n*. *See also* Medical Taylorism
Technological change, 28, 59, 60, 119, 197–98
Terris, M., 117–19, 132, 209
Third-party payment: medical practice and, 6–7; choice of physicians and, 98; health-care costs and, 172–73
Titles, authority and, 84–85
Toxicology: occupational medicine and, 70, 178–79, 218; clinical role and, 115, 116
Toxic substances. *See* Hazards
Trust issue: employee relations and, 146–54, 168–70, 173; with management, 170
Twaddle, A., 140

U.S. Government, Bureau of Health Professions, 65
U.S. Steel, 23
Union-busting managers, 158
Union Carbide, 22, 72
Unions. *See* Organized labor
United Mine Workers of America, 72, 84
United Technologies, 22
Upjohn Co., 23
USX, 23
Utilitarian calculus, 14–16

Veblen, T., 71
Vinyl chloride, 213
Visual display terminals (VDTs), 76

Waldron, H. A., 32
Walsh-Healey Public Contracts Act of *1936*, 56
Walters, V., 21
War: history of field and, 27, 29. *See also* World War I; World War II
Weber, M., 10, 85–88
Welfare capitalism, 34
Welfare work, 47–48
Wellness revolution 119–20, 132–33
Westinghouse Electric, 23
Whittaker, A. H., 45, 208
Wilensky, H. L., 138, 176*n*
Wolfe, T., 142–43
Work, views of, 3–4
Worker's advocates, overstatement of hazards and, 124–25
Worker's compensation laws: history of field and, 28–29, 35–38, 41, 54, 200; occupational disease and, 50, 145; preplacement physical examinations and, 145. *See also* Compensation claims; Medical adjudication
Worksite wellness programs, 132–33
World War I, 42–51
World War II, 29, 45, 56–60
Wright, C. C., 148*n*

Xerox Corporation, 72, 76–77, 188

Yeager, C., 142–43, 144